PARTISAN
INTERVENTIONS

PARTISAN

INTERVENTIONS

EUROPEAN PARTY POLITICS AND

PEACE ENFORCEMENT IN THE BALKANS

Brian C. Rathbun

Cornell University Press

ITHACA AND LONDON

Copyright © 2004 by Cornell University

First published 2004 by Cornell University Press

Printed in the United States of America

Library of Congress Cataloging-in-Publication Data

Rathbun, Brian C., 1973–
    Partisan interventions : European party politics and peace enforcement in the Balkans
  Brian C. Rathbun.
      p. cm.
    Includes bibliographical references and index.
    ISBN 0-8014-4255-9 (alk. paper)
     1. European Union countries—Foreign relations—Decision making. 2. Political parties—European Union countries—Influence. 3. Humanitarian intervention—Balkan Peninsula. 4. Kosovo (Serbia)—History—Civil War, 1998–1999—Participation, European. 5. Yugoslav War, 1991–1995—Peace. 6. Peacekeeping forces—Balkan Peninsula. I. Title.
  JZ1570.R37   2004
  327.117—dc22   2004012142

Cloth printing   10 9 8 7 6 5 4 3 2 1

For Ernie

Contents

Acknowledgments

This book is about partisan military interventions—partisan in two senses. First, partisanship means taking sides. The subject is peace enforcement, in which a group of countries resorts to armed action against an ethnic group or nation to prevent or end its suppression of another. Second, I explore the role of political parties in determining foreign policy. Peace enforcement is also partisan because political parties disagree about what constitutes the national interest and whether humanitarian intervention is a worthwhile endeavor. Parties are driven in the international arena, I believe, by the same ideologies that define their domestic agenda. They are "policy-seekers" whose purpose is to implement a program, not just win elections. Leftist party support for humanitarian intervention reflects an "inclusive" foreign policy ideology consistent with a domestic emphasis on equality. Without this same commitment, rightist parties may instrumentalize peace enforcement operations to realize other nonhumanitarian purposes, but they do not exhibit the same consistent support for such operations.

Like any other, this book is the product of an idea, lucky breaks, and good advice. My original inclination to study partisan cleavages in foreign policy arose from a dual interest in European party politics and international relations. I was fascinated as an undergraduate in a class with Herbert Kitschelt by his framework for understanding party cleavages, and noted that it might also provide a means for explaining interparty and intraparty differences on the question of European integration. The international relations theory I had been exposed to, however, offered no way of integrating these insights from comparative politics. Ernst Haas, my dissertation chair, provided the intellectual scaffolding that I needed to connect these two literatures.

Numerous academics and analysts were skeptical of my thesis. I would never have persevered without the encouragement of Ernst Haas. Ernie's patience and his interest and confidence in me helped me through the difficult years of graduate school. His own work is not cited once in these pages, yet his influence is present throughout: his recognition of the importance of domestic politics, his understanding that the national interest is not simply given but created by political actors, and his commitment to striking a careful balance between the need for social scientists to find common patterns across countries and to remain sensitive to and explain in systematic ways those features unique to particular cases.

Just recently, after Ernie's passing, I discovered a letter he had sent to me in response to a progress report on my fieldwork. I had expressed frustration that instead of a simple generalizable process, I was finding different partisan cleavages across countries and that ideology was interacting with both historical experience and recent events. I thought I was failing. Ernie felt otherwise. He wrote, "I am particularly impressed with your growing theoretical sophistication and tolerance for ambiguity . . . Good social science is not nailing down simple propositions with incontrovertible data (though that is nice too) but dealing with ambiguity in a creative way." By ambiguity, Ernie meant the importance of context. I read his letter primarily looking for the encouragement I needed at the time and have only recently noted that Ernie provided five suggestions, every one of which I had taken without realizing that I had done so. The result is a much more interesting book. I dedicate it to him.

Others also helped enormously. Beth Simmons provided a necessary skeptical reader, and I count convincing her that party ideology made a difference as one of my greatest accomplishments. Jonah Levy was more enthusiastic about the project than almost anyone and read the manuscript thoroughly and insightfully. Philip Tetlock left perhaps the most significant intellectual mark on the book, as his ideas about how politicians resolve value conflicts were the framework I needed to put the phenomena I was seeing into words. Elizabeth Kier was a role model and enthusiastic supporter from start to finish. Joseph Grieco was a committed mentor at Duke and without his help I would have never entered graduate school. Mike Colaresi, John Duffield, Rick Herrmann, Jacques Hymans, Marcus Kurtz, Kevin Narizny, John Sides, and Don Sylvan all provided invaluable comments. Audiences at Ohio State University, the University of Texas, the University of British Columbia, Princeton University, Catholic University, McGill University, Georgetown University, and the College of William & Mary helped me sharpen the argument. I owe a special debt to Nicolas Jabko and Daniel Ziblatt for their help in orienting myself in foreign countries and for use of their comfy couches. Marc

Howard was my trusted counselor about those things no one teaches you in graduate school, such as how to get a grant and how to find a publisher. Alvaro Artigas proved deft at sweet-talking French secretaries to convince them to schedule interviews with their bosses. I owe much to Roger Haydon at Cornell University Press, who took a chance on a first-time author. Heike MacKerron, Amaya Bloch-Lainé, and Craig Kennedy at the German Marshall Fund, Nicole Gnesotto, and Nelson Polsby were invaluable sources of contacts. Finally, my profound thanks to all those I interviewed either anonymously or on the record for their forthrightness, availability, and time.

I am grateful for the support provided by the Institute for International Studies Macarthur Research Grant, the Center for German and European Studies at Berkeley, the Institute for Global Conflict and Cooperation, and the Berlin Program of the Social Science Research Council. The Friedrich Ebert Foundation also helped financially and allowed access to records of the private deliberations of the Social Democratic Party during the 1990s. The Heinrich Böll Foundation allowed me to look through unpublished Green documents. The Labour Party office in London sent me numerous texts. Karl Kaiser at the Deutsche Gesellschaft für Auswärtige Politik in Berlin generously offered an office. The Mershon Center at Ohio State awarded me a postdoctoral fellowship that enabled me to revise the work. Jeff Anderson offered a home at the Center for German and European Studies at Georgetown University to make the final changes.

My parents, Chris and Josette Rathbun, always told me that it is the duty of each generation to selflessly provide the means for the next to accomplish all it can. They believe that tradespeople, like my grandparents, hope that their children will be lawyers and doctors. They in turn raise poets and artists. My parents include professors in this last category. I am not so sure, but I hope I have made them proud. Finally, all my love to my wife, Dr. Nina Srinivasan Rathbun, who is intellectual, romantic, and life companion all in one. I have no idea how anyone finishes a book without someone like her in their life.

Brian C. Rathbun

Washington, D.C.

PARTISAN
INTERVENTIONS

CHAPTER I

Contesting the National Interest:
Political Parties and International Relations

rimat der Aussenpolitik. Raison d'état. These concepts capture the conventional wisdom that partisan politics and foreign policy are best kept at a distance. The "primacy of foreign policy" conveys the high stakes involved in international affairs. The pursuit of the national interest is too important to allow petty domestic politics to interfere, even in democracies, for the prosperity and even the lives of a country's citizens are at stake. The kaiser said famously during the First World War, "I know no parties anymore, only Germans." *Raison d'état* evokes the Machiavellian notion that the ends always justify the means. In foreign policy, politicians must often depart from the legal and moral norms that mark their domestic politics. Elected officials and diplomats may prefer a different course, but powerful forces dictate otherwise. Both reason of state and the primacy of foreign policy treat "low politics" and "high politics" as separate areas of policy-making in which different rules apply. The prevalence of these concepts in thinking about international relations goes a long way toward explaining why there have been so few analyses of the domestic politics of foreign and security policy, and even fewer of the role of political parties.

More often than not, however, references to the primacy of foreign policy, by politicians and academics alike, are exhortations rather than characterizations of actual policy-making. When Senator Arthur H. Vandenberg talked of politics stopping at the water's edge, he was pleading rather than describing. The same structural theorists who argue that a state's position in the international system largely forecloses its policy choices also lament the inconsistencies that pluralistic systems of government create in international affairs. Kenneth Waltz writes: "The tendency of politicians to draw foreign policy into the arena of party contention is . . . widely deplored and feared."[1] Why feared, if so infrequent? Is foreign policy partisan and if so, under what conditions? Do parties disagree about the same issues across countries?

This book analyzes the role of political party ideology in defining the national interest. I take issue with the notion that governments pursue a consistent hierarchy of goals.[2] Parties "defend the national interest," but different parties define the national interest in different ways. The national interest is not given objectively. Its identification depends on the subjective viewpoints of political parties. In order to answer the question *what* the national interest is, it is necessary to recognize *who* is defining it. Parties contest the national interest. Politics does not always stop at the water's edge—neither at the banks of the Rhine, nor at the shores of the English Channel.

Political parties are "policy-seekers"—groups of like-minded individuals whose goal is to implement agendas that reflect their values. Their sets of policies and ideas are marked by a coherence that enables us to identify them as ideologies. The values that parties represent in domestic politics, which rest on particular moral understandings of how society should be ordered, are often the values underlying their foreign policy as well. The domestic and foreign policy–making processes are not completely separate spheres.

This may not come as a surprise to those who are unfamiliar with the theoretical debates in the field of international relations or acquainted with the insights of comparative politics. In some sense we know that rightist parties are more inclined to use force and that leftist parties are more supportive of international aid. The right is somehow "tougher" than the left. Yet, strikingly, no one has moved beyond those intuitions toward a comprehensive explanation of what it means to be on the left or right in terms of foreign policy.

Partisan debates can generally be reduced to fundamental disputes about the importance of equality and liberty, whether at home or abroad. The left's stress on equality manifests itself in a general pattern of concern for minorities and the underprivileged. The international counterpart of this agenda encompasses the promotion of human rights and liberal values in other countries. I call this an *inclusive* foreign policy.[3] Such a program indicates a broader conception of political community to which the left

---

1. Kenneth N. Waltz, *Foreign Policy and Democratic Politics: The American and British Experience* (Boston: Little, Brown, 1967), p. 63.

2. Stephen D. Krasner, *Defending the National Interest: Raw Materials Investments and U.S. Foreign Policy* (Princeton: Princeton University Press, 1978).

3. I adopt the phrase from William O. Chittick and Annette Freyberg-Inan, "The Impact of Basic Motivations on Foreign Policy Opinions Concerning the Use of Force: A Three-Dimensional Framework," in Philip Everts and Pierangelo Isernia (eds.), *Public Opinion and the International Use of Force* (New York: Routledge, 2001), pp. 31–56.

believes it has more obligations than the right does. This is also evident in a more pronounced *multilateralism*. Egalitarianism also leads the left to oppose the use of force since military action is the imposition of an unequal hierarchy of power. This *antimilitarism* is reinforced by the left's stress on liberty and its resistance to coercive state action.

Parties cannot always translate their ideological positions into policy, however, and different institutional configurations affect the ability of parliamentary parties to implement their agendas. Presidential systems tend to be insulated from parliamentary and therefore from party pressure. Heads of state in such countries often ignore the will of their parties in a way that prime ministers do not. In France, such autonomy was an explicit goal of the constitutional changes that produced the Fifth Republic. In parliamentary systems, coalition partners in multiparty governments must also negotiate compromises.

The role of parties in defining the national interest illuminates a relatively unexamined empirical phenomenon—military intervention for humanitarian purposes. My focus is *peace enforcement,* the use of military coercion by third parties to impose peace among conflicting groups or force an improvement in humanitarian conditions.[4] This is different from peacekeeping, in which soldiers serve as impartial mediators using force only for self-defense. I deal with nine cases: British, French, and German responses to the ethnic conflicts in Bosnia and Kosovo, as well as to the creation of a European Union (EU) capacity for undertaking these types of operations. In each case study, I seek to answer two questions. Who favored the use of military force for humanitarian purposes, and the creation of new multilateral institutions for the purposes of such operations? And who opposed these steps?

The answers are not the same for all countries. Peace enforcement creates value conflicts, particularly within leftist parties that are forced to choose between the peaceful resolution of conflicts and the protection of human rights. Politicians support different policies depending on their positions on the ideological spectrum and their country's histories in armed conflict. Some individuals, mostly on the extreme left or in countries such as Germany where force has never served inclusive ends, argue that human rights and pacifism are inextricable, and oppose all military action. Others just as stridently insist that recourse to force is sometimes necessary to ensure adherence to leftist values. These are generally moderates and those in countries such as Britain

---

4. My use of the phrase "peace enforcement" is restricted to operations where the primary stated purpose is humanitarian. Therefore operations like the Gulf War do not fall under this rubric. I use the term "humanitarian" broadly to include not only actions designed to provide tangible relief such as food and medicine, but also those intended to protect civilians' rights. "Humanitarian intervention" is a broad term that encompasses both peacekeeping and peace enforcement.

and France where the military has in the past brought about what are regarded as positive outcomes. These positions are not set in stone, however. Events often create the perception of a disjuncture between values and policies that parties subsequently attempt to fix. Nor are humanitarian concerns the only issues at stake. Parties, particularly on the right, often use these operations to realize other goals such as gaining international influence or maintaining regional stability.

A focus on party ideology helps explain changes in national policy crucial for understanding significant outcomes in contemporary international relations. How was Germany able after years of vacillation to take part in peace enforcement? Why was the British Labour government the most fervent supporter of committing ground troops to Kosovo and of a crisis management capacity for the EU when its Conservative predecessor had strenuously resisted enforcement in Bosnia and had been the major roadblock for a security role for the EU? Parties are vital for understanding why NATO was more determined to end humanitarian suffering through the use of force in Kosovo than in Bosnia, and how NATO was able to win the war after two months of ineffective bombing. Parties are also necessary for explaining why after ten years of negotiations the major European powers finally agreed on a new institutional framework for directing peacekeeping and peace enforcement operations under the EU, the most significant step to date in turning it into a global political actor. These important events have been the subject of much descriptive analysis, but they have received little theoretical treatment. The argument also has implications beyond humanitarian intervention. In the conclusion, I discuss its application to the American-led war against Iraq in 2003.

THE SYNTHESIS: DOMESTIC POLITICS AND IDEAS IN THE STUDY OF INTERNATIONAL RELATIONS

The field of international relations has recently turned toward the examination of the role of both domestic politics and ideational factors in national interest formation. Strangely, however, these two new directions are almost never combined.[5] Studying the role of parties in national interest formation enables us to synthesize ideational and domestic-level approaches. In most advanced democracies, domestic politics means party politics; and parties are the logical place to start in any exploration of the role of ideas in domestic politics, for they represent particular visions of what society should look like.

5. For a rare exception, see Elizabeth Kier, *Imagining War: French and British Military Doctrine between the Wars* (Princeton: Princeton University Press, 1997).

In the field of international political economy, scholars are increasingly looking to domestic politics to explain outcomes, relying less on the structural variables that until recently dominated debate.[6] Parties have formed an important part of these explanations. Partisan effects have been found in trade and exchange rate policy, complementing earlier findings on partisanship in domestic macroeconomic policy, and in European economic integration.[7] However, there has been little systematic work on the effect of parties on the "high politics" of security and defense policy. Nor have there been many efforts to explain systematically the role of parties in *political* integration, the process of building a European Union with foreign and security policy responsibilities loosely resembling those of states, which has taken on increasing importance with the completion of the single market and monetary union.

Where party effects are discovered, scholars typically do not go beyond establishing the difference between the left and the right on a particular issue to explaining the fundamental source of those diverging preferences.[8] Where such effects are not found, it is often because there is no developed theory of what parties would or would not support in the first place.[9] For those scholars who do provide a complete mechanism, parties serve primarily as the political representatives of the social classes that form the backbone of their political support, aiming at tilting the distribution of material benefits in their favor.[10] But European security policy in the 1990s does not have different material consequences for the constituencies of different political parties. It involves public and not private goods.[11] Why then would parties conceive of the national interest differently? A focus on another function of parties, as vehicles of ideology, helps answer this question.

6. Most notably, see Peter B. Evans, Harold K. Jacobson, and Robert D. Putnam (eds.), *Double-Edged Diplomacy: International Bargaining and Domestic Politics* (Berkeley: University of California Press, 1993).

7. On exchange rate policy, see Beth Simmons, *Who Adjusts: the Domestic Sources of Foreign Economic Policy during the Interwar Years* (Princeton: Princeton University Press, 1994). On trade policy, see Daniel Verdier, *Democracy and International Trade: Britain, France and the United States, 1860–1990* (Princeton: Princeton University Press, 1994). On domestic macroeconomic policy, see R. M. Alvarez, Geoffrey Garrett, and Peter Lange, "Government Partisanship, Labor Organization and Macroeconomic Performance," *American Political Science Review,* Vol. 85, No. 2 (1991), pp. 539–556. On the role of parties in monetary integration, see Thomas Oatley, *Monetary Politics: Exchange Rate Cooperation in the European Union* (Ann Arbor: University of Michigan Press, 1997).

8. Why, for instance, did leftist parties support decolonization while rightist parties generally resisted it? See Miles Kahler, *Decolonization in Britain and France: The Domestic Consequences of International Relations* (Princeton: Princeton University Press, 1984).

9. Joanne Gowa, "Politics at the Water's Edge: Parties, Voters and the Use of Force Abroad," *International Organization,* Vol. 52, No. 2 (1998), pp. 307–324.

10. See Kevin Narizny, "Both Guns and Butter, or Neither: Class Interests in the Political Economy of Rearmament," *American Political Science Review,* Vol. 97, No. 2 (2003), pp. 203–220.

11. On public goods theory, see Mancur Olson, *The Logic of Collective Action: Public Goods and the Theory of Groups* (Cambridge: Harvard University Press, 1965).

The most important strand of the growing literature on the role of ideational factors in international relations is constructivism, an approach critical of the assumption that states are preoccupied with the material concerns of security, power, and wealth.[12] Constructivists question, rather than assume, state preferences, and they argue that nonmaterial variables such as norms, principles, values, and culture help states "define," or constitute, the national interest.[13] The national interest is what politicians believe it is. I depart, however, from those who focus predominantly on the global diffusion of norms in the international community. They pay particular attention to the role of transnational advocacy groups and international organizations in helping or forcing states to redefine their interests.[14] Since international norms define universally legitimate behavior, these constructivists typically look for cross-national policy convergence.

This tendency leaves these scholars ill-equipped to explain national variation in state interests and foreign policy, and leads them to neglect the domestic level of analysis, an arena in which ideational variables also play a role.[15] For instance, Finnemore explains the growing number of humanitarian military operations by great power democracies as a result of a changing international normative context, particularly the increasing acceptance of the idea that all humanity is endowed with basic rights.[16] I do not dispute the emergence of this norm. Indeed it is crucial in the empirical case studies that follow. Equally important, however, is cross-national and cross-temporal variation in its embrace. Who takes up these principles and puts them into practice? While Risse-Kappen correctly maintains that "ideas do not flow freely," he does not have a theory of persuasion.[17] Policy-makers are exposed

12. The two most cited works in this tradition are collections: Judith Goldstein and Robert Keohane (eds.), *Ideas and Foreign Policy: Beliefs, Institutions and Political Change* (Ithaca: Cornell University Press, 1993); and Peter Katzenstein (ed.), *The Culture of National Security* (New York: Columbia University Press, 1996). The ontology and epistemology of constructivism are best explained by Alexander Wendt, *Social Theory of International Politics* (Cambridge: Cambridge University Press, 1999).

13. The phrase "defining the national interest" is from Martha Finnemore, *National Interests in International Society* (Ithaca: Cornell University Press, 1996), chap. 1.

14. Kathryn Sikkink, "Human Rights, Principled Issue-Networks, and Sovereignty in Latin America," *International Organization,* Vol. 47, No. 3 (1993), pp. 411–441; Audie Klotz, "Norms Reconstituting Interests: Global Racial Equality and U.S. Sanctions Against South Africa," *International Organization,* Vol. 49, No. 3 (1995), pp. 451–478; Finnemore (1996), chap. 2.

15. This has also been noted by Chaim D. Kaufmann and Robert A. Pape, "Explaining Costly International Moral Action: Britain's Sixty-Year Campaign against the Atlantic Slave Trade," *International Organization,* Vol. 53, No. 4 (1999), p. 641.

16. Martha Finnemore, "Constructing Norms of Humanitarian Intervention," in Katzenstein (1996), pp. 153–185.

17. Thomas Risse-Kappen, "Ideas Do Not Flow Freely: Transnational Coalitions, Domestic Structures, and the End of the Cold War," *International Organization,* Vol. 48, No. 2 (1994), pp. 185–214.

to numerous sets of sometimes diametrically opposed ideas. Why do they choose one set over another? A focus on party ideology helps rebut the realist critique that ideational arguments cannot specify which ideas matter.[18] International norms are more likely to take root when they land on fertile soil. Particular ideas resonate and cohere with others. Parties become the domestic vehicles of international norms.

THE PARTISAN ARGUMENT AND ITS COMPETITORS

Ideas through the Front Door: Parties as Policy-Seekers

Predating the recent interest of international relations scholars in nonmaterial causal factors is a body of work that puts a particular ideational variable front and center—party ideology. While focusing on the role of transnational groups and epistemic communities, international relations scholars have overlooked the most direct route for ideas to influence policy. Parties bring ideas with them through the front door.[19] The "policy-seeking" literature in comparative politics has demonstrated that parties put together sets of policies, present them to the electorate, and carry out those promises.[20] In addition to their role as the representatives of particular social constituencies, they also serve as vehicles for ideologies. As Peter Hall writes: "Political parties are the agents of collective purpose in a democracy . . . [T]hey distill the multiple stands of social sentiment into concrete programs backed up by a particular moral vision."[21] Not all policies go together. Party programs are reflections of the basic principles and values for which parties stand. Policies are "packaged by ideology."[22] The most fundamental feature

18. Legro also attempts to solve this problem. See Jeffrey Legro, "Which Norms Matter? Revisiting the 'Failure' of Internationalism," *International Organization,* Vol. 51, No. 1 (1997), pp. 31–63.

19. On epistemic communities, see Peter M. Haas (ed.), *Knowledge, Power and International Policy Coordination* (Columbia: University of South Carolina Press, 1992).

20. Hans-Dieter Klingemann, Richard I. Hofferbert, and Ian Budge, *Parties, Policies and Democracy* (Boulder: Westview Press, 1994) is the most ambitious test of the policy-seeking argument. They have found through quantitative analysis of government spending that parties give priority, when in government, to issues that they stress in their campaigns and manifestos.

21. Peter Hall, *Governing the Economy* (New York: Oxford University Press, 1986), p. 91. Lipset and Rokkan write that parties primarily have an "expressive function. They develop a rhetoric for the translation of contrasts in the social and cultural structure into demands and pressures for action or inaction." See Seymour M. Lipset and Stein Rokkan, "Cleavage Structures, Party Systems, and Voter Alignments: An Introduction," in S. M. Lipset and S. Rokkan (eds.), *Party Systems and Voter Alignments: Cross-National Perspectives* (New York: Free Press, 1967), p. 5.

22. See Lipset and Rokkan (1967), p. 3; Klingemann et al. (1994), p. 24. Partisan ideology is also crucial for explaining coalition formation, as parties will not select just any partner. See Abram de Swaan, *Coalition Theories and Cabinet Formations* (San Francisco: Jossey-Bass, 1973); Robert Axelrod, *Conflict of Interest* (Chicago: Markham, 1970).

of any ideology is its coherence. An ideology is a "belief system," "a configuration of ideas and attitudes in which the elements are bound together by
some form of constraint or functional interdependence."[23] Certain policies
assume others. In the next chapter, I will specify more precisely which domestic and foreign policies tend to go together.

My policy-seeking argument makes two central and testable claims, each
of which runs counter to an established school of thought in comparative
politics and international relations. First, parties articulate and implement
very different policies in the areas of humanitarian intervention and European defense cooperation due to their different ideological fundamentals.
This proposition calls into question the assumption of consistent national
approaches to international affairs that has long been the dominant tradition
in the policy literature found in such journals as *International Affairs, Politique Etrangère,* and *Internationale Politik,* and that has recently been given
firmer theoretical and conceptual foundations. I call theories based on this
assumption, which have been applied to country propensities both to use
force as well as to seek collaborative solutions under the framework of international institutions, *cultural* theories. Second, the policy-seeking argument
maintains that by and large parties win elections to formulate policies rather
than formulate policies to win elections. The latter office-seeking view is the
starting point for almost all formal work on electoral competition and is
increasingly utilized in studies of the domestic politics of foreign policy,[24]
including systematic theorizing about military intervention. Below I review
these sets of arguments and their weaknesses.

Consensual Constitution: Culturalists and the National Interest

There have been a growing number of explicitly cultural analyses of foreign policy that point to the crucial role played by shared sets of beliefs, ideas,
and values within particular countries that generate unique national approaches
to international relations.[25] Culture is not objectively given, but rather a

23. Philip E. Converse, "The Nature of Belief Systems in Mass Publics," in David Apter (ed.),
Ideology and Discontent (New York: Free Press, 1964), p. 207.

24. See for instance, Helen V. Milner, *Interests, Institutions and Information* (Princeton: Prince-
ton University Press, 1997). For a review of office-seeking and policy-seeking arguments see Kaare
Strom, "A Behavioral Theory of Competitive Political Parties," *American Journal of Political Science,*
Vol. 34, No. 2 (May 1990), pp. 565–598.

25. The best explications of culturalist logic in international relations can be found in books deal-
ing with German and Japanese antimilitarism. See Thomas Berger, *Cultures of Antimilitarism: National
Security in Germany and Japan* (Baltimore: Johns Hopkins University Press, 1998); John Duffield,
*World Power Forsaken: Political Culture, International Institutions, and German Security Policy after
Unification* (Palo Alto: Stanford University Press, 1998); Peter Katzenstein, *Cultural Norms and National
Security: Police and Military in Postwar Japan* (Ithaca: Cornell University Press, 1996).

subjective consensus, the result of a particular interpretation of major historical experiences that becomes institutionalized. In the case of security policy, that experience is war. Culture defines and constitutes the fundamental goals of political actors. Once consolidated, it is extremely difficult to change. Absent a significant shock, culture serves as a filter or lens through which subsequent events are evaluated, and points towards particular responses deemed more appropriate than others. Culturalists argue there are distinctly national norms regarding the utility of force as well as particular national instincts governing a country's relationships with the EU and NATO.

While the individual country chapters that follow will draw out these arguments much more thoroughly, I will briefly review their claims here. Germany, it is argued, has a uniquely antimilitarist and multilateralist approach to international affairs due to its tragic history with militarism. Even after the end of the Cold War and reunification, Germany has sought to bind itself into international institutions such as the EU and demurred when asked to play a role in military missions other than collective defense. France, continually inspired by de Gaulle's quest to restore French greatness following the humiliation of the Second World War, pursues an activist foreign and defense policy aimed at keeping it front and center in decisions on the major issues of international relations. Historically this has meant a prickly relationship with NATO and sometimes with the EU. In the post–Cold War environment, however, France's desire for *grandeur* requires participation in international peace operations, and hence cooperation with both organizations. Britain is the most loyal NATO ally, eager to participate in out-of-area operations, but does not see them so much as the mark of a great power. It is openly hostile to European integration, however, consistently resisting encroachments on its national sovereignty to an extent not found in Germany or even France.

Culturalists offer important insights on the role of the past in explaining the present, but nevertheless have difficulties explaining change over time. Shared cultures are extremely stable and constraining, and are said to transcend partisan divides, so that government turnover leads to only cosmetic changes in foreign policy. Thomas Berger writes: "While a particular group may reject the prevailing political reality for some time, ultimately it is forced to either make compromises or it runs the risk of becoming politically marginalized."[26] For culturalists, a German Christian Democrat has more in common with a German Social Democrat than with a British Conservative. Cross-national variations between countries in foreign policy are larger than variations over time within countries.

---

26. Berger (1998), p. 12.

This means that even while stressing the importance of the domestic level of analysis, culturalists still do not incorporate domestic *politics* into their work. Their explanations are strangely apolitical. The policy-seeking literature, however, unlike the ideational literatures in international relations stressing cultural consensus or normative convergence, stresses conflict." 'Party' has throughout the history of Western government stood for division, conflict, and opposition within a body politic," write Lipset and Rokkan.[27] I will show that cultural factors particular to countries present obstacles to policy change, but that these do not prove insurmountable. In fact, the historical experiences so central to cultural analyses sometimes create contestation rather than suppress it.

Culturalists ultimately share the same view of parties as realists, although the logic is different. Realists generally dismiss the role of ideological factors in international politics because of the power of systemic, rather than cultural, constraints. I purposely neglect realism here because, unlike cultural theories, it has never offered any expectations about humanitarian intervention, and those that it might possibly offer are unsatisfactory. First, realists might see such interventions as an effort to create regional stability, avoid refugees, or establish influence, all instrumental motivations that I take into account but which I find are generally concerns of the right side of the political spectrum. Even if realism is stretched to include these factors, it cannot explain why all parties would not behave similarly. Merely noting the importance of these factors for some but not all leaders in the same country is not enough. Second, realists might see humanitarian intervention as a luxury of larger powers. In this case, it remains silent and does not expose itself to theoretical testing. Finally, under a very broad reading, realists might see any humanitarian action as surprising since morals putatively play no significant role in world affairs. In this case realism disqualifies itself as an explanatory possibility by virtue of the very occurrence of the phenomenon. This is not to say that events beyond a state's borders do not affect foreign policy. I will show they demand a response and force change, but they do not determine the reaction. Experience is interpreted through partisan lenses.

The factors that culturalists identify—the influence of Gaullism in France, pacifism in Germany, and Euroskepticism in Britain—are much more relevant to the phenomena under study, which makes their claims much more credible alternatives. They note what is unique about each case and illuminate key features of the domestic debates over peace enforcement, even if I argue they misspecify the extent of culture's reach. They make specific

27. Lipset and Rokkan (1967), p. 3.

predictions about state behavior. This enables culturalists to write about national responses to Bosnia and Kosovo. Realists have not done so.

Ideas out the Window: Parties as Office-Seekers

Parties are virtually synonymous with elections. Therefore, no investigation of the role of political parties in international affairs would be complete without taking into account the possible electoral motivations behind their behavior. For office-seeking theories of party politics, the ideas that underlie political programs are merely instruments for obtaining power. In Anthony Downs's famous formulation, "[P]arties formulate policies in order to win elections, rather than win elections in order to formulate policies."[28] Afterward, ideas can go out the window. Office-seeking and policy-seeking motivations are extremely difficult to disentangle, as obtaining office requires articulating policies and implementing policies requires obtaining office. However, there are times when parties are forced to choose. If parties are motivated primarily by winning and maintaining office, parties in opposition should attempt to take advantage of their rivals, even when the political consequence would be to bring about a foreign policy outcome they do not support. For instance, Schultz argues that opposition parties oppose military action when they believe that it will fail.[29] In addition, if they change their policies, it is with the expectation that in so doing they will reap electoral windfalls. Policy reversals are not genuine changes of heart brought on by new experiences, but rather calculated moves to improve prospects for power. Variation in foreign policy over time and across countries reflects differences in public opinion.

I find that in the empirical cases under study, parties are guided primarily by principle, not electoral profit. This is not to say that office-seeking motivations never play a role in politics, only that they are fairly marginal in the cases I explore.[30] Elections affect the relative attention that parties focus on particular issues and the times at which their policies are revealed, but not their actual preferences. Politicians do try to conceal and distract from their true beliefs at

28. Anthony Downs, *An Economic Theory of Democracy* (New York: Harper Collins, 1957), p. 28.

29. Kenneth A. Schultz, *Democracy and Coercive Diplomacy* (Cambridge: Cambridge University Press, 2001).

30. Another aspect I considered but decided to exclude was the role of Yugoslav expatriates and their lobbying influence. The Croatians in particular played a role in the German decision to recognize Croatia and Slovenia. However, my argument, designed to address the question of the use of force, offers no hypothesis about how ideology would affect parties' decisions on this issue. In addition, the effect of the Croatian lobby should have been to make Germany one of the most active in putting troops on the ground to counter the Bosnian Serbs, but this was emphatically not the case. Since Germany is the only country in which these groups are electorally significant, I do not treat this as a full-fledged alternative.

times when they might do political harm, as posited by what is sometimes called the salience theory of political competition.[31] This is particularly true of opposition parties. Elections do not determine party interests, however. Party leaderships, those with the most to gain from being or staying elected, are the most susceptible to these tendencies, but they are not successful unless they can bring the broader party along. This requires persuasion, for which ideology is best suited. Parties also try to shape public opinion in their favor. They lead rather than follow. Although the claim that parties take advantage of rivals for simple political gain or that they quickly reframe policies in response to changing political winds is not a full-fledged theory of humanitarian intervention, it provides important, testable challenges to a policy-seeking argument. My finding about the ultimate insufficiency of office-seeking assumptions serves as an important challenge to the formal literature on the domestic politics of international conflict, which goes so far as to explain the entire democratic peace literature on the basis of politicians' fears of losing office.[32]

Auerswald does offer a comprehensive theory of military intervention on the basis of office-seeking assumptions.[33] He maintains that the domestic institutional configuration of states is critical for explaining their propensity to use force. These propensities are consistent regardless of the distribution of dovish or hawkish preferences in the legislature and the executive because governments are primarily concerned with maintaining their hold on power.[34]

31. See Ian Budge and Dennis Farlie, "Selective Emphasis or Direct Confrontation? An Alternative View with Data," in Hans Daalder and Peter Mair (eds.), *Western European Party Systems: Continuity and Change* (London: Sage, 1983), pp. 267–306. Gaubatz has discovered a tendency of democracies to avoid initiating or escalating wars as elections approach, a very similar approach. See Kurt Taylor Gaubatz, *Elections and War: The Electoral Incentive in the Democratic Politics of War and Peace* (Stanford: Stanford University Press, 1999). I do not, however, find in the cases studied here any correlation between hawkish or dovish party positions and election cycles and therefore do not make this an explicit counterargument. In Germany, the CDU was becoming increasingly interventionist before the 1994 election. In France, the Gaullists campaigned on a tougher line against the Bosnian Serbs, but actually began reducing the French presence in the Balkans immediately following their election. The British Conservatives and French President Mitterrand pursued an unvarying dovish policy regardless of season. The "diversionary" literature on warfare might also be considered relevant, but operations of the type discussed here do not provide enough of a "rally around the flag" effect to distract from domestic problems. Nor is it clear that governments actually engage in this behavior. For a review, see Gowa (1998).

32. Bruce Bueno de Mesquita, James D. Morrow, Randolph M. Siverson, and Alastair Smith, "An Institutional Explanation of the Democratic Peace," *American Political Science Review,* Vol. 93, No. 4 (1999), pp. 791–807.

33. David P. Auerswald, "Inward Bound: Domestic Institutions and Military Conflicts," *International Organization,* Vol. 53, No. 3 (1999), pp. 469–504; David P. Auerswald, *Disarmed Democracies* (Ann Arbor: University of Michigan Press, 2000).

34. He writes, "The effect on executive behavior of partial or complete agenda control does not depend on variations in executive and legislative preferences. Expectations regarding conflict behavior and accountability are also relatively unaffected by the convergence or divergence of executive-legislative preferences." Auerswald (1999), p. 408.

No theory of foreign policy beliefs or preferences is necessary. Of particular importance is the balance of power between the executive and legislature. Fearing domestic political failure that could cost them their jobs, government leaders in the executive branch are reluctant to intervene when their accountability is high and agenda control is low since these factors increase the costs and likelihood of failure, respectively. Crucial for accountability is the dependence of the executive on the confidence of the legislature. Critical for agenda control is the role of the legislature in determining foreign policy.

Countries with presidential systems where government leaders have fixed tenure and the legislative branch plays little role in policy are the most willing to intervene. Parliamentary governments, regardless of their ideological hue, are more cautious, as failure could upset their backbenchers and trigger revolts that bring governments down. Coalition governments have to contend with multiple parliamentary parties, magnifying this concern. Government leaders in presidential systems do not face these constraints, as the sanctions for failure rarely include losing office. According to this set of hypotheses, France since the establishment of the presidential mandate in foreign policy under the Fifth Republic should be consistently the most interventionist of European states. Given the parliamentary character of its executive, Britain should be more reluctant. Germany, consistently governed by a coalition of parties, should be even more so.

In fact, however, institutional conditions offer varying opportunities for "voice" on the part of parties, influence that they utilize to put forward the positions hypothesized in the theory of party preferences I offer below.[35] If parties are policy-seekers, then their primary goal is to have their concerns heard. The role of parties is more pronounced in parliamentary systems because the prime minister is more accountable to the legislature. However, systems in which party influence is higher are not predisposed towards less interventionist policies, for that depends on partisan ideologies. Party preferences have to be built into the model. Parties can push parliamentary executives just as easily in a more interventionist (or integrationist) direction. Coalition governments have to strike a compromise between the two partners, so a minor coalition partner can pull the major coalition partner in any direction it wants to go. Presidential institutions provide executives with a higher degree of autonomy that they may or may not use to depart from the party line,

35. On voice as a strategy of influence, see Albert O. Hirschman, *Exit, Voice and Loyalty: Responses to Decline in Firms, Organizations, and States* (Cambridge: Harvard University Press, 1970). Immergut offers a similar argument that institutions create "veto points" at which parties can affect the policy-making process. Ellen Immergut, "The Rules of the Game: The Logic of Health Policy-Making in France, Switzerland and Sweden," in Sven Steinmo, Kathleen Thelen, and Frank Longstreth (eds.), *Structuring Politics: Historical Institutionalism in Comparative Analysis* (Cambridge: Cambridge University Press, 1992), pp. 55–89.

whatever that may be. If a president's parliamentary party is more interventionist, he may ignore it.

Continuing the argument in this introduction that parties are driven by their ideologies, the next chapter will specify the content of these different visions for society, both domestic and international. Policy-seeking theorists, while providing a useful corrective to purely office-seeking arguments, have been less successful in conceptualizing the values that underlie ideologies— those principles that give them coherence and inspire policies. For the most part, they have proceeded atheoretically, asking voters to identify themselves or experts to rank parties on a left-right scale without specifying a meaning of "left" and "right."[36] Scholars have also coded party manifestos according to party stands on particular issues, then searched for statistical associations between sets of positions, defining a single dimension of party competition through pure induction.[37] They have found, for instance, that parties of the right stress law and order and traditional morality, while parties of the left advocate the extension of social services and internationalism. Although this description seems intuitively correct, it offers no theoretical answer to the question of why particular sets of positions go together and what common thread binds them, and consequently no way of deriving hypotheses about foreign policy positions. I aim to better clarify what it means to be on the left and on the right in terms of foreign policy.

36. On self-identification, see John D. Huber, "Values and Partisanship in Left-Right Orientations: Measuring Ideology," *European Journal of Political Research*, Vol. 17, No. 5 (1989), pp. 599–621; Ronald Inglehart and Hans-Dieter Klingemann, "Party Identification, Ideological Preference and the Left-Right Dimension among Western Mass Publics," in Ian Budge, Ivor Crewe, and Dennis Farlie (eds.), *Party Identification and Beyond: Representations of Voting and Party Competition* (Chichester: Wiley, 1976). For expert evaluations, see Francis Castles and Peter Mair, "Left-Right Political Scales: Some Expert Judgments," *European Journal of Political Research*, Vol. 12 (1984), pp. 73–88; Michael Laver and W. Ben Hunt, *Policy and Party Competition* (New York: Routledge, 1992).

37. Matthew J. Gabel and John D. Huber, "Putting Parties in Their Place: Inferring Party Left-Right Ideological Positions from Party Manifestos Data," *American Journal of Political Science*, Vol. 44, No. 1 (2000), pp. 94–103; Ian Budge, David Robertson, and Derek J. Hearl, *Ideology, Strategy and Party Change: Spatial Analyses of Post-War Election Programmes in 19 Democracies* (Cambridge: Cambridge University Press, 1987).

CHAPTER 2

Partisan Lenses and Historical Frames: Ideology, Experience, and Foreign Policy Preferences

I t is not enough to argue that parties matter. Merely noting that foreign policy changes following an election does not amount to a theory. It offers no explanation about what parties stand for and how that translates into international relations. Nor is it satisfactory to stipulate that leftist parties are antimilitarist and rightist parties are unilateralist, and to point to their respective pacifist and go-it-alone policies as evidence. This borders on tautology. It is necessary to explain the origins of those beliefs. *Why* are leftist parties more inclusive, antimilitarist, and multilateralist than their rightist counterparts? It is because these values emerge logically from the core fundamentals that distinguish left from right at the domestic level. Herbert Kitschelt writes that the "universe of possible political demands and programs in the modern age is captured in the slogan of the French Revolution . . ."[1] This is a bold claim, but contestation over these values underlies most of the partisan debates of the past and the present.[2] Antimilitarism, humanitarianism, and multilateralism are the foreign policy manifestations of liberty, equality, and fraternity.

Four theoretical tasks are involved in building a theory of foreign policy preferences. The first is defining what it means to be on the left and the right domestically. The second is to suggest a three-dimensional model of foreign policy beliefs that improves upon the existing literature. The third is to offer hypotheses about what it means to be on the left or on the right in terms of foreign policy, that is to connect fundamental domestic political

---

1. Herbert Kitschelt, *The Transformation of European Social Democracy* (Cambridge: Cambridge University Press, 1994), p. 9.
2. Milton Rokeach, *The Nature of Human Values* (New York: Free Press, 1973), chap. 6.

values with their foreign policy equivalents. These first three tasks help identify the particular lenses through which parties view the world. The fourth task is to hypothesize how and whether politicians make value trade-offs. Some issues, peace enforcement in particular, expose parties to value conflicts that they can resolve in several ways. How they do so determines how the partisan debate within a country is framed. Historical experience is of primary importance in this regard.

Defining the Fundamental Values of Political Conflict

Kitschelt is correct to start with the French revolution. The terms "left" and "right" are thought to have originated during France's experiment with democracy.[3] The left was the advocate of political equality and liberty against an *ancien régime* based on a strict hierarchy of power concentrated in the hands of a church and state that restricted individual freedom. In contemporary advanced democracies, leftists are still more egalitarian and, at least in the social and political spheres, more libertarian than their rightist opponents who have a more exclusive conception of political, economic, and social rights and are more authoritarian.

The definition of the left-right cleavage as between a left advocating social change toward greater political and economic equality and a right favoring a more hierarchical economic order is generally accepted.[4] It is important to note that in many cases, the modern right is not anti-egalitarian so much as unwilling to take active steps to create greater equality. I define the right negatively rather than positively. Nevertheless, the difference regarding equality is pronounced enough to have real ramifications for foreign policy.

The notion that leftist parties emphasize the importance of liberty while rightists underscore the necessity of authority is more controversial because of rightist support for free-market mechanisms.[5] The confusion arises from

3. Roger Eatwell, "The Rise of 'Left-Right' Terminology: The Confusions of Social Science," in Roger Eatwell and Noel O'Sullivan (eds.), *The Nature of the Right* (London: Pinter Publishers, 1989), pp. 33–46.

4. Lipset writes, "By 'left' we shall mean advocating social change in the direction of greater equality—political, economic, or social; by 'right' we shall mean supporting a traditional, more or less hierarchical social order, and opposing change toward greater equality." See Seymour M. Lipset, "The Psychology of Voting: An Analysis of Political Behavior," in *Handbook of Social Psychology* (Cambridge: Addison-Wesley, 1954), p. 1135. This definition of "left" has stood up over the course of decades. See also Robert Putnam, *The Beliefs of Politicians* (New Haven: Yale University Press, 1973), p. 213; John Gerring, *Party Ideologies in America, 1828–1996* (Cambridge: Cambridge University Press, 1998).

5. Kitschelt argues that the social organization that best fosters liberty is the marketplace. Kitschelt (1994), p. 9; also Rokeach (1973), chap. 6.

a failure to distinguish between the economic sphere on the one hand and the sociopolitical sphere on the other. In the economic arena, liberty and equality conflict. The extreme form of enforced equality, communism as practiced in the Soviet bloc, means the complete absence of liberty.[6] Most governmental behavior, indeed law itself, is coercive and restrictive of choice, so efforts by the left to establish material equality require restrictions on economic freedom. For the democratic left, this does not stem from a belief in the importance of state authority per se, but rather from a conviction of the importance of economic and social equality. The right is more economically libertarian, but this does not extend into the social and political fields. On nonmaterial issues, rightists stress obedience to the authority of the state and often the family and church by advocating tough criminal justice policies and traditional morality.[7] In the parlance of American politics, social conservatives tend to be economic conservatives while economic liberals tend to be social liberals.

The particular issues on which the left does battle with the right have steadily changed over time, as has the relative salience of liberty and equality in partisan conflicts. After the establishment of democracy and the consolidation of political liberties in Western European countries, attention turned to economic equality. The left favored the redistribution of wealth and government intervention in the economy to create employment opportunities for the working class. On issues of social and political liberties, left and right were in broad agreement. The success of the postwar economic period in generating unprecedented levels of material parity between the classes led some to declare the "end of ideology," but the political terrain shifted again.[8] A "new left" emerged in the late 1960s trumpeting postmaterial issues such as civil liberties and freedom of expression, and thereby reestablishing the salience of the libertarian-authoritarian dimension.[9] This phenomenon has met with a reaction from a "new right" stressing firmer law-and-order policies and a more exclusive conception of political and social entitlement evident in its calls to restrict citizenship and welfare benefits

6. Rokeach (1973), chap. 6.

7. Psychologists identify these tendencies as "submission" and "aggression," two of the three central values of authoritarianism. See T. W. Adorno, Else Frenkel-Brunswick, Daniel J. Levinson, and R. Nevitt Sanford, *The Authoritarian Personality* (New York: Harper, 1950).

8. Daniel Bell, *The End of Ideology: On the Exhaustion of Political Ideas in the Fifties* (Glencoe: Free Press, 1960).

9. On postmaterialism, see Ronald Inglehart, *The Silent Revolution: Changing Values and Political Styles among Western Publics* (Princeton: Princeton University Press, 1977). For instance, in one of the few attempts at systematic, cross-national coding, leftist parties in all three countries are more supportive of permissive social policy, the best indicator of libertarianism offered. Michael Laver and W. Ben Hunt, *Policy and Party Competition* (New York: Routledge, 1992), Appendix B.

for immigrants.[10] These trends, combined with the repoliticization of the role of the welfare state in an internationalized economy by the neoliberal right, means that both the libertarian and egalitarian dimensions have become salient in party competition in advanced democracies in recent decades.

Green parties did not redefine the meaning of left and right, however, as some have suggested.[11] Their new libertarian issues fit well with the traditional leftist emphasis on equality. For instance, to fight for the ability of homosexuals to make their own choices about their sexuality means to advocate their equal protection. The new left simply introduced new issues into the political arena and co-opted them for the left, all the while continuing to support most of the program of its leftist forefathers such as the welfare state.[12] The older social democratic left has gradually co-opted these new issues as well, although at varying speeds.[13] Although some center-left parties have reacted to the new right phenomenon by advocating tougher law-and-order and immigration policies, showing that party positions are also subject to change when events overtake them or they prove disastrous electorally, it is extremely rare that rival parties overtake one another on either of these two dimensions.

DEFINING THE FUNDAMENTAL VALUES OF FOREIGN POLICY CONFLICT

What does it mean to be on the left or on the right in terms of foreign policy? While cognitive researchers have tried to identify key variables that form the fundamental bases of foreign policy belief systems, they have not connected them to particular partisan approaches or values.[14] Nor have they

---

10. See Herbert Kitschelt, *The Radical Right in Western Europe* (Ann Arbor: University of Michigan Press, 1995); Hans-George Betz, "The New Politics of Resentment: Radical Right-Wing Populist Parties in Western Europe," *Comparative Politics,* Vol. 25, No. 4 (1993), pp. 413–427.

11. Inglehart (1977).

12. Kitschelt and Hellemans find that new left parties graft new leftist issues onto old leftist issues, as opposed to Inglehart's hypothesis that new leftist parties simply do not care about traditional left-right issues. Herbert Kitschelt and Staf Hellemans, "The Left-Right Semantics and the New Politics Cleavage," *Comparative Political Studies,* Vol. 23, No. 2 (1999), pp. 210–238. Green parties "link libertarian commitments to individual autonomy and popular participation with a leftist concern for equality." Herbert Kitschelt, "Left-Libertarian Parties: Explaining Competitive Innovation in Competitive Party Systems," *World Politics,* Vol. 40, No. 1 (1988), p. 195.

13. Kitschelt (1994).

14. See E. R. Wittkopf, *Faces of Internationalism: Public Opinion and Foreign Policy* (Durham, N.C.: Duke University Press, 1990). Holsti and Rosenau show some associations between domestic and foreign policy attitudes but do not provide a framework for explaining them. Ole R. Holsti and James N. Rosenau, "Liberals, Populists, Libertarians and Conservatives: The Link Between Domestic and International Affairs," *International Political Science Review,* Vol. 17, No. 1 (1996), pp. 29–54.

tried to demonstrate their translation into actual government behavior, focusing primarily on American mass public and elite attitudes. I propose instead a theory of partisan preferences based on three foreign policy continua that can be traced to the fundamental values of equality and liberty. My more theoretically grounded approach to conceptualizing the cleavages that divide parties also makes it possible to generate hypotheses about the types of foreign policies that parties will pursue.

The first continuum measures the inclusiveness or exclusiveness of the national interest. To what extent does an individual or a party believe its country should preoccupy itself with the internal processes of other countries when they have few tangible consequences for the country in question? An inclusive conception considers the promotion of the welfare of other countries to be part of the national interest, whether it be their economic development or the extension of basic rights to all of their citizens. An exclusive conception makes room only for those matters directly pertaining to a country's own well-being. This is similar to what Eugene Wittkopf calls cooperative internationalism and William Chittick et al. call multilateralism, a term that generally carries other connotations that I will discuss below.[15]

The second dimension concerns positions on the appropriateness of using forceful measures for pursuing the national interest. While in advanced democratic societies there are no longer true militarists, there are hawks who consider the use of force as a more acceptable and more necessary instrument. Hawks think about force in a way very similar to what Robert Jervis calls the "deterrence model" of international politics.[16] Goals are best reached through military superiority and willingness to take military action. If adversaries are not met with credible threats or actual punishment, they will only increase their demands. Appeasement never pays. Toughness, credibility, and resolve are critical. The model could just as easily be called the "compellence" model since the same thinking applies to the best means of making other countries do what is desired, as opposed to preventing them from doing what is undesired.

Antimilitarists, or doves, stress the efficacy and morality of civilian methods of conflict resolution, such as diplomacy and sanctions. Doves argue in

15. Wittkopf (1990); William O. Chittick, Keith R. Billingsley, and Rick Travis, "A Three-Dimensional Model of American Foreign Policy Beliefs," *International Studies Quarterly*, Vol. 39 (1995), pp. 313–331. Another similar concept is Hurwitz and Peffley's "ethnocentrism," which captures feelings of national superiority that are only one part of a broader package of how countries define their relations to others. Jon Hurwitz and Mark Peffley, "How are Foreign Policy Attitudes Structured? A Hierarchical Model," *American Political Science Review*, Vol. 18, No. 4 (1987), pp. 1101–1120.

16. Robert Jervis, *Perception and Misperception in International Politics* (Princeton: Princeton University Press, 1976), chap. 3. For similar discussions, see Glenn H. Snyder and Paul Diesing, *Conflict among Nations* (Princeton: Princeton University Press, 1977), pp. 209–309; John A. Vasquez, *War Puzzle* (Cambridge: Cambridge University Press, 1993), chap. 6.

terms captured by the "spiral model" of international politics. The threat or use of force only increases tension and leads to arms races or escalations in violence. Each side, fearing a loss in its credibility or enraged by the injustice of the other's actions, ratchets up the conflict. Publics rally around the flag, hardening positions during war and making negotiations and settlements more difficult. The use or threat of force is inefficient, dangerous, and for some, even immoral. Peaceful, sometimes called "civilian," means of conflict resolution such as political dialogue are more likely to yield results.[17]

The final continuum concerns the framework within which states pursue their interests, a dimension bounded at opposite ends by multilateralism and unilateralism. Multilateralism is "an institutional form which coordinates relations among three or more states on the basis of 'generalized' principles of conduct—that is, principles which specify appropriate conduct for a class of actions, without regard to the particularistic interests of the parties or the strategic exigencies that may exist in any specific occurrence."[18] Multilateral institutions are attempts to bring order to international relations, making them more predictable and less arbitrarily based on power. They are based on the idea of diffuse reciprocity—the principle that a state will benefit from cooperation in the long run but not necessarily each time and on every issue.[19]

The cost of this coordination is limitation of a state's ability to determine its policy itself—its sovereignty. Although multilateral institutions vary in the degree to which they bind the hands of their members, even organizations that merely provide forums for consultation force countries to hear the demands of others and justify their own, thereby exposing them to political pressure they would not have felt otherwise. The converse of multilateralism is therefore unilateralism, the choice to avoid institutional commitments and preserve freedom of decision. The choice between unilateralism and multilateralism is particularly politicized in the case of European integration, whose essence is the gradual delegation of authority to multilateral decision-making bodies. It is the most pronounced form of multilateralism. Other scholars have noted the integration cleavage but not its

---

17. This is the most common continuum identified in the belief system literature. Hurwitz and Peffley (1987) call it a "morality of warfare" dimension, Wittkopf (1990) a "militant internationalist" dimension, Chittick et al. (1995) a "militarist" dimension. They do not connect it to these two models of international politics, however.

18. John Gerard Ruggie, "Multilateralism: Anatomy of an Institution," *International Organization*, Vol. 46, No. 3 (1992), p. 571.

19. James A. Caporaso, "International Relations Theory and Multilateralism: The Search for Foundations," *International Organization*, Vol. 46, No. 3 (1992), p. 602. On diffuse reciprocity see the chapter on reciprocity in Robert O. Keohane, *International Institutions and State Power: Essays in International Relations Theory* (Boulder: Westview Press, 1989).

affinity with domestic cleavages in European societies or with the more general concept of multilateralism.[20]

CONNECTING DOMESTIC AND FOREIGN POLICY

The next task is to offer hypotheses about what it mean to be on the left or on the right in terms of foreign policy—to connect fundamental political values with their foreign policy manifestations. Due to their ideological stress on equality, individuals on the left are more inclusive than individuals on the right. There is a clear coherence between a political program that seeks to abolish hierarchies, thereby ensuring equal rights for all citizens at home, and a foreign policy that seeks to uphold rights for citizens in other countries. Both are marked by a pronounced concern for others. Domestically a stress on equality is visible through support for ending discrimination and closing the income gap between rich and poor. Internationally it is evident in the left's advocacy of human rights, promotion of democracy, and international aid.[21] An emphasis on equality has typically made leftists champions of the weak against the strong, fighting for the underprivileged. They apply this inclusive agenda at the international level as well. Leftists are marked by a broader conception of political community both at home and abroad and can be said to be more genuine believers in an international society.[22] Rightists are more hierarchical, stressing the importance of self-reliance at home, and circumscribing their conception of the national interest abroad so as to take into account primarily the needs of the national community.[23] All politicians can be expected to pursue an exclusive foreign policy in the sense that they will engage in self-defense. However, this leaves much still undetermined concerning the extent to which parties will push agendas at the expense or to the benefit of others.

20. Liesbet Hooghe and Gary Marks, "The Making of a Polity: The Struggle over European Integration," in Herbert Kitschelt, Peter Lange, Gary Marks, and John D. Stephens, *Continuity and Change in Contemporary Capitalism* (Cambridge: Cambridge University Press, 1999), pp. 70–100.

21. David Halloran Lumsdaine, *Moral Vision in International Politics: The Foreign Aid Regime, 1949–1989* (Princeton: Princeton University Press, 1993); Alain Noël and Jean-Philippe Thérien, "From Domestic to International Justice: The Welfare State and Foreign Aid," *International Organization,* Vol. 49, No. 3, pp. 523–553.

22. Chittick and Freyberg-Inan note the importance of community as a factor in foreign policy beliefs but do not connect it to domestic political values. See William O. Chittick and Annette Freyberg-Inan, "The Impact of Basic Motivations on Foreign Policy Opinions Concerning the Use of Force: A Three-Dimensional Framework," in Philip Everts and Pierangelo Isernia (eds.), *Public Opinion and the International Use of Force* (New York: Routledge, 2001), pp. 33–56.

23. It should be noted that I am not making a value judgment. Rightists often posit moral reasons, for instance, for their opposition to income redistribution, maintaining that it removes incentives for self-help and thereby perpetuates poverty.

Leftists are also more antimilitarist for two reasons. Due to their general resistance to the use of coercive means by the state for realizing political and social (if not economic) outcomes, leftists are more reluctant to use force in international relations as a means of resolving conflicts. International hard-liners are domestic hard-liners as well. They are more likely to agree that both individuals and states respond to threats and punishment. For instance, a belief that tough sentencing helps prevent crime is the logical counterpart to the attitude that the best way to reach foreign policy objectives is to intimidate other nations through military superiority.[24] Egalitarianism also contributes to antimilitarism. The use of force is an act of subordination in which a hierarchy, an unequal order of weak and strong, is imposed. In fact for E. H. Carr, the creation of equality among states, in which the good of the whole is considered above the good of the parts, is the precondition for a just and moral international society. Force, however, interferes with the creation of an international order in which the strong are not as privileged over the weak. "The constant intrusion, or potential intrusion, of power renders almost meaningless any conception of equality between members of the international community," he writes.[25]

Finally, leftists are more multilateralist than rightists due to their ideological stress on equality. Concern for others is evidence of an identification with and obligation to a broader community, both domestically and internationally. This means that leftists are more likely to consider national needs to be similar to those of the international community and consequently are more comfortable limiting discretion over policy. Leftists are more likely to recognize the legitimacy of interests of other states at the international level, while rightists are inclined to see the demands of their states as more important and more justified than those of others. Among the latter, for their state to delegate control over decisions in particular areas will be perceived as allowing other states to take advantage of it, and they will be loath to cooperate in the forums of international organizations, sometimes even when this serves party purposes. This, of course, does not mean that leftists want no say in their own policy-making, or that they support all international institutions, only that collaboration on issues they care about comes easier to them. Leftist objections to international cooperation tend to focus on those organizations, such as the International Monetary Fund, that are seen to be fostering global inequalities and benefiting the few at the expense of the many.

24. Again, I avoid a moral judgment. It can be argued that toughness at home and abroad actually does help prevent crime and war.
25. E. H. Carr, *The Twenty Years' Crisis, 1919–1939* (New York: Harper and Row, 1964), p. 68; Hans J. Morgenthau, *Politics among Nations* (New York: Alfred A. Knopf, 1954), p. 162.

This typology should hold true at the level of both the individual and the party. The more politicians or parties as a whole are egalitarian and libertarian, the more inclusive, more antimilitarist, and more multilateralist they should be, ceteris paribus. This explains not only interparty, but also intraparty differences between moderate and extreme factions. Moderate rightists will have a more exclusive conception of the national interest than leftists, and extreme rightists even more so. This theory of preferences should be of use for generating expectations about party positions on a wide range of policy issues not under investigation here, including alliance formation, nuclear proliferation and missile defense, economic sanctions, and international courts.

Distinguishing Means from Ends: Integration and Intervention as Interests and Instruments

Cognitive theorists sometimes refer to antimilitarism and unilateralism as *dispositions,* implying that they are goals or interests in themselves, rather than instruments to achieve certain purposes. This is not always the case, however, and the extent to which it is true for politicians and parties as a whole is critical for generating hypotheses about party choice when liberty and equality inspire contradictory policies. Antimilitarism can be an approach to conflict resolution, and therefore a means to an end. As one moves to the extreme left, it becomes more of a goal in itself. For pacifists, the use of force is not merely objectionable on efficiency grounds, it is immoral. In practice, these arguments tend to go together. Those most opposed to the use of force in principle are generally the least sanguine about its possible utility in realizing the national interest.

Multilateral institutions are generally considered means to an end, rather than ends in themselves.[26] They allow collaborative solutions to mutual problems. In the case of European defense cooperation, countries that cannot perform certain security functions on their own seek to do so in tandem with others.[27] Again this does not mean that ideology is unimportant to international cooperation. Although multilateral institutions are instruments

---

26. This is the understanding of "functional" theories of cooperation. Functionalism is a broader category encompassing both neoliberal institutionalism, which applies to international cooperation, and liberal intergovernmentalism, which applies to European integration. Robert O. Keohane, *After Hegemony: Cooperation and Discord in the World Political Economy* (Princeton: Princeton University Press, 1984); Lisa L. Martin, "Interests, Power, and Multilateralism," *International Organization,* Vol. 46, No. 4 (1992), p. 767; Kenneth Oye, "Explaining Cooperation under Anarchy: Hypotheses and Strategies," in Kenneth Oye (ed.), *Cooperation under Anarchy* (Princeton: Princeton University Press, 1986), pp. 1–24.

27. Andrew Moravcsik and Kalypso Nicolaïdis, "Explaining the Treaty of Amsterdam: Interests, Influence and Institutions," *Journal of Common Market Studies,* Vol. 37, No. 1 (1999), p. 61.

for realizing collective outcomes, particular groups of politicians are more likely to make use of them than others. Before governments make a choice among institutions, they must choose to institutionalize. They must grant a particular multilateral organization competence in a new area, which is not just a function of a perceived need. As noted by Liesbet Hooghe and Gary Marks, this has become increasingly controversial as the European Union has developed beyond a free trade area and single market into an organization resembling a nation-state in many ways.[28]

Rightist parties are more inclined to resist European political integration due to their more narrow conception of political community. They often view unilateralism as an end in itself.[29] Leftist parties, less encumbered by this ideological opposition, are better able to evaluate each new step in the integration process in an instrumental way. For them, multilateralism is a means for reaching particular goals, although they are also more likely to support the general goal of political integration. Their ease with multilateralism is seen in their advocacy of building Europe-wide institutions that resemble those of nation-states as a way of promoting peaceful and stable relations among member countries. In some countries such as Germany, parties are indeed more inclined towards integrationist solutions than their ideological counterparts in Britain and France, but there are significant enough differences within such countries to make for partisan debate.

Even a humanitarian intervention itself can be a means for reaching a narrower, more exclusive goal than protecting minority and civilian populations. This is obvious for those countries that are directly affected by the transnational effects of nearby ethnic conflicts or civil wars. But the inclusive ideas that provide the moral justification for humanitarian interventions can be put to other purposes as well. This is a more nefarious process of instrumentalization. As will be seen, this is particularly true for the right. In this way, my argument departs from most ideational arguments to date, which tend to resist the notion that ideas are used as pretexts for governments with ulterior motives, since this lessens the causal importance of nonmaterial

28. "The accretion of authoritative competencies at the European level has raised the issue of national sovereignty in ever more transparent fashion," with fewer decisions "resolved by rational-scientific methods, by ascertaining the most efficient means to given ends" and more decisions involving "political contention concerning fundamental goals of European integration." Particular issues of European cooperation are not "compartmentalized," but rather seen as "interconnected." Hooghe and Marks (1999), p. 72.

29. Functionalists largely miss this. Ceding sovereignty, in this approach, is not especially problematic. It is merely "a special case of the more general problem of institutional choice or institutional design: Why does a group of actors collectively decide upon one specific set of institutions rather than another to govern their subsequent interactions?" Mark Pollack, "Delegation, Agency, and Agenda Setting in the European Community," *International Organization*, Vol. 51, No. 1 (1997), p. 103.

determinants of the national interest.[30] If anything, however, this shows the power of ideas, rather than demeaning them. Carr and Morgenthau both refer to ideas and principles as powerful "weapons," not as insignificant epiphenomena.[31] Nor does it necessarily mean that ideas are not instrumentalized to realize other ends that are equally ideological.

RESOLVING VALUE CONFLICTS . . .

The theory of partisan preferences is not enough on its own to develop empirical expectations for party positions and government behavior since values can conflict. The recognition that inclusiveness, antimilitarism, and multilateralism can serve as both means and ends helps to develop better expectations for party positions and behavior when they are confronted with issues that expose difficult trade-offs, as is the case for the left in both of the empirical phenomena under study. Military intervention for humanitarian purposes forces leftist parties to choose between their interests in antimilitarism on the one hand and promoting human rights or multilateral defense cooperation under the framework of European institutions on the other.

Psychological researchers argue that the key to understanding how and whether politicians make value trade-offs depends on what is known as their *level of differentiation,* measured by the number of dimensions that actors take into account when determining their positions on particular issues.[32] This concept applies not to the content, but to the structure of beliefs, although differences in the latter can lead to diametrically opposed policy choices. A lack of differentiation is evident when actors adopt a single rule for determining their positions on a policy, avoiding value tradeoffs.

Less differentiated leftist party members judge military interventions and multilateral cooperation in defense only along the antimilitarist continuum.

30. Krasner calls this using ideas as "hooks." See Stephen D. Krasner, "Westphalia and All That," in Judith Goldstein and Robert Keohane (eds.), *Ideas and Foreign Policy: Beliefs, Institutions, and Political Change* (Ithaca: Cornell University Press, 1993), p. 257. For the constructivist dissent, see Mark M. Blyth, " 'Any More Bright Ideas?' The Ideational Turn of Comparative Political Economy," *Comparative Politics*, Vol. 29, No. 2 (1997), pp. 229–250. For an example of the instrumentalization of ideas, see Ido Oren, "The Subjectivity of the 'Democratic' Peace," *International Security*, Vol. 20, No. 2 (1995), pp. 147–184.

31. Carr (1964), p. 68; Morgenthau (1954), p. 82. See also Jack Snyder, *Myths of Empire: Domestic Politics and International Ambition* (Ithaca: Cornell University Press, 1991).

32. This is sometimes called "cognitive complexity," which has the unfortunate implication that those who differentiate less are less intelligent. This is not necessarily the case. Philip E. Tetlock, "Learning in U.S. and Soviet Foreign Policy: In Search of an Elusive Concept," in George W. Breslauer and Philip E. Tetlock (eds.), *Learning in U.S. and Soviet Foreign Policy* (Boulder: Westview Press, 1991), pp. 20–61. Philip E. Tetlock, "Monitoring the Integrative Complexity of American and Soviet Policy Rhetoric: What Can Be Learned?" *Journal of Social Issues*, Vol. 44, No. 2 (1988), p. 103.

They reject all actual and potential uses of force and the institutional means to carry them out. They determine their position by simply asking whether the military will be engaged. Their arguments use the spiral model. They claim that all military operations escalate, a position that allows them to deny the existence of a value conflict since intervention would have been ineffective. For such leftists, pacifism is not only a means but also an end in itself.

More differentiated individuals and parties use more ideological dimensions to help them make their choice. They take into account the inclusivist-exclusivist and the unilateralist-multilateralist dimension, evaluating the purpose for which force will be used or situating European cooperation in defense matters in the larger integration process that they support. They ask themselves not only whether the military will be involved, but also whether the goal for which force is being applied is consistent with their inclusive conception of the national interest.[33] They become more pragmatic, approaching each military intervention on a case-by-case basis, taking into account attributes of what "interactionist" psychologists call the strategic *situation* as well as their antimilitarist disposition.[34] They also recognize the necessity of maintaining institutions to perform such operations. They sincerely regret the need for peace enforcement, as they share a commitment to antimilitarism that is evident in their position on other issues, such as arms control. However, they believe in some instances it is a necessary means to an end. This position is accompanied by the use of deterrence and compellence language as a marker of their commitment though not a hawkish disposition.

The right is presented with a value conflict as well, but it is not as severe. Even if peace enforcement is not in the national interest, once national troops are committed a nation's credibility and prestige are implicated. Failure might indicate a lack of resolve in other, more vital aspects of foreign policy. The country must finish what it started. These concerns are more important to rightist parties because they are dispositionally hawkish. An undifferentiated approach to peace enforcement leads rightist politicians to simply consider an operation along the inclusivist-exclusivist continuum, rejecting military missions that do not affect tangible national interests. The more differentiated position for the right incorporates the hawk-dove dimension. This leads

33. Jentleson and Britton stress this as the most important factor for determining public support as well. Bruce Jentleson and Rebecca L. Britton, "Still Pretty Prudent: Post–Cold War American Public Opinion on the Use of Force," *Journal of Conflict Resolution*, Vol. 42, No. 4 (1998), pp. 395–418.

34. On this distinction, see Richard K. Herrmann, Philip E. Tetlock, and Penny S. Visser, "Mass Public Decisions to Go to War: A Cognitive-Interactionist Framework," *American Political Science Review*, Vol. 93, No. 3 (1999), pp. 522–524.

to a more interventionist position even in humanitarian cases, although the timing of support differs from that of the left. Rightists generally do not support peace enforcement at the beginning. However, once enforcement is underway, those politicians who differentiate more will fall in line beyond the armed forces.

Of course, there are countless other, nonideological dimensions that individuals and parties can consider when determining their position on a humanitarian operation. For instance, they can judge whether it will be costly or cheap, feasible or hopeless. It is my empirical finding, however, that for each individual case of humanitarian intervention, different beliefs as to the likelihood of success and other factors that might enter into a decision-making calculus are largely determined by an individual's position on the ideological spectrum. In other words, values are causally prior.

. . . At the Country Level

While there are leftist antimilitarists and interventionists in each country, historical experience determines the overall balance between pragmatists and ideologues on the use of force. In countries where coercive foreign policy means are seen to have in the past helped realize inclusive goals, leftist parties generally regard the military as an instrument that can (but will not necessarily) serve their version of the national interest. These parties in countries with what I will call a "positive" experience with the use of force generally support peace enforcement and European defense cooperation. Positive historical experiences also provide leftist parties with the endurance they need to escalate militarily if the initial application of force is ineffective. In countries in which force has negative associations and has only served as a vehicle for narrower, exclusive purposes, leftists by and large consider antimilitarism an end in itself and inconsistent with other inclusive goals such as promoting human rights. In these instances of a "negative" experience with the use of force, they oppose all interventions.

In all the countries under study, the touchstone was the Second World War. Crudely stated, for the victors, even though as much a battle for survival as for principle, it provided a salient example of how force was and is sometimes necessary for battling aggressors who seek to spread an antidemocratic ideology antagonistic to human rights. For the losing country, it created a visceral connection between war and terrible destruction and crimes against humanity. The countries studied in this book are the polar extremes. In the conclusion, I discuss more ambiguous cases. It is important to note that history does not present itself objectively but is the product of a kind of negotiation over time. For instance in France, the lesson of its initial defeat and subsequent collaboration could easily have led to the conclusion that force should not remain an instrument of foreign policy. De Gaulle's achievement was to restore a feeling of pride and efficacy to his humiliated country. His country's humiliation led him to frame historical experience. Nor is history's function that of an all-purpose analogy.[35] Leftist parties in the victorious Allied countries do not apply the Munich example to all instances of conflict. They merely draw from it the possibility of using force for something they believe in.

Therefore, in Britain, and (due to de Gaulle's efforts) France, where the use of force had more positive associations, an inclusive left was more willing to commit national resources to promote domestic values abroad in Bosnia and Kosovo. Its multilateralism also enabled it to support European defense cooperation. Antimilitarist ideology, more powerful in Germany than the left's inclusive inclinations, held that all uses of military force were inherently escalatory and ill suited to preventing human rights violations. Antimilitarism was also more important than the left's multilateralist leanings, leading it to oppose creating military structures that would make the European Union capable of intervening in such conflicts.

With a more exclusive conception of the national interest, parties of the right do not face the same value conflicts, at least at the outset of armed conflict for humanitarian purposes. Although they have less difficulty resorting to arms, they do not conceive of these types of operations as necessary, at least in countries not tangibly affected by such conflicts. Humanitarian intervention and multilateral cooperation in defense affairs present the right not with a challenge but with an opportunity. As will be shown, rightist governments in both Germany and France used the intervention in Bosnia instrumentally to achieve other ideological purposes.[36] The German right used humanitarian and multilateral justifications to increase German involvement in military operations so as to make the use of force "normal" again. In addition, the right was affected by the prospect of refugee inflows and fears about regional stability due to Germany's geographical proximity to Bosnia (although the left was not). The French right instrumentalized humanitarian operations

35. Yuen Foong Khong, *Analogies at War: Korea, Munich, Dien Bien Phu, and the Vietnam Decisions of 1965* (Princeton: Princeton University Press, 1992).

36. Some might object that the possibility of instrumentalization makes it difficult to falsify the argument. If the right intervenes in a humanitarian crisis, self-interested motivations can always be mustered to explain the anomaly. I set the bar high, however. The possible instrumental motivations I point to are either well-established factors in a country's history (such as the influence of Gaullism) and therefore decidedly not ad hoc, or those that resonate with the basic ideological values that drive the right (such as the desire to have a free hand to deploy a state's armed forces). Ultimately, the true test is the empirical evidence. The fact that I find the same instrumental factors at play consistently within each country in both the Balkans and European Security and Defense Policy (ESDP) cases, and also in other countries such as Japan, suggests that they are highly significant.

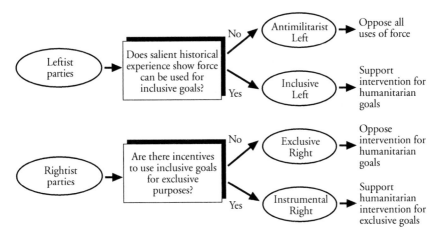

Figure 1. Historical experience and political party positions on humanitarian intervention

and European defense cooperation as part of a new twist on an old Gaullist ideological goal of promoting France's international standing. Participation in multilateral military operations for instrumental purposes, however, means a shallower commitment. This fact became clear in both cases when, in the case of France, costs rose, or in the case of Germany, when the party completed its normalization project.

The argument is summarized in Figure 1. The final outcome, support for or opposition to humanitarian intervention, is meant broadly to also encompass positions on building European institutions to undertake these operations. This is a different role for history than that foreseen by the culturalists reviewed above. The experiences considered so critical for defining political culture do not stifle foreign policy discussion. Instead they help frame the debate differently in each country. History is crucial for understanding along which of the foreign policy continua the partisan battle will be fought. It parochializes the domestic discussion. Culturalists should be credited for bringing to light the importance of the past for the present, and history plays a role in all the cases that follow. However, as David Laitin writes, "Culture instills not values to be upheld but rather points of concern to be debated."[37] In Germany, the fight over humanitarian intervention, at least initially, pitted an antimilitarist left against a more hawkish right. The German experience with militarism made intervention more controversial rather than less. "No such passion and vehemence were provoked in any other NATO

37. David Laitin, "Political Culture and Political Preferences," *American Political Science Review,* Vol. 82, No. 2 (1988), p. 589. I should stress that my use of the word "parochial" is not meant pejoratively. I am using the concept to make an empirical rather than a normative distinction.

country whose troops were to be deployed," observe Andrei Markovits and Simon Reich.[38] In Britain, and to a lesser extent, France, an inclusive left did battle with a more reluctant and exclusive right that questioned the extent to which national interests were at stake in the Balkans. In this way, the argument resembles the classic formulation by Seymour M. Lipset and Stein Rokkan on domestic political cleavages in European society.[39] Particular historical experiences at critical junctures such as the Reformation or the Industrial Revolution structure partisan divides along different axes.

. . . At the Individual Level

Differentiation also has determinants at the individual and party levels. Three elements are crucial for determining an individual's and a party's level of differentiation in the aggregate. As individual members, factions or parties as a whole move to either extreme of the political spectrum, they become less willing and able to make value trade-offs because they hold on to values more intensely.[40] While pragmatists and ideologues might share a common ideology that puts them on the left or right side of the political spectrum, it is more painful for more extremist politicians to admit contradictions.[41]

Second, those actively engaged in issues of foreign and defense policy, such as members of parliamentary committees devoted to international affairs, are more likely to demonstrate a capacity for differentiation than those who are not.[42] All parties have speakers for and experts on foreign and defense policy who are more actively involved in international affairs than other party members. Their in-depth consideration of topical issues

38. See Andrei Markovits and Simon Reich, *The German Predicament: Memory and Power in the New Europe* (Ithaca: Cornell University Press, 1997), p. 11.

39. Seymour M. Lipset and Stein Rokkan, "Cleavage Structures, Party Systems, and Voter Alignments: An Introduction," in S. M. Lipset and S. Rokkan (eds.), *Party Systems and Voter Alignments: Cross-National Perspectives* (New York: Free Press, 1967).

40. Tetlock (1988), p 107. Putnam argues that cognitively complex characteristics are found in more "pragmatic," as opposed to "ideological" politicians, a concept identical to Tetlock's. Centrist and extreme wings of a party would differ in terms of their ideological "style," or how they pursue their policy goals, rather than in the goals themselves. See Putnam (1973), p. 5.

41. Some also argue that those on particular sides of the political spectrum are more capable of learning. Tetlock (1988) holds that center-left politicians are more capable of learning than rightist politicians, while Carr (1964) argues the opposite, claiming that "radicals" are wide-eyed idealists without the clarity to see international relations for the dangerous game it is. I argue instead that the strength of those beliefs, not the substance, is what is important.

42. Cognitive psychologists argue that individuals with more knowledge about a subject have a better appreciation for the conditions under which particular principles apply. See Paul Sniderman, Philip E. Tetlock, and Laurel Elms, "Public Opinion and Democratic Politics: The Problem of Non-Attitudes and the Social Construction of Political Judgment," in James Kuklinski (ed.), *Citizens and Politics: Perspectives from Political Psychology* (New York: Cambridge University Press, 1999), pp. 254–288; Herrmann et al. (1999).

makes them more likely to appraise each case individually rather than adopt standard rules. Experts will evaluate issues along several different dimensions before they form a position. Their attention to detail also makes them more likely to recognize the trade-offs sometimes demanded among competing values. This is true regardless of their substantive ideological starting points.

Third, differentiation will increase as individuals move from the party grassroots to the parliament, and within parties as a whole as they move from opposition into government. This is because as individuals and parties make these transitions, they are more politically accountable for their positions.[43] They therefore see the need to anticipate all potential shortcomings, which requires a careful weighing of advantages and disadvantages. Differentiation is most advanced among individuals and parties in office because international policies have direct consequences for those in other countries. Whether the government acts militarily or not, it is accountable for the outcome that follows. More thorough reviews of policy will result.

. . . Over Time

The model is not completely static, however. First, parties adjust their positions in response to changing geopolitical circumstances. The end of the Cold War was a decisive break that required new strategies to meet old objectives, particularly for the right in France and Germany. These structural changes do not account for change over the course of the 1990s, however. Second, the content of leftist and rightist political programs changes over time, as a part of society's normative evolution. Specific politicians sometimes act as entrepreneurs, drawing attention to new issues and linking them to party values where no connection previously existed. In France, for example, the question of humanitarian intervention was first identified as a leftist issue by a smaller group within the Socialist Party. Third, policy change can occur when events seem to expose shortcomings in previously held beliefs, a process that some scholars identify as learning.[44]

Belief systems are highly resistant to reevaluation and change, as individuals tend to interpret experience so as to conform to their value structures. Events must be truly tumultuous to have an effect, such as wars, revolutions, and economic depressions. A number of factors make policy

43. Philip E. Tetlock, "Accountability and Complexity of Thought," *Journal of Personality and Social Psychology*, Vol. 45 (1983), pp. 74–83. I combine Tetlock's (1988) hypotheses that complex thought increases as politicians enter into the executive branch and into the majority in the legislature, an argument that is constructed with the U.S. system in mind. See p. 107.

44. Jack S. Levy, "Learning and Foreign Policy: Sweeping a Conceptual Minefield," *International Organization*, Vol. 48, No. 2 (1994), p. 283.

change more likely. First, politicians learn more from failures than successes.[45] Second, politicians learn more from their own personal experiences
than from those of others. Vicarious experience is generally not enough to
induce belief change.[46] For this reason, the Second World War had different effects. For France, the United States, and Britain in particular, it
provided a positive example of using force to realize objectives the left could
support. In Germany it instilled a belief in the hopelessness of all war. Third,
policy change is more likely when a new and appealing replacement policy
is readily available.[47]

For the antimilitarist left, Bosnia had all of these elements. The Europeans
and Americans eventually found a diplomatic solution to the conflict but not
before over two hundred thousand people lost their lives, many as a result of
ethnic cleansing massacres, all despite the presence of the largest United
Nations peacekeeping operation in history. For the Europeans in particular,
that failure was even more bitter because they were on the ground and invested
in the conflict. Even ordinary parliamentarians made frequent trips to the
region and saw the conflict firsthand. It received an extraordinary amount of
television coverage. This made the atrocities even more vivid for the antimilitarist left than those in Rwanda where a UN force was only belatedly sent,
with just a small European contribution, the media intensity was much less
intense, and the conflict was much further away. The choice not to intervene
in Rwanda can of course also be partly attributed to the previous failure at
peace enforcement in Somalia.[48] Following Bosnia and the Srebrenica massacre in particular, the antimilitarist left could turn to a new policy of inter-
ventionism based on human rights that was equally in line with its ideological
values, even if it marked a 180-degree turn.

Change does not occur uniformly across parties, however. It is led by those
more disposed towards differentiation in the first place: foreign and defense
policy experts, moderates, and governing leaders. Political psychologists note
that more differentiated thinkers are more capable of adjusting their beliefs
to lessons drawn from new experiences.[49] They are more capable of incorpo-
rating new information because they are more accountable in the case of party
and government leaders, find it less painful in the case of the moderates, or

45. Dan Reiter, "Learning, Realism and Alliances: The Weight of the Shadow of the Past," *World Politics,* Vol. 46, No. 4 (1994), pp. 490–526; Levy (1994), pp. 304–306.

46. Levy (1994), p. 305; Reiter (1994), p. 494.

47. Jeffrey Legro, "The Transformation of Policy Ideas," *American Journal of Political Science,* Vol. 44, No. 3 (2000), pp. 419–432.

48. Michael Barnett, *Eyewitness to a Genocide: The United Nations and Rwanda* (Ithaca: Cornell University Press, 2002).

49. Janice Gross Stein, "Political Learning by Doing: Gorbachev as Uncommitted Thinker and Motivated Learner," *International Organization,* Vol. 48, No. 2 (1994), pp. 163–166; Tetlock (1991).

are exposed to it more often in the case of the experts. This type of learning should not be confused with a more accurate reading of the geopolitical environment. These politicians did not find *the* answer to dealing with ethnic conflicts. NATO tried to use force the next time in the Balkans with meager success at the outset, which provided another learning experience. If subsequent events confirm antimilitarist fears about spiraling conflicts, parties and individuals can decrease their differentiation level as well. Those on the extreme left, without extensive experience in foreign affairs, or not in the senior leadership of the party are the first to turn back to their old positions.

THE RESEARCH DESIGN

Empirical Expectations: The Partisan Policy-Seeking Argument versus the Cultural and Office-Seeking Arguments

In this section, I tease out propositions that can be used to test opposing claims, focusing first on the contrast between partisan and culturalist theories and second on differences between office-seeking and policy-seeking theories. Culturalists make behavioral predictions on the issues of humanitarian intervention and European defense policy at the levels of both the party and the state. The relative merits of these expectations can be evaluated by their ability to account for (1) cross-sectional variation across the party spectrum within each country, (2) longitudinal variation in government policy over time within each country, and (3) cross-national differences in government policy. The units of analysis for (1) are all parties represented in parliament and the factions within them; for (2), parties in power; and for (3), countries. Table 1 provides a summary.

Table 1 Empirical expectations: The party ideology versus the culturalist argument

	Party ideology	Culturalists
Cross-sectional variation in party positions	*Divergence* between major centrist parties	*Convergence* between major centrist parties
Cross-temporal variation in national behavior	*Vacillation* over time	*Consistency* over time
Cross-national variation in national behavior	*Varying* national differences	*Stable* national differences

Cultural explanations of foreign policy are structural. Parties operate under constraints that prevent them from articulating and implementing contrasting policies. Room for political agency is limited. Therefore, culturalists expect convergence in political party positions on these issues within each country—at least among the major centrist parties, as they share common historical experiences. The partisan argument expects divergences based on the foreign policy typology developed above. Leftist parties are policy-seekers that pursue an antimilitarist, multilateralist, and inclusive agenda. When they are confronted with value conflicts, those who deny them will be drawn from more extremist factions and parties. They will oppose the use of force even for humanitarian purposes and therefore also any multilateral institutions designed for this purpose. The relative balance between antimilitarists and interventionists will be determined by a country's history with force. In Britain and France, the left as a whole will be more interventionist than in Germany. It will be more inclined to escalate in the case of initial failure and to support European defense cooperation. Excluding the antimilitarist left, willingness to contemplate stronger military measures will increase toward the left side of the political spectrum as the intensity of preferences increases.

Rightist parties, in contrast, pursue a more hawkish, unilateralist, and exclusive agenda. They will largely oppose humanitarian intervention, particularly peace enforcement, although members of these parties more inclined toward differentiation will change their minds when their country's reputation is at stake. They will have serious concerns about sovereignty. These two tendencies will increase toward the right side of the political spectrum. To the extent that rightist parties depart from these expectations, they do so in order to instrumentalize foreign policy ideas for narrower purposes. However, their behavior will show that their commitment to inclusiveness and multilateralism is shallower than that of the left.

Cultural arguments expect consistency in government policy across time within each country. The constraining effects of culture are stable across government turnovers. The partisan argument expects vacillations in line with the theory of foreign policy preferences. Parties both articulate and attempt to implement their alternative foreign policy agendas. Finally, culturalists expect stable national differences in government policy. France, driven by a Gaullist consensus on increasing France's influence on world affairs, should be consistently the most interventionist and the most supportive of European defense cooperation. Germany, culturally hesitant to use force, should be the least interventionist but the most integrationist. Britain, a former great power somewhat less sure of its role, falls somewhat behind France in terms of intervention but is implacably opposed to European defense cooperation. In stark contrast, the partisan argument expects national differences to vary over time, depending on who is governing.

Office-seeking and policy-seeking motivations are extremely difficult to disentangle. In those cases in which both arguments expect the same

Table 2 Empirical expectations: Office-seeking versus policy-seeking

	Office-seeking	Policy-seeking
Opportunities for opportunism	Seized regardless of policy consequences	Only take advantage of opponents when disagreements emerge over policy
Policy change	Parties change policies primarily to win elections	Parties change policies when they do not correspond to values
Who leads?	Party leadership	Experts, moderates, and politicians in office
How do they justify it?	Electoral necessity	Staying true to core values
When do they change?	Prior to elections	After events that threaten ideological coherence
Effect of institutions	Directly determine preferences by exposing government to sanctions	Constrain opportunities for voice by parlimentary parties and coalition partners
Presidential	Most interventionist	Presidential prerogative
Parliamentary	Less interventionist	Depends on governing party ideology
Coalitional	Least interventionist	Balance struck between major and minor party in government

behavior, I rely on in-depth interviewing to establish motivations. However, I also offer several ways of testing these arguments against each other on the basis of different behavioral expectations (see Table 2). First, if parties are motivated primarily by the desire to win and maintain themselves in office, this means that they will take advantage of their rivals in periods of difficulty, even if it might bring about unwelcome policy changes. For instance, if the opposition does not pledge support to the government, the latter may be pulled further in the direction of its more extreme wing. Policy-seekers, on the other hand, will not sacrifice policy goals for political gain.

Second, policy change provides another opportunity to differentiate among these motivations. The most prominent example of policy change in this book is the gradual acceptance of peace enforcement and European defense cooperation by the antimilitarist left. For office-seeking theorists, if parties change their policies, it is with the expectation that in so doing they will reap electoral windfalls. In the policy-seeking view, such changes are a response to a perceived lack of correspondence between policies and ideological values, a recognition most often triggered by events that seem to expose contradictions in belief systems.

I use three indicators to distinguish between office-seeking and policy-seeking change. First, *when* does change occur? Office-seeking arguments expect parties to be more sensitive to voter concerns immediately prior to elections if there is an incentive to shift policies. In contrast, among leftist parties, I expect change in a pro-intervention and pro–defense cooperation direction when events demonstrate the ineffectiveness of peaceful methods of conflict resolution. When these new hopes prove unfounded, however, leftist parties have a reason to revert to their antimilitarist position.

Second, *who* leads the process in favor of peace enforcement and developing institutions to conduct it? Among leftist parties, it will be led by those more highly predisposed toward recognizing and accepting value trade-offs. Above I identified moderates and experts as less likely to deny such conflicts. In addition, accountability means leftists should be more inclined toward peace enforcement and European defense cooperation after they move from opposition into government. Office-seeking theorists expect the party leadership to be the driver of the process as it benefits the most from being elected.

Third and finally, *how* do converts to intervention justify their change in position? The office-seeking argument expects parties to justify new positions on the basis of their electoral consequences, at least privately. Interventionists would argue that supporting humanitarian military operations and European defense cooperation are necessary as part of a broader move toward the political center. In contrast, the policy-seeking argument expects interventionists to defend these policies as being in keeping with party values in light of new information.

Office-seeking theories also expect behavior to reflect the institutional conditions in which governments operate, in particular whether they face sanctions that threaten their ability to stay in power in case of foreign policy failure. Parties fear losing office. Although based on a different logic, these expectations of stable cross-national differences are identical to those in the cultural argument. France, due to its presidential system, will be the most interventionist, regardless of the party in power. Britain's parliamentary system will make the government more cautious as a misstep could provoke the backbenches. Coalitional governments in Germany make the executive branch even more hesitant. There is no explicit office-seeking theory of European integration although it is implicit in intergovernmentalism, since the theory is based on a pluralist model of interest aggregation in which governments implement the policies that powerful societal groups prefer. Presumably they do this to curry favor with those groups and remain in power—at least, no other rationale is provided by the theory. In the case of defense cooperation, intergovernmentalists presume that this interest group is society itself.[50] They

---

50. Andrew Moravcsik, *A Choice for Europe: Social Purpose and State Power from Messina to Maastricht* (Ithaca: Cornell University Press, 1999).

would maintain that any departure from the national consensus on European defense could cost parties dearly at the polls. Electoral and cultural concerns work in tandem.

In contrast, the policy-seeking argument foresees variations in national behavior based on the extent to which institutions offer opportunities for politicians to voice the preferences I hypothesized earlier. In parliamentary systems, parties will be able to more effectively push their governments in the direction they prefer, which will depend on their ideological point of view. In coalition governments, the voices of minor parties will also have to be considered, which could just as easily make such governments more rather than less interventionist. In presidential systems, heads of state will be able to ignore parliaments and their own parties to a greater degree than in Westminster systems. However, this does not mean that presidents will be more forceful in humanitarian interventions than prime ministers. Nevertheless, in cases in which the former try to buck their own parties, departures from the party line will provoke significant, if ultimately ineffective, outcries.

Different derivations of office-seeking arguments are tested in each chapter. In Britain, I am able to assess the degree to which parties exploit their opponents' weaknesses, particularly in the case of the extremely weak Major government. In Germany, I weigh the relative ability of electoral considerations to explain policy change. In France, I consider whether the lower exposure of the executive branch to voter sanctions in case of failure makes it more interventionist than in other countries.

Case Selection

The choice of Germany, Britain, and France provides adequate cross-national cultural and institutional variation on the independent variables to appraise the counterarguments. In all three countries, there were governments of the left and the right during the time period under investigation, which allows for an evaluation of cross-temporal change. For this reason, the United States was excluded, since the Republicans were in office for only two years of the Balkans crises and not during the period that receives most attention.[51] I do, however, treat the United States in chapter 7. Selecting three smaller powers also provides a more difficult test for the argument, as their foreign policies are generally regarded as highly circumscribed by systemic constraints, particularly by how the United States defines its interests. This makes the success of the partisan hypothesis that much stronger. They

51. In addition, since the United States is not a member of the EU and not a party to the negotiations over ESDP, adding it would add an imbalance to the investigation. Also, the American story has been told by numerous firsthand observers. See chapter 7.

are also considered to have much stronger and more restrictive political cultures than the United States. The latter has been marked by struggles between an exclusive, often isolationist, right and an inclusive internationalist left throughout the century.

The empirical cases of intervention under study are Bosnia and Kosovo, although I refer to others to the extent they are necessary to establish a partisan pattern in each national case. Bosnia and Kosovo are the most striking examples of an increasing number of multilateral military operations for humanitarian purposes driven predominantly by moral concerns. Although such operations have been arguably the most salient security issue in the immediate post–Cold War period, they have received very little theoretical attention. The mission in Bosnia was the largest in the UN's history, involving almost forty thousand troops, and the air campaign against Serbia was the first major operation in NATO's fifty-year existence. Adding the negotiations on European defense cooperation allows for another demonstration of the applicability of the argument as well as providing insights into the EU's first steps toward becoming a major political player. I dissect all the cases into smaller subcases so as to increase the number of observations and better enable the establishment of definitive patterns.[52] This also increases variation in the dependent variable. For instance, at various points in the Bosnian conflict the preferences of some states in the peace operation can be characterized as "nonintervention," at least in terms of peace enforcement.

Claims can be made that Bosnia and Kosovo are too different to adequately compare or that they are not independent observations. The international community was much less forceful in its dealings with the Bosnian Serbs, at a time when the three European powers were all at some point led by rightist governments, than with the Yugoslavian Serbs, when leftist governments were in power. Bosnia, it could be argued, was more of an intractable situation and the United States was less interested in helping, at least until summer 1995. The left also benefited from the experience gained in Bosnia. Nevertheless, these problems can be managed by establishing partisan patterns of propensity to intervene consistent across cases, even if parties, countries, and the West as a whole were more hesitant in Bosnia than in Kosovo. For instance, if the right in a particular country was less willing than the left to engage in enforcement in both Bosnia *and* Kosovo, I can establish that a partisan divide existed.

In terms of cross-national comparison, constraints existed but were common to all sides so that variation can be attributed to partisan factors.

52. On the use of this strategy of case multiplication, see Gary King, Robert O. Keohane, and Sidney Verba, *Designing Social Inquiry: Scientific Inference in Qualitative Research* (Princeton: Princeton University Press, 1994).

U.S. reluctance to send ground troops into Bosnia created an asymmetry in the risk of retaliation if air power were to be used that sometimes fostered transatlantic frictions with the British and French, as I discuss in the conclusion. Despite this common restraint, however, Britain and France responded very differently. The same can be said of the role of the military and the UN. Both the French and British armed forces and the UN Secretariat were pushing central decision-makers away from peace enforcement, but this cannot explain the variation in outcome. The governments knew that the military and the UN were being less than forthright about what was possible on the ground. They discounted this when they wanted to follow a tougher line, and hid behind it when they did not. This does not mean that UN preferences in Bosnia were not important for deciding for instance when to use air strikes to protect peacekeepers. However, the decision by troop contributors to partially delegate to the UN secretary general the authority to call in NATO fighter planes was made consciously to make air strikes less likely. The authority was later usurped when national positions on intervention changed.

It should be pointed out that the argument is not meant to provide a comprehensive theory of humanitarian military intervention capable of predicting government action in all cases precisely, although it surely helps. Numerous other factors intrude into the decision-making calculus such as the ferocity of the fighting, troop availability, or whether countries contemplating involvement have recently had their hands burned in previous conflicts.[53] I merely intend to show that parties articulate different enough policies to make for very different international outcomes, keeping in mind that other factors might militate across the political spectrum against intervention.[54]

The key questions, i.e. the dependent variables, for each case are somewhat different, although in both instances they boil down to the willingness of particular parties and governments to use force. In Bosnia, I decipher who was willing to consider military action at the beginning of the conflict and later when a strategy of conciliation and diplomacy had not succeeded in stemming the Bosnian Serb tide. The Bosnian war began when the Bosnian Serbs, fearful of becoming a minority in the former Yugoslavian province follow-

---

53. See for instance Patrick Regan, *Civil Wars and Foreign Powers: Outside Intervention in Intrastate Conflict* (Ann Arbor: University of Michigan Press, 2000).

54. Nevertheless, there is nothing particularly surprising in the patterns of responses by leftist and rightist parties to other ethnic conflicts. In Rwanda, for instance, the U.S. Democrats were deterred from intervention by the fact that they had tried peace enforcement in Somalia, over the objections of Republicans, with disastrous results. The British Conservatives were already in deeper in Bosnia than they wished to be. The French Gaullists and President Mitterrand used the intervention for public relations purposes, but made no real commitment to stopping the genocide. In the latter two cases, governments were heavily criticized by leftist parliamentary parties, but the opposition groups had no voice in policy.

ing the secession of Croatia and Slovenia, began an offensive with Serbian help to seize territory in spring 1992, with a view toward joining these ethically cleansed gains to what remained of Serb-dominated Yugoslavia.[55] By early 1993, they controlled over 70 percent of Bosnian territory, and with this strong negotiating hand they consistently thwarted efforts by the EU and the UN to negotiate a political solution with Bosnian Croats and Muslims.[56]

The United Nations Protection Force (UNPROFOR), composed of national forces under UN military command, was initially sent to escort and use "all necessary means" to defend humanitarian convoys providing aid to suffering civilians in areas of fighting. At the same time, these "blue helmets" were deployed under a peacekeeping resolution that stipulated that they were supposed to remain impartial in the conflict as a whole. It was passed under Chapter VI of the UN Charter, not Chapter VII, which permits enforcement tasks. The force was increasingly ineffective in the face of Bosnian Serb intransigence, and the UN Security Council added growing numbers of enforcement tasks directed primarily against the Bosnian Serbs. The key question is: How did various parties and governments respond to this deterrence failure? Who wanted to increase the mandate of UNPROFOR to include peace enforcement, or thought that the mandate already allowed and required such action?

In Kosovo, I investigate both the initial willingness of particular parties to use force against Yugoslavia as well as to contemplate a potentially very costly escalation following the initial failure to expel Yugoslav forces from Kosovo. In 1998, Yugoslav president Slobodan Milosevic began a crackdown on the Albanian civilian population in Kosovo, which was struggling for independence, causing tens of thousands to flee their homes. Following a series of ultimatums and failed negotiations, NATO began a full-scale air campaign against Serb-dominated Yugoslavia in March 1999. Milosevic responded brutally with a massive and seemingly systematically planned military sweep that forced over three-quarters of the Albanian population out of their villages, with roughly 800,000 seeking refuge in neighboring countries and another 500,000 internally displaced in Kosovo by the end of April. A key question is how did parties and governments respond to this compellence failure? Who favored increasing the pressure by accelerating bombing or using ground forces?

Sources and Measurement

I use a combination of public and private sources for measuring independent and dependent variables and establishing the causal mechanism. The

---

55. The most thorough account of the war is Steven L. Burg and Paul S. Shoup, *The War in Bosnia-Herzegovina* (London: M. E. Sharpe, 1999).

56. On the peace process, see David Owen, *Balkan Odyssey* (San Diego: Harcourt Brace, 1995).

public material I rely upon is overwhelmingly drawn from primary sources, including parliamentary debates, government statements, and party platforms and resolutions. The types of sources available are themselves functions of important independent variables in the study. In France, the relative insulation of foreign policy from the National Assembly means that there is a very small parliamentary record compared to that in Britain and Germany, a shortcoming made up for by reliance on public statements reported in the press. In these instances I rely on politicians' comments themselves, not their subsequent interpretation in the reports. In addition, the French Foreign Ministry, eager to demonstrate the importance of French contributions to world affairs, provides a record of ministers' statements more comprehensive than those available for the other countries.

Documenting national foreign policy preferences as to multilateral military operations and the creation of structures for performing such missions cannot be done with public sources alone. One cannot infer a single country's preference from the outcome of the negotiations or the actions taken by NATO or the UN as both require consensus. There is a natural tendency for governments to stress publicly that they are in agreement with their alliance and negotiation partners so as to demonstrate solidarity vis-à-vis an adversary. Party preferences in multiparty governments are also difficult to ascertain because coalitions often feel the same need to present a unified front. Electoral concerns also influence the extent to which real positions are revealed. Quite often I found that the need to maintain party, coalitional, or international consensus obscured very different positions, some of which are only first uncovered in this book. Motivations are also sometimes veiled. Parties that instrumentalize interventions do not trumpet their true efforts. Even when motives are more straightforward, the causal process—from party ideology, filtered through historical experience, to party or government position—is also difficult to see.

For these reasons, matching public with private sources was critical to measuring independent and dependent variables and tracing the causal process. This project is based to a great extent on roughly a hundred in-depth interviews conducted between May 2000 and August 2001 with senior politicians, diplomats, and military officers including former foreign and defense ministers, heads of the armed services, ambassadors to NATO and the United Nations, and foreign and defense policy spokespersons of political parties. Special care was taken to find subjects close to the decision-making process so as to ensure they were offering more than mere opinions. I was also able to gain access to the private minutes of numerous opposition political parties, which provided a window into the considerations that went into both policy determination and policy change.

Public sources are nevertheless extremely useful in measuring both the independent and the dependent variables. Regarding the latter, the deterrence literature has argued that words are extremely important because public statements send signals of resolve to adversaries. Rational choice scholars have noted the deterrent effect of public proclamations of determination in democracies. By drawing attention to crises, democracies raise the costs of potential failure, thereby signaling their resolve to their opponents.[57] Consequently, strong public statements do give an indication of the commitment of a country to peace enforcement. Talk is not cheap. The converse is also true. Being irresolute in public statements undermines credibility. I can therefore partially measure preferences, the dependent variable, by analyzing language. Arguing in spiral model terms by expressing fears of a cycle of violence indicates a lack of resolve, while using deterrence and compellence concepts such as credibility and signaling show the opposite. Given that rightist parties have a hawkish and leftist parties a dovish disposition, when the former adopt spiral and the latter compellence/deterrence argumentation, this is extremely revealing.

So far as independent variables are concerned, I utilize numerous indicators to place parties and individuals along a left-right spectrum. First, I rely on a qualitative reading of the domestic policy party programs in manifestos, since measuring ideology on the basis of foreign policy positions would of course be tautological. Second, I tested the reliability of my judgments with numerous quantitative measures.[58]

Parties are arrayed from left to right as follows:

- Britain: Labour, Liberal Democrats, and Conservatives.
- France: Communists, Greens, Socialists, Union for French Democracy (UDF), Rally for the Republic (RPR), and National Front.[59]
- Germany: Party for Democratic Socialism (PDS), Greens, Social Democrats (SPD), Free Democrats (FDP), Christian Democratic Union (CDU), and Christian Social Union (CSU).

For individuals, I identify their membership in particular factions of the party through profiles, self-identification and self-conceptualization of the meaning of "left" and "right," or categorization as such by other members

57. James Fearon, "Domestic Political Audiences and the Escalation of International Disputes," *American Political Science Review*, Vol. 88, No. 3 (1994), pp. 577–592.

58. Francis Castles and Peter Mair, "Left-Right Political Scales: Some Expert Judgments, *European Journal of Political Research*, Vol. 12 (1984), pp. 73–88; John D. Huber, "Values and Partisanship in Left-Right Orientations: Measuring Ideology," *European Journal of Political Research*, Vol. 17 (1989), pp. 599–621; Laver and Hunt (1992).

59. Recently the vast majority of the UDF and RPR have merged in a new party, the Union for a Popular Movement (UMP).

of their parties.[60] Parties in all cases use these labels to describe themselves and others. So as to ensure that my understanding of "left" and "right" echoed with the parties' own understanding, I consistently asked in interviews how politicians understood the meaning of these terms. Individuals on the left or right wings of the parties are referred to as "left-wingers" or "right-wingers," not to be confused with "leftists" and "rightists" or "the left" and "the right," by which I mean individuals and parties on a particular side of the spectrum, respectively.

While it is easy to establish a correlation between national experience and leftist party positions on peace enforcement and European defense cooperation, more is needed to show that this is in fact the result of differentiation and history. The existence of multiple dimensions can be seen in positions that parties take on other foreign policy issues. The extent of differentiation is evident from whether politicians explicitly acknowledge or deny value trade-offs. The importance of history is ascertained by the role it plays in justification of policies. If the same experience is cited overwhelmingly both in public and in private and both during the time of decision-making and well afterward, we can be comfortably sure of its causal role.

Often, however, the true cause of action is hidden or combined with other arguments. Equality is a "valence issue," meaning that individuals or parties often do not voice their opposition to humanitarian military action on the grounds that it is not in the national interest, or that protecting minority or human rights is none of their business, for fear of appearing callous.[61] They might instead claim that a military operation is impossible or question why other parts of the world are not more deserving of attention. Or they might add those arguments on top of an explicitly exclusivist rationale. Nevertheless, it is often possible to read between the lines of public sources. An ideological opposition can be detected if politicians display low levels of what cognitive psychologists call evaluative complexity.[62] For those who lack this, the policy they prefer is always the best in all aspects. It is the most moral, the least costly, the most likely to succeed. All good things go together. What is sometimes called "belief system overkill" is evident when particular individuals of a particular party or faction of a political party tend to pile on reasons for pursuing or not pursuing a given course.[63]

60. For instance, Roth and Criddle provide a wealth of information in a compendium of the personal histories of British MPs. Andrew Roth and Byron Criddle, *Parliamentary Profiles* (Bristol: Cedric Chivers, 1998).

61. See Ian Budge and Dennis Farlie, "Selective Emphasis or Direct Confrontation? An Alternative View with Data," in Hans Daalder and Peter Mair (eds.), *Western European Party Systems: Continuity and Change* (London: Sage, 1983), pp. 267–306.

62. Tetlock (1991).

63. Jervis (1976), p. 131.

This is generally more common among those at extreme ends of the political spectrum. Low evaluative complexity is evidence of an intense ideological preference and can be used as a measurement tool. In complex peacekeeping and peace enforcement operations such as in the Balkans, there are rarely unambiguous answers. Some factors push toward intervention while others militate against it. An operation may be moral, but illegal. It may demonstrate a certain selective indignation, but be military feasible. Given this fact, the more reasons that politicians marshal for or against and the less they acknowledge possible drawbacks of their position, the more an individual or a party is opposed to or supports a particular path.

Given that there is often no logical connection between many of the possible considerations, when they all tend to work in favor of an individual or a party's position some arguments are inevitably instrumental. If an operation is deemed unlikely to succeed due to geographical terrain, there is no necessary reason to also believe that no side is deserving of more help than another. Yet these beliefs tend to cluster together, indicating that they are subservient to more fundamental ideological objections. As will be seen, both fervent interventionists and fervent noninterventionists debate in this fashion.

I use a number of techniques to examine the arguments to decipher which are the underlying causes of action. The first is logical consistency. For example, rightist politicians often argued that humanitarian intervention was not in the national interest because their countries had no vital and tangible stake in the Balkans. Simultaneously they claimed that intervention there would demonstrate a double standard because their nations had in the past turned a blind eye to other human rights violations in Turkey or Tibet. It is safe to conclude that if intervention in Bosnia was not in the national interest, this "selective outrage" argument was instrumental and merely piled onto the first, as these individuals were surely not advocating worldwide intervention to right wrongs.

Secondly, when elements of the left and right both oppose intervention, I look to see which arguments are used by both sides and which are unique to one side or the other. I find that although both sometimes claim that intervention is infeasible, illegal, or selective, the left almost never says it is not in the national interest, or that all purely humanitarian aid operations should stop, whereas the right does make these claims. The right, in contrast, almost never declares that the use of force is immoral. This has led me to conclude that to the extent that the right objects to humanitarian intervention, its doubts center on the importance of protecting human rights. The left's misgivings are over the use of force as a means of foreign policy. Finally, during interviews I simply asked which arguments were genuine and which were contrived. After the dust settled, politicians were more comfortable identifying their real concerns. Rightists were more forthright in indicating that their opposition centered on a lack of a tangible national interest, and leftists in admitting their objection was due to pacifism.

Plan of the Book

The next three empirical chapters treat the question of military intervention by country, evaluating the relative ability of the partisan argument and its office-seeking and culturalist competitors to account for national foreign policies. I begin with an analysis of the most clearly partisan case—Great Britain. Labour and the Tories differed about whether the national interest included the Balkans. The German chapter adds a layer of complexity, as the German left gradually changed its antimilitarist position while the German right instrumentalized intervention. However, by the end of the 1990s, following the success of the CDU strategy and the reorientation of the SPD and Greens in favor of peace enforcement, the partisan cleavage resembled that in Britain. Finally, France adds two new twists, a somewhat unique rightist ideology and a different set of institutions that appears at first to make France a true exception to the argument. The French left was led by a president with little inclination to intervene for inclusive purposes. The right was driven by a unique Gaullist ideology that instrumentalized military operations to increase French status. As the conflicts progressed, however, the French right reverted to a more exclusive conception of the national interest similar to that of the right in Britain and Germany, and the left shook off Mitterrand's monopoly on policy for a more forceful approach. The final empirical chapter on European defense serves as a recapitulation of the same themes seen in the intervention case studies. In the conclusion, I review the major empirical findings and draw links between the phenomena uncovered in these pages and similar experiences with peace enforcement in four other cases—the United States, Canada, Japan, and Italy. I also demonstrate the relevance of the argument beyond humanitarian intervention to the war against Iraq in 2003.

CHAPTER 3

A Faraway Place of Which We Know Little? The Politics of Humanitarian Intervention in Great Britain

Britain under the Labour Party was the most vehement advocate of the use of force in Kosovo. When it appeared that an air war alone would not be sufficient to realize NATO's goal of preventing human rights violations in the Serbian province, U.S. President Bill Clinton even chided Prime Minister Tony Blair for lobbying for a ground invasion of Kosovo.[1] Just a few years earlier, however, the same U.S. administration had complained that the Conservative government was not forceful enough in its dealings with the Bosnian Serbs.[2] "You just don't understand what bastards those Brits are," Clinton reportedly said.[3] This was quite a statement from the leader of a country with no forces on the ground. Nevertheless, of the major troop contributors, Britain was the least willing to strengthen the UN and NATO mandate in Bosnia. It was France, of all countries, that urged greater NATO involvement in the Balkans. What accounts for this difference? Why did NATO's most loyal European member vary so much in its steadfastness to the missions of the Atlantic Alliance?

This variation, I maintain, was due to a turnover in government. A leftist Labour Party that considered upholding human rights a part of the national interest replaced a rightist Conservative Party that questioned the extent to which British interests were at stake in the Balkans. Labour had

---

1. Rhiannon Vickers, "Blair's Kosovo Campaign: Political Communications, the Battle for Public Opinion and Foreign Policy," *Civil Wars,* Vol. 3, No. 1 (2000), p. 68.

2. James Gow, *Triumph of the Lack of Will: International Diplomacy and the Yugoslav War* (New York: Columbia University Press, 1997), p. 175.

3. Samantha Power, *"A Problem from Hell": America and the Age of Genocide* (New York: Harper Collins, 2002), p. 326.

a more inclusive ideology because of its egalitarianism, and this led to a more robust approach to humanitarian intervention. The party made an explicit connection between the values reflected in its domestic policy agenda and its foreign policy program. The left-of-center Liberal Democratic Party did the same. A political culture loyal to NATO meant little. Partisan definitions of the national interest varied widely and were the real motivating force.

This marked a complete role reversal from the Cold War, during which the Labourites had gone as far as advocating unilateral disarmament in the 1980s. In an international environment in which more traditional and tangible interests were at stake, most notably the threat posed by the Soviet Union, the Conservatives were more hawkish. The collapse of the Eastern Bloc ushered in a new era with a new set of international problems, including an explosion of ethnic conflicts and failed states generally accompanied by gross violations of human rights. These problems had few direct consequences for Britain. The Labour and Liberal Democratic parties became more hawkish than the right in cases of military intervention for humanitarian purposes. The two could draw from the example of their country using force for inclusive purposes during the Second World War. Although there are leftist politicians in Britain with antimilitarist dispositions who reject all uses of force regardless of the objective of the operation, unlike in Germany they are confined overwhelmingly to the extreme left of the Labour Party. This meant that the interparty debate over military action was fought along an inclusive-exclusive continuum, as opposed to the Cold War battles between hawks and doves.

Positions on the utility of military force for realizing foreign policy objectives were completely subordinate to these different conceptions of the national interest. The language of the parties revealed their preferences. In Bosnia, the Conservative government adopted the spiral model in both its rhetoric and its actions, refusing to arm British forces in ways that might make them more capable of performing their mission but which it feared might provoke the Bosnian Serbs. The Labour Party's criticism while in opposition centered on signaling resolve and living up to commitments made by Britain and the UN, elements of the deterrence model. The party brought this strategy into office, matching words with deeds.

Each approach had its pitfalls. The arguments used by the Conservative government, meant to convey to its restless backbenches that the government had no intention of going beyond peacekeeping in Bosnia, had the effect of signaling a lack of resolve to the Bosnian Serbs, who were the largest impediment to peace. This helped create the conditions for failure in Bosnia, in particular the taking of UN hostages and the fall of the safe areas. When the air campaign in Kosovo was initially ineffective, Labour believed successful compellence necessitated an escalation of the war, including the use of ground troops. The Blair government was constrained by its more reluctant allies, however, and the need to show a united NATO face left Labour publicly supporting a strategy it did not privately believe in.

The opposition responded differently in each instance. The parties of the left did not take advantage of their domestic opponent's failures, contrary to the expectations of office-seeking theories of party competition. Labour and Liberal Democratic support actually helped the Conservative government maintain the British peacekeeping presence in Bosnia when pressure from the parliamentary party for withdrawal was the greatest. The Conservative Party did later, however, seek to capitalize on Labour and NATO's early failures in Kosovo. This is evidence not that rightist parties are more opportunistic office-seekers, but that parties are policy-seekers that contest the national interest. The Tories' position reflected their lack of support for humanitarian intervention in general. Although the Liberal Democratic Party had an even greater need to distinguish itself from Labour, it backed the government.

In this chapter, I will demonstrate that Labour and the Liberal Democrats were more supportive of the use of force for the protection of human rights than the Conservatives during both interventions. In the sections that follow, I first review the security policies of the three major British parties during the Cold War, and demonstrate the changes in partisan alignments brought about by the end of the bipolar era and the emergence of a new security issue in Bosnia. This provides an initial topography of the party landscape on foreign policy issues. Subsequently, I will review each government's approach and its ideological underpinnings, the role of backbench pressure, and both government and opposition responses to failures during the two interventions.

Role Reversal in the Post–Cold War World: Lib-Lab Hawks and Tory Doves

During the 1980s, the Labour and Liberal Democratic parties were more antimilitarist than the Conservatives, as evident in their embrace of the spiral model. Peace, both parties believed, was more likely attained through efforts at reducing suspicion than by demonstrating strength. Both parties feared the escalation dynamics created by the nuclear arms race. Labour argued that "Mrs. Thatcher's insistence on retaining permanently a British nuclear weapon invites other countries to conclude that they are only safe with a nuclear capability of their own."[4] It instead advocated policies to ameliorate the security dilemma,

4. Labour Party, "A Power for Good: Report of the Policy Review Group on Britain in the World," in *Meet the Challenge, Make the Change: A New Agenda for Britain* (1989), p. 87. Most of the Labour documents cited in this chapter were provided by the party's central office.

writing that "ultimately, the best defence of Britain lies not in armaments . . . but an end to the mutual distrust and hostility that have bedeviled both East and West since the end of the Second World War."[5] The Liberal Democrats shared this approach. In 1982, they advocated a "doctrine of common security" to "replace the present expedient of deterrence through armaments."[6] Both argued for a more defensive and less provocative military posture.[7] Since 1990 Labour and the Liberal Democrats have championed freezing the number of nuclear warheads, more intrusive verification procedures for the Chemical and Biological Weapons Conventions, the ratification of the Comprehensive Test Ban Treaty, a prohibition on the use of land mines, and embargoes on sales of arms to violators of human rights.[8] This shows that when not faced with value trade-offs, both parties have more dovish dispositions.

The Conservatives, in contrast, embraced the deterrence model during the Cold War. Their 1983 electoral program read: "The Western Alliance can keep the peace only if we can convince any potential aggressor that he would have to pay an unacceptable price. To do so, NATO must have strong conventional forces backed by a nuclear deterrent."[9] The party criticized Labour's disarmament proposals, arguing that the Soviet Union would see them as a sign of weakness and exploit them. The Conservatives identified NATO's military buildup as the cause of Soviet disarmament in the late 1980s and even of the end of the Cold War.[10]

As a result of these partisan differences, the left's support for and the right's opposition to humanitarian intervention have puzzled scholars and practitioners alike. Auerswald writes that "surprisingly" it was the right wing of the Conservative Party that most opposed greater military involvement in

5. Ibid., p. 85.

6. Quoted in Liberal Democratic Party, "Shared Security: Security and Defence in an Uncertain World," *Policy Paper* No. 6 (1994), p. 8.

7. Labour took a more extreme approach, advocating unilateral steps to reduce hostility. The party sought to prevent the deployment of cruise or Pershing missiles in Europe and opposed the doctrine of flexible response—that the West had to be superior to the Soviet Union at all levels of combat so as to be able to win a nuclear war. See Labour Party, *The New Hope for Britain* (1983 election manifesto), and "Power for Good," p. 86. The more moderate Liberal Democrats called for a "no first use" policy, a mutual rather than a unilateral freeze on nuclear weapons, and the cancellation of the next generation of nuclear submarines. Liberal-SDP Alliance, *Working Together for Britain* (1983 election manifesto).

8. On Labour's policies, see their *Policy Briefing Handbook* (1992), chap. 26.1; *Road to the Manifesto: Labour's Strategy for Britain in the Modern World* (1996); *Report to Conference,* Brighton (24–28 September 2000); and *Policy Handbook* (2001). On Liberal Democratic policy, see *Changing Britain for Good* (1992 election manifesto); "Shared Security" (1994); *Make the Difference* (1997 election manifesto).

9. Conservative Party, *The Challenge of Our Times* (1983 election manifesto). See also Conservative Party, *The Next Moves Forward* (1987 election manifesto).

10. Conservative Party (1983); Conservative Party (1987); Conservative Party, *The Best Future for Britain* (1992 election manifesto).

Bosnia.[11] Politicians have echoed his confusion. During the Kosovo war, the right-wing Conservative Andrew Robathan called it a "paradox" that "in this war . . . former soldiers such as myself, who are occasionally accused of being somewhat bellicose, are asking the questions and expressing concern, whereas old CND hands such as the Prime Minister appear to be enthusiastic in their pursuit of war."[12] Even Prime Minister John Major was confused.[13] The position of the Liberal Democrats was also surprisingly warlike. The left-wing Labourite George Galloway remarked: "Once upon a time, Liberal Democrats were men who wore beards, sandals and long, woolly jumpers. They believed in the United Nations and they believed in peace. Increasingly, with each campaign, they come before us not in woolly jumpers but in ever-grander military uniforms. 'War war' is the Liberal Democrat slogan."[14]

The positions of the parties cannot be understood without reference to the objective sought. Labour could overwhelmingly support the use of force in Bosnia and Kosovo, as opposed to other uses of the military by Britain in the post–Cold War period, because it regarded the aims of the former interventions as consistent with its inclusive ideology. Support for the interventions in Bosnia and Kosovo was an explicit extension of the leftist parties' domestic political values into the foreign policy arena. A Labour election document read: "We only bring our nation contempt if we apply double standards to the values we demand for ourselves compared to the treatment we are prepared to condone for the citizens of other countries. Labour believes that the values that inform our domestic programme must also form the basis of our foreign relations. That is why this statement puts forward a strong commitment by Labour to promote human rights. . . . We cannot pride ourselves on our democratic traditions if we fail to help those who are demanding the same democratic rights for themselves."[15]

Robin Cook, who would become foreign secretary, and David Clark, Labour's shadow defense secretary, also drew the direct link between domestic political equality and Labour's policy on Bosnia. Backbenchers echoed those sentiments, talking of using interventions to "extend freedom" and

11. David P. Auerswald, *Disarmed Democracies* (Ann Arbor: University of Michigan Press, 2000), p. 73.

12. *Hansard* (19 April 1999), col. 639. *Hansard* is the record of parliamentary debates. The CND (Campaign for Nuclear Disarmament) was a movement that revived in the 1980s for British unilateral reductions in nuclear weapons. Edwina Currie noted that "the loudest voices from Labour Back Benchers urging military action are the same voices that were urging that we should do nothing in the Gulf." *Hansard* (29 April 1993), col. 1182.

13. John Major, *The Autobiography* (London: Harper Collins, 1999), p. 535.

14. *Hansard* (25 March 1999), col. 591.

15. Labour Party (1996), p. 2.

"create uniform rights"[16] across the globe. The foreign and defense affairs spokesperson for the Liberal Democrats, Menzies Campbell, when asked why the party supported military interventions in the Balkans, responded with an inclusive statement: "Tradition. Gladstone said, 'Remember that the sanctity of life in the hill villages of Afghanistan among the winter snows is as inviolate in the eye of Almighty God as can be your own.'"[17] For both parties, human rights were a part of the national interest.[18]

Leftist critics saw narrower, more exclusive national interests behind other military interventions, which explains why some of the most vehement opponents of the Gulf War were major proponents of intervention in Bosnia. The disparity between the Conservative government's lack of resolve in Bosnia and its vigorous backing of the liberation of Kuwait was a constant theme. Paddy Ashdown, leader of the Liberal Democratic Party, asked during question time in Parliament: "If . . . it was considered right to risk lives in defence of the United Nations and international law in the Gulf, why is it wrong to do the same in Bosnia? Are we so cynical that our answer to that question is that the only difference between the two regions is oil? I hope not."[19]

The Intraparty Debate over Bosnia: The Extreme Inclusive Left versus the Extreme Antimilitarist Left

During the Bosnian war, there were Labour Party members who objected to any use of force beyond peacekeeping on antimilitarist grounds. They were located overwhelmingly in the far or "hard" left of the party, and were predominantly members of the Campaign Group, an informal club of politicians who took extreme positions on domestic issues.[20] Under its former

16. In *Hansard,* see Robin Cook (19 July 1995), col. 1752; David Clark (19 July 1995), col. 1778; Ernie Ross (23 February 1993), col. 812; (25 September 1992), col. 157.

17. Interview with the author (18 July 2001). A Liberal Democratic foreign policy adviser made the same case: "Liberties are not just for us but for all people. If we are representing these values, we should hold others to those values as well." Interview with the author (11 July 2001).

18. "International morality, an international community and Britain's interests all coincide," said shadow foreign secretary Jack Cunningham at a Labour Party conference. *Report of Conference,* Annual Conference 1994/Special Conference 1995, p. 177. "A commitment to universal human rights is fundamental to Labour's political philosophy." Labour Party (1996), p. 23.

19. *Hansard* (29 April 1993), cols. 1192–1193. Galloway was more polemical, claiming that "if oil was flowing in the streets of Srebrenica rather than just blood, 29 countries would quickly have assembled a vast armada of armies and air forces to come to the rescue of a sovereign state and a member of the United Nations that is being invaded and subjected to brutal aggression . . ." (12 July 1995), col. 960. See also comments by Liberal Democrat Russell Johnston (25 September 1992), col. 147, and left-wing Labour MP Ken Livingstone (19 July 1995), col. 1742.

20. I identify membership in a wing of a party using Andrew Roth and Byron Criddle, *Parliamentary Profiles* (Bristol: Cedric Chivers, 1998), a compendium of the positions and histories of all members of parliament.

leader, Tony Benn, the faction had played a major role in the party's move to the left in the 1980s. Benn was one of the most vocal critics of any peace enforcement action in Bosnia, arguing throughout that the mission should restrict its mandate to the delivery of humanitarian aid.[21] This group did not differentiate between different types of military operations, objecting to all uses of force.

Opponents marshaled numerous arguments that showed their intense opposition to military intervention in Bosnia. The first argument stressed that Bosnia was a civil war, an internal matter that neither Britain nor any other state should become involved in. The second argument maintained that all sides were morally equivalent and therefore undeserving of Western support, a position that led to accusations of anti-Muslim feeling. Third, Labour antimilitarists asked how any government could justify peace enforcement in Bosnia when there were more egregious human rights violations in other parts of the world. Finally, leftist opponents doubted the probability of success of any military operation given the terrain, the putatively intractable ethnic hatreds that fueled the fighting, and the guerrilla fighting style of the warring sides. Some went as far as to doubt the government's humanitarian intentions, claiming that it was driven by the "grandeur of an imperial past."[22]

These arguments masked a more fundamental objection to military action. While it is possible for politicians to oppose interventions based on their probability of success, when these individuals tend to cluster on a particular side of the political spectrum, it indicates that these estimates are not based on objective analysis alone. Nor was there any logical reason for politicians fearful of failure to believe all sides were equally guilty of crimes. Ultimately, their resistance was to the military means and not the ends of the operation. While Labour opponents claimed that military intervention was wrong because all sides were morally equivalent, the true logic of their position was actually the reverse. Antimilitarists argued that all sides were morally equivalent because they believed the use of force was wrong. "After all, the people I describe in derogatory terms as appeasers and pacifists are hardly any less committed to racial equality than I am," said Labour MP and avid interventionist David Winnick. "It would be nonsense to argue otherwise. But they will always find

21. See in *Hansard* (29 April 1993), col. 1172; (10 March 1994), col. 405; (12 April 1994), col. 28; (31 May 1995), col. 1001.

22. Dennis Skinner, *Hansard* (7 December 1994), col. 318. On the civil character of the war, see Tony Benn (18 April 1994), col. 646; (31 May 1995), col. 1020; Robert Wareing (31 May 1995), cols. 1088–1089. On the moral equivalence of all sides, see Robert Wareing (29 April 1993), cols. 1230–1232; (12 April 1994), col. 27; (31 May 1995), cols. 1088–1089; (12 July 1995), col. 958. On the impossibility of the task, see Tam Dalyell (31 May 1995), cols. 1047–1050; (19 July 1995), cols. 1776–1777.

a justification for not taking military action by demonizing the victims of what is happening."[23]

Their other arguments betrayed this. Fears of military spirals generally accompanied references to moral equivalence and intractability. Opponents argued that any use of force would lead to an escalation of the war. This more basic antimilitarism was also evident in their opposition to any new role for NATO in crisis management and their complaints about the military alliance usurping the role of the UN as it gradually took on peace enforcement tasks.[24]

Nevertheless, left-wing opponents were outnumbered by Labour supporters of intervention, even on the extreme left. The most strident supporters of more robust military action in Bosnia were also drawn from the Campaign and Tribune Groups, the leftist factions of the party, and included the party's left-wing leader during the 1980s, Michael Foot. Most had been members of the Campaign for Nuclear Disarmament and had supported unilateral reductions in nuclear weapons during the Cold War. Now they argued that only military engagement would prevent further aggression, particularly by the Bosnian Serbs. The Labour chairman of the Defence Committee in Parliament, Bruce George, explained: "You had a lot on the left, very interestingly, who throughout the 1970s and 1980s and early 1990s were anti-defense, but were very gung-ho because they were pro–human rights. Even Ken Livingstone was very pro-NATO for the first time in his life. So it caused a lot of personal conflicts. Most of the left of the Labour Party was really gung-ho about stuffing the Serbs."[25] For these politicians, inclusive principles came before antimilitarism. This seems to discount the possible assertion that the key factor in the role reversal was not a changing international context, but a change in the Labour Party itself. The party under Blair was indeed different but this was not significant for its position on peace enforcement. Although the party's move to the center might have reduced the number of hard leftists in the party, due to Britain's history they were equally if not more likely to be fervent interventionists than radical pacifists.

The strong support for armed action in Bosnia by some of the most left-wing Labour politicians stands in great contrast to the attitude of the German left, as will be seen in the following chapter. This was due to the vastly

23. Interview with the author (24 July 2001).

24. See, for instance, comments by left-winger Alice Mahon, *Hansard* (31 May 1995), cols. 1080–1082. For fears of spirals, see comments by Jim Marshall (12 July 1995), col. 966; Dennis Skinner (26 July 1993), col. 871; and Robert Wareing (24 May 1993), col. 579. All are considered to be part of the "hard left" and were members of the Campaign Group or the other leftist grouping, the Tribune Group. For general antimilitarism, see Tony Benn (12 April 1994), col. 28; (18 April 1994), col. 646; (31 May 1995), cols. 1019–1022.

25. Interview with the author (May 2000).

different experiences of each country with the military, particularly during the Second World War. The Labour left drew parallels between Hitler's fascism and the ethnic cleansing prosecuted by the Bosnian Serbs and Britain's failure to stop either through diplomacy. Livingstone said: "[T]his is what it must have sounded like as, year after year, weasel-worded people . . . said, 'Czechoslovakia is a long way away. It is a small country of no significance to us.'"[26] John Home Robertson declared: "It is clear from today's speeches that some honourable Members regard Bosnia-Herzegovina as what might be described as a faraway place of which we know little, to borrow a phrase from another era of appeasement."[27] By invoking appeasement, Labour was indicting both the Tories' narrow conception of the national interest and their refusal to take tougher military action. Labour was also signaling its belief that force could be used for inclusive purposes.

In the case of humanitarian intervention, these left-wingers embraced the deterrence model. Chris Mullin, a member of the Campaign Group, said: "It is clear, is it not, that aggression for the Serbs unhappily has paid? The only time that it will not pay is when they realise that the UN is serious."[28] Not acting would send a message to fascist dictators, argued the left-wing MP Clare Short.[29] Appeasement was also a powerful and pervasive rhetorical weapon, the embodiment of deterrence logic. David Winnick complained in a Commons debate that "the air of Munich pervades this place."[30] Max Madden also smelled "the stench of appeasement."[31] These members of parliament supported the Conservative government at all times during the war when either the UN or NATO took more forceful action. Other members of the Campaign Group who spoke out in favor of military action included Harry Barnes and "Red" Ken Livingstone. They were joined by members of the slightly more moderate "soft left," including Tony Banks and Malcolm Wicks. Some went so far as to call for a ground invasion of Bosnia.[32] In their "peace

26. *Hansard* (29 April 1993), col. 1219.

27. *Hansard* (31 May 1995), col. 1029.

28. *Hansard* (29 April 1993), col. 1169.

29. *Hansard* (29 April 1993), col. 1237.

30. *Hansard* (7 December 1994), col. 321. Other parliamentary references to appeasement include Andrew Faulds (29 April 1993), cols. 1203–1210; (31 May 1995), cols. 1061–1063; Max Madden (7 December 1994), col. 322; Malcolm Wicks (1 March 1994), col. 794; David Winnick (24 May 1993), col. 576. The Liberal Democrats also made historical allusions. Ashdown said: "It is as logical to claim that this is a civil war as to claim that the events in Sudentenland [*sic*] in the 1930s was [*sic*] a civil war." (29 April 1993), col. 1191.

31. *Hansard* (29 April 1993), col. 1223.

32. In *Hansard*, see Tony Banks (12 July 1995), col. 964; Harry Barnes (24 May 1993), col. 578; Ken Livingstone (29 April 1993), cols. 1217–1219; (19 July 1995), col. 1742; Malcolm Wicks (1 March 1994), col. 794; David Winnick (24 May 1993), col. 576; (7 December 1994), col. 321. For the advocates of action on the ground see Chris Mullin (29 April 1993), cols. 1203–1205; (18 April 1994), col. 651; Max Madden (29 April 1993), cols. 1222–1223.

through strength" strategy during the Cold War, the Tories sought to deter the Soviets through credible threats of military action. In the post–Cold War period, the Labour Party advocated protecting human rights through strength.

Although left-wing interventionists engaged in more differentiation than their pacifist counterparts, evaluating the issue of peace enforcement along both the hawk-dove and the inclusivist-exclusivist continua, they displayed just as little evaluative complexity. As the partisan argument predicts, provided leftist politicians make the trade-off between their values of inclusiveness and antimilitarism, support for intervention increases toward the extreme left of the ideological spectrum in domestic politics. This makes them less willing to admit the potential costs of or difficulties in realizing their policies. The extreme left argued just as stridently that Bosnia was not a civil war and that the Serbs bore the overwhelming degree of blame for the conflict.[33] They also tended to avoid designating precise military alternatives, leaving themselves open to Foreign Secretary Douglas Hurd's moniker, the "something must be done school." To the extent they did address the question of means, they insisted that action would be effective. Faulds said it was "outrageous" to suggest that military objectives could not be achieved.[34]

The Exclusive Right: A Lack of Interest

Conservative opposition to British involvement in Bosnia focused on the lack of a tangible British interest in the Balkans. It was most transparently expressed by the right wing of the party. MP Nicolas Budgen was the most explicit:

> [T]he risk of danger to the British national interest is an argument that we, as Tories, have always advanced to justify any risk to British soldiers. That was certainly felt about the Falklands. . . . The strength of feeling . . . when we debated the Falklands war surprised . . . many of the people detached from ordinary emotions, who see these things in terms of legalistic peacekeeping, with references to the United Nations, the European Union and the concept of international law. . . . There was the feeling that British people and British territory had been conquered; that the wrong must be righted as quickly as possible; and that to that end it was justifiable to suffer casualties and the loss of lives. There is at present no such feeling about our involvement in Bosnia.[35]

---

33. In *Hansard,* see Andrew Faulds (31 May 1995), cols. 1061–1063; Ken Livingstone (29 April 1993), cols. 1217–1219; Calum Macdonald (26 July 1993), cols. 837–840; Clare Short (29 April 1993), cols. 1235–1239; (31 May 1995), col. 1020; (19 July 1995), col. 1740.

34. *Hansard* (29 April 1993), col. 1210.

35. *Hansard* (31 May 1995), cols. 1075–1076. See also (19 April 1993), col. 30; (14 July 1993), cols. 966–967; Terry Dicks (18 April 1993), col. 651; Nigel Forman (29 April 1993), col. 1230; Andrew Robathan (31 May 1995), cols. 1077–1079; Sir Peter Tapsell (13 May 1995), col. 1053.

Other right-wingers were also disdainful of the left's argumentation. Andrew Robathan said: "In my experience, few soldiers fight for international law. They fight for Queen and country, family, mates, pay, leave and even for excitement; but I doubt that many would fight for international law. . . . For what noble cause could our troops die in Bosnia? It appears that the noble cause may be keeping two bands of cut-throats apart."[36]

Most hostility to intervention in the Balkans was not so explicit, however. Opponents also marshaled more politically palatable arguments identical to those of the antimilitarist left, framing the conflict as a civil war in which all sides were morally culpable taking place in a region that historical precedent had shown was impervious to intervention. Conservatives asked how any government could justify peace enforcement in Bosnia when there were more egregious human rights violations in other parts of the world.[37] The intention here is not to contest the validity of those claims. Bosnia was indeed an extremely complicated situation and not as deadly as other conflicts in more remote locations. Instead I seek to explain why particular factions or political parties were more inclined to use those arguments as reasons for inaction than others. It seems more likely that these arguments provided publicly acceptable reasons to oppose involvement in Bosnia than a genuine meeting of the minds on the practicality and morality of intervention between the extreme left and the right.

The fact that these other reasons for not using force were often accompanied by explicitly exclusive statements, of a kind never made by antimilitarists, indicates that their use reflects a more basic objection to intervention based on ideological fundamentals rather than concerns about its feasibility or legitimacy. For instance, Peter Tapsell said: "Let us bring some hard-headed realism into the practical conduct of our Balkan policy. *No important British national self-interest is involved.* That is the basic point." However he went on immediately to say: "[I]f humanity is to be the determining factor in British foreign policy, why are not we sending troops to Angola,

36. *Hansard* (31 May 1995), col. 1068. Bismarck's dictum that the Balkans were not worth the bones of a single Pomeranian grenadier was a common refrain. See John Biffen (12 July 1995), col. 953.

37. On the civil character of the war, see comments in *Hansard* by Sir Anthony Grant (24 May 1993), col. 575; (12 July 1995), col. 960; Archibald Hamilton (18 April 1994), col. 649. On the culpability of all sides, see Ian Duncan-Smith (29 April 1993), col. 1171; Peter Tapsell (31 May 1995), cols. 1050–1054; Peter Viggers (29 April 1993), col. 1232. On the lack of viable military options, see comments by Julian Brazier (24 May 1993), col. 579; (18 April 1994), col. 655; Winston Churchill (25 September 1992), cols. 162–163; Roger Gale (18 April 1994), col. 654; Jim Spicer (7 December 1994), col. 320; Peter Tapsell (10 March 1994), col. 405; John Townend (19 July 1995), col. 1741. On the abundance of other possible areas for intervention, see Peter Tapsell (31 May 1995), col. 1009.

Rwanda, Cambodia, Kurdistan, Tibet and Chechnya, to mention just a few? What is so very different about Bosnia?"[38] He added that intervention would be impossible and that all sides were guilty of atrocities.

One can assume that if right-wing MPs did not favor intervention in Bosnia for reasons of national interest, they would have been loath to intervene in areas more distant from Bosnia in what were considered more intractable civil wars that often involved great powers. Conservative interventionists, typically in the moderate wing of the party, recognized that opponents' arguments did not express the core of their objections. The moderate Sir Patrick Cormack said: "The fiercest opponents I had were on the right of the Conservative Party who did not want to get involved in the Balkans and trotted out all sorts of specious excuses like recycled and inaccurate accounts of what happened in the Second World War, mouthing platitudes about Vietnam and body bags. There were people on the right of the party like Tapsell who were very, very opposed but on the right of me when it comes to most political issues."[39]

PLAYING IT CONSERVATIVE: THE MAJOR GOVERNMENT AND THE TORY PARTY IN BOSNIA

The exclusivist right wing of the Tories and the interventionist left wing of the Labour Party defined the extremes of the debate over Bosnia. Although there were pacifist opponents of intervention, the exclusivist Conservatives were the more powerful force. According to ministers and their advisers, hostility was not reserved to the right wing. The Conservative government was very cognizant of a "silent but significant disaffection among Tory backbenchers," said Pauline Neville-Jones, political director at the Foreign and Commonwealth Office (FCO), and the point person during the Bosnian conflict. "They did not like the nature of the conflict. Defense is for serious power conflicts. Tories will fight Saddam Hussein with great risks but did not want to get involved in other people's affairs that do not engage Britain's interests."[40] Vocal Tory supporters of a stronger line in Bosnia, the moderates Cormack and Quentin Davies, found themselves isolated. When asked how many supporters there were for more determined action, Cormack said:

38. *Hansard* (31 May 1995), col. 1053 (emphasis added). See also Archibald Hamilton (18 April 1994), col. 649.
39. Interview with the author (24 July 2001).
40. Interview with the author (19 July 2001). An adviser to Foreign Secretary Hurd said the same: "Within the Conservative Party, the pressure was much more for disengagement and not getting stuck in." Interview with the author (2 July 2001).

"In my own party, very, very, very few indeed. I was on occasion the sole voice in my party. For long periods, I was on my own."[41]

Auerswald suggests that at significant moments during the Bosnian conflict, the government was constrained by its own party—that fears of losing office kept it from taking a tougher line in Bosnia.[42] Ministers and civil servants reject this theory. An adviser to Foreign Secretary Hurd calls backbench grumbling "the dog that did not bark."[43] However, this is not because the party did not have the power to constrain the government.[44] Political Director Neville-Jones said that Prime Minister Major "could not afford" to ignore the parliamentary party. "It would have been suicide. He had to know that the Cabinet was behind him. That was the way to ensure that the backbenchers could be kept in line."[45] Defense Secretary Malcolm Rifkind, who became foreign secretary in summer 1995, said the government never felt inhibited, "[n]ot because there were not such constraints in existence. If we had wanted to make any radical changes in terms of stepping up our involvement, it would have involved considerable opposition from our own party and also some on the other side."[46] The prime minister complained to U.S. officials that escalation would bring down his government.[47]

Exclusivist opposition was not a problem primarily because the government itself had a basically exclusivist ideological approach and devoted significant efforts to reassuring those who were uneasy. The Cabinet shared the views of the parliamentary party. Backbench opposition "was never a serious issue, because we did not want to go in that direction anyway," said Defense Secretary Rifkind. "A constraint implies we would have liked to. Right from day one, the government was very cautious. We had our own doubts. We had our own serious questions about whether the balance of the public interest lay in terms of being there or not."[48] Foreign Secretary Hurd put it more bluntly: "There was no serious British national interest involved. No strategic. No commercial."[49] The cracks

41. Interview with the author (24 July 2001). Davies remembered: "I would say there was a very strong feeling against any kind of involvement at all. I would say I was in the minority." Interview with the author (27 June 2001).

42. David Auerswald, "Inward Bound: Domestic Institutions and Military Conflicts," *International Organization,* Vol. 53, No. 3 (Summer 1999), p. 493.

43. Interview with the author (2 July 2001).

44. For this reason, it would have been difficult even for former prime minister Margaret Thatcher, a prominent voice for air strikes, to have led Britain into a broader war against the Bosnian Serbs (especially given the fact that the right-wing Thatcherite faction of the party comprised some of the most implacable critics of involvement). Tellingly, her justification of her position centered more on credibility than human rights violations.

45. Interview with the author (19 July 2001).

46. Interview with the author (19 July 2001).

47. Richard Holbrooke, *To End a War* (New York: Modern Library, 1999), p. 227.

48. Interview with the author (19 July 2001).

49. Interview with the author (28 June 2001).

in the larger parliamentary party were mirrored in the Cabinet, with tough questions from the chancellor of the exchequer, Kenneth Clarke. The foreign secretary said of the resistance by moderates: "Ordinary people approaching this *de novo* including people like Michael Heseltine and Kenneth Clarke, who were normally very cooperative with everything I was trying to do, did not see it. Why should we get further involved?"[50]

At least initially a consensus existed within the government to deploy British forces to help protect aid convoys delivering humanitarian assistance to the suffering civilian populations while the UN and EU diplomatic envoys attempted to negotiate a political solution. In August 1992, the government agreed to deploy eighteen hundred troops for that purpose. As the situation in Bosnia deteriorated and the warring parties prevented the delivery of humanitarian aid, pressure to do more grew. UNPROFOR forces were repeatedly turned back in their efforts to reach civilian populations. The government gradually sent more troops, whose numbers reached thirty-six hundred in 1995, but insisted throughout that UNPROFOR had a peacekeeping and not a peace enforcement mandate.

Any movement beyond this threatened the consensus in the party, according to sources within the government.[51] Foreign Secretary Hurd defended the government's approach as balanced, placing it in the mainstream: "It would be possible for us in Britain to say . . . that none of these conflicts are anything to do with us: that . . . no specific British interest exists. . . . Alternatively, we could take the view . . . that, wherever there is injustice or intolerable suffering, it is part of our duty as a nation to do our best to bring it to an end. . . . Somewhere between those two extreme answers . . . , somewhere between the saloon bar and Gladstone, lies the policy that any British Government would in practice seek to follow."[52] Pauline Neville-Jones later suggested that the government's approach was closer to that of exclusivist backbenchers. "It is part of the problem of any government. Where on the spectrum of opinion does it place itself? I want to suggest to you that the government was always doing a balancing act, but the drag had always been in the direction of 'What the hell are you there for?'"[53]

50. Interview with the author (28 June 2001). Neville-Jones says that his aversion "was not financial." Instead, Clarke "represents some kind of guts about the party on this one." Interview with the author (19 July 2001).

51. On the mandate see comments in *Hansard* by Douglas Hogg (24 May 1993), col. 575; Malcolm Rifkind (18 April 1994), col. 643; (21 November 1994), cols. 341–348. On the limits of the consensus, an adviser to Hurd remembered: "There was not much opposition up to the level of peacekeeping assuming there was a peace to keep. It is when you start to get into the level of peace enforcement where difficult questions of rules of engagement would come into operation that some people started peeling away from the consensus, some people from the Conservative Party, a few from the Labour Party." Interview with the author (26 June 2001).

52. *Hansard* (23 February 1993), col. 774.

53. Interview with the author (19 July 2001).

The government's sympathy with the views of right-wing backbenchers was evident in its adoption of the their argumentation. Foreign Secretary Hurd had identified the Serbs as the primary aggressors in September 1992 and sanctions against the former Yugoslavia to deter Serbia from providing military assistance to its sympathizers in Bosnia were a de jure recognition that the war was not only civil in nature.[54] By April 1993, however, with international pressure to do more growing, Hurd was fending off detractors by declaring in Parliament that "No side has the monopoly on evil" and that Bosnia was a civil war that was not amenable to outside intervention and was no worse than numerous other conflicts. These arguments became the refrain of other speeches as well.[55] Other ministers would continue this approach. Defense Secretary Rifkind took the position the furthest, arguing that the "UN can make no moral distinction between intervening in Bosnia and intervening in Angola or Cambodia. . . . Those . . . who called for UN intervention, but sought to imply that it must be made in Bosnia even if not elsewhere, displayed an inappropriate inconsistency."[56]

An adviser to the foreign secretary said later that the characterization of the conflict as a civil war helped remove some of the pressure for intervention. "To see it as a civil war made it much more acceptable that one should be seeking to play a honest-broker role rather than taking any one head on." Although the adviser did "not think the interpretation was completely phoney," he added that "it was not that people realized later that all along it was a war of aggression. At any point there were elements of civil war

54. Douglas Hurd, *Hansard* (25 September 1992), col. 121.

55. *Hansard* (29 April 1993), col. 1167. Most notably the foreign secretary made a speech at the Travelers Club in September 1993 denouncing the "something must be done" school. Douglas Hurd, "The Power of Comment—Government and the Media," Speech at the Travelers Club, London (9 September 1993). "No one is blameless," said Hurd of Bosnia. In most other ethnic conflicts, the suffering is "substantially greater than anywhere in Europe." Douglas Hurd, "Speech at the Defence and Security Forum Ltd.," London (26 May 1993). Hurd implied that all were at fault when he stated: "There will be no decisive victory in this war where Bosnian Serbs shell Bosnian Muslims, Bosnian Muslims attack Bosnian Croats, Bosnian Muslims fight Bosnian Muslims, and across an ethnic map which denies any of them the chance of settled military success." Douglas Hurd, "Culture and Cultural Diplomacy," speech at Marlborough House, London (26 January 1994).

56. *Hansard* (29 April 1993), col. 1245. Rifkind also noted the more serious ethnic conflicts in other regions in speeches. Malcolm Rifkind, "Peace and Stability—the British Military Contribution," speech at Carnegie Council on Ethics and International Affairs, New York (13 April 1994) in *The Framework of UK Defence Policy: Key Speeches on Defence Policy by the Rt. Hon. Malcolm Rifkind 1993–1995* (London: Centre for Defence Studies), No. 30/31 (1995). For other ministers' comments on the moral equivalence of the warring parties, see statements in *Hansard* by Under Secretary Douglas Hogg (26 July 1993), col. 870. On the characterization of the conflict as a civil war, see remarks by Douglas Hogg (23 February 1993), col. 856; (24 May 1993), col. 573; (26 July 1993), col. 872; Douglas Hurd (12 April 1994), cols. 21–29. The defense minister made reference to the other internal conflicts more serious than Bosnia. Malcolm Rifkind (29 April 1993), col. 1244–1248.

and Milosevic pursuing his own agenda concurrently."[57] Conservative MP Cormack, who wanted a more forceful British policy, called this "a very convenient excuse." He added: "I must be careful in saying that it was insincere. But they did not want to listen to any facts that did not fit in with their theory that it was a simple civil war."[58] Another adviser to the foreign secretary captured the commitment to that characterization when he called it an "absolute, fundamental, theological distinction."[59]

Although the government claimed that the international community would not acquiesce to territorial gains by Bosnian Serbs, the Major government's hesitance to engage in any activities akin to peace enforcement was clear at all major crisis points during the war when the UN and NATO considered strengthening UNPROFOR's mandate.[60] The British originally opposed the imposition of a no-fly zone over Bosnia and were extremely reluctant to apply air power to break the siege of Sarajevo, later accomplished through the "Sarajevo ultimatum" in February 1994 at France's initiative. A French NATO official described the British as being "absolutely out of their minds" when they heard of this plan for air strikes.[61] Temporarily riding the wave of outrage in world opinion, the government appeared more sanguine about the role of force following the ultimatum's initial success, with Defense Secretary Rifkind claiming that it had "transformed" the prospects for diplomatic success. Yet the government made no effort to sustain public support. One month later, Rifkind was stressing that the "circumstances of Sarajevo were unique," and that the ultimatum was not a general formula to be applied elsewhere in Bosnia.[62]

Most crucially, the Conservative government was the least willing of the major troop contributors to commit to the creation of safe areas for predominantly Bosnian Muslim civilian populations in June 1993. Pressure from the international community eventually proved overwhelming. Rifkind said later: "We went along with it because we were in the minority, and we did not want to bugger up everything just because we took a different view."[63] The British insisted, however, that the wording of the resolution state that UNPROFOR's mandate was to "deter against attacks" on the peacekeepers themselves rather than to "defend" the safe areas—the formulation that the

57. Interview with the author (2 July 2001).
58. Interview with the author (24 July 2001).
59. Interview with the author (26 June 2001).
60. Hurd, "Speech at the Defence and Security Forum" (1993); Douglas Hogg, *Hansard* (24 May 1993), col. 575.
61. Interview with the author (6 April 2001).
62. Compare the statements of Malcolm Rifkind in *Hansard* (10 March 1994), cols. 399–410; and (18 April 1994), col. 645.
63. Interview with the author (19 July 2001). Hurd and his advisers confirmed this in interviews with the author.

French preferred, as will be seen in the coming chapters.[64] This would later have severe repercussions.

Contesting Conservative Policy: Labour and the Liberal Democrats in Opposition

The Labour and Liberal Democratic parties took a more hawkish position at every moment during the conflict at which the UN and NATO considered an escalation in force. Both Labour backbenchers and shadow cabinet members called for the actual defense of the safe areas, disputing the government's interpretation of the UNPROFOR mandate.[65] Although the frontbench of the party was more dubious of the prospects for a larger intervention, agreeing with the government that a military solution could not be imposed, it did argue for stronger military measures, including the bombing of supply lines from Serbia into Bosnia.[66] Shadow foreign secretary Jack Cunningham called the government's threats "threadbare," and stated that if his party was a member of the "something must be done" school, the Conservatives followed the maxim that "something must be said."[67]

The Labour frontbench was not as interventionist as the Liberal Democratic leadership, however. Paddy Ashdown, the leader of the party, was consistently ahead of the government, calling for a no-fly zone and the creation of safe areas before the government took such steps.[68] He went further than the Labour leadership as well, both publicly and privately advocating a significant increase in ground forces.[69] Menzies Campbell, a foreign policy

---

64. Douglas Hogg said: "[W]e have the concept of safe areas and the agreement to use air action to defend UNPROFOR troops should they be attacked within those safe areas. . . . On the question of safe areas, we have made it plain that, if UNPROFOR troops in the safe areas are attacked, air assets will be deployed to support them." *Hansard* (24 May 1993), col. 572, 575.

65. For backbencher opinion, see statements in *Hansard* by Harry Barnes (24 May 1993), col. 578; Max Madden (1 March 1994), col. 790; Mike O'Brien (21 November 1994), col. 348; Clare Short (29 April 1993); cols. 1235–1238. Frontbencher statements include George Robertson (24 May 1993), cols. 571–572. Calls became more vocal following attacks on safe areas, such as against Bihac in December 1994. See shadow foreign secretary Cook's comments in *Hansard* (7 December 1994), cols. 313–314. On the mandate see Menzies Campbell (31 May 1995), col. 1037; Kate Hoey (31 May 1995), col. 1056; Calum Macdonald (26 July 1993), cols. 837–838.

66. In *Hansard,* see John Cunningham (25 September 1992), cols. 131–137; (29 April 1993), cols. 1776–1784; David Clark (18 October 1993), col. 50. See also deputy defense spokesperson George Robertson's comments: (26 July 1993), cols. 866–871. However, Cunningham called for an ultimatum: (29 April 1993), cols. 1176–1184. Labour defense spokespersons advocated this strategy as other times as well. See David Clark (18 October 1993), col. 50; George Robertson (26 July 1993), cols. 866–871.

67. Jack Cunningham, "Speech at the RIIA" (1993); Jack Cunningham, "Britain in the World," *Conference Report* (30 October 1993), p. 217.

68. See Paddy Ashdown, *The Ashdown Diaries* (London: Allen Lane, 2000), p. 211.

69. *Hansard* (25 September 1992), col. 123; (29 April 1993), cols. 1189–1199; Ashdown (2000).

spokesperson for the party, said: "We were arguing for the use of air power. We were arguing for the use of armor. We were essentially arguing for peace enforcement while we were still at peacekeeping at other people's speedometer."[70] Ashdown's statements were lent more credibility by his extensive experience in military affairs. Fervent Labour advocates of a more forceful approach attributed the less robust positions of the Labour leadership to electoral considerations. Although a strident left-wing interventionist, even Labour MP David Winnick said apologetically: "[A]fter four election defeats, the Opposition frontbench had to be a little careful not to give the impression that we were yearning for a war in which many British soldiers would come back in body bags. We were leading up to a situation where we knew how crucial the next election was, because if we had been defeated a fifth time, what was the future for the Labour Party? Those are factors that any responsible party leader has to take into account."[71] Without a serious prospect of electoral victory, it is likely that the Liberal Democrats could be more strident.

The fact that both leftist parties were more interventionist than the Conservatives, and that Labour most likely would have been even more so if it had not been worried about exposing itself to political criticism in the case of failure, demonstrate the clear differences between the two sides of the political spectrum. This was not due to disparities in information. Leaders of the official Opposition had access to classified information in the Privy Council that was not available to other members of the party. The Conservatives considered this a useful tool to manage criticism. Foreign Secretary Hurd said: "It is a considerably useful device for governments because once you tell them the kind of considerations in your mind, such as facts and intelligence reports he did not previously know, it does inhibit him from saying you are the worst prime minister that has ever been."[72] Despite these briefings, however, both parties still believed the government should intervene more forcefully. The failure of the briefings to dampen criticism led to resentment on the Tory backbenches. The Liberal Democrat Menzies Campbell recalled: "There was a certain amount of resistance in the Conservative Party. Why brief us when we are trying to knock spots off you in the House of Commons?"[73]

Sending Signals at Home: The Conservative Government and Domestic Opposition

Given that the stated aim of the British government and the international community in general was to prohibit any territorial gains through

---

70. Interview with the author (18 July 2001).
71. Interview with the author (24 July 2001).
72. Interview with the author (28 June 2001).
73. Interview with the author (18 July 2001).

the use of force, why did the British government more than others so publicly insist on the maintenance of strict impartiality, which they interpreted
as preventing them from using force, and characterize the situation as
intractable and no more desperate than others in the world? After all, these
served as demonstrative signals of a lack of commitment to resolving the
conflict. The Conservative's own former defense secretary Tom King criticized the government for this.[74]

The Major government did perceive this problem of sending signals to
both its opponents and its domestic audience. While it was not advocating
a policy much different from that preferred by the party, the latter was restive
enough that the government deemed reassuring its own backbenchers to be
more important than sending messages to the Bosnian Serbs. An adviser to
the foreign secretary said of the public nature of deterrence in democracies:
"That's the dilemma. That defined what Hurd was doing. The pressure on
him was a Conservative Party that was very afraid of being dragged in."[75]
When the author asked Foreign Secretary Hurd whom these statements about
the intractability and moral ambiguity of the conflict were directed toward,
he answered: "Our colleagues in the Cabinet were more skeptical. They certainly did not believe in air strikes. Above all they did not believe in further
involvement. . . . The same was true in the parliamentary party, the majority party. People were viscerally opposed to deeper risk-taking."[76]

These public statements, however, contributed significantly to the two
most serious crises of the Bosnian war—the taking of UN hostages in May
1995 and the fall of the safe areas to the Bosnian Serbs in July 1995. As Philip
Towle noted, "[T]he attempt to explain to the British public that the armed
forces in Bosnia were highly vulnerable weakened their deterrent effect against
Serbian forces."[77] In response to NATO air strikes in May 1995, the Bosnian
Serbs took hundreds of UN peacekeepers hostage, chaining them to potential military targets as "human shields" to prevent military reprisals. At Britain's
initiative, major troop contributors responded by creating a Rapid Reaction
Force that reinforced the UN forces with heavier weapons. The government
did not welcome the step. The diplomat Neville-Jones said of the hostage crisis: "We had to do this thing that we never really wanted to do, but clearly
was now unavoidable, which was bring in heavy armor."[78] As the prime minister said in Parliament, the force "will provide the protection forces, *for the*

74. *Hansard* (29 April 1993), col. 121.
75. Interview with the author (2 July 2001).
76. Interview with the author (28 June 2001).
77. Philip Towle, "The British Debate about Intervention in European Conflicts," in Lawrence
Freedman (ed.), *Military Intervention in European Conflicts* (Oxford: Blackwell, 1994), p. 101.
78. Interview with the author (19 July 2001). Although the French seized on the initiative and
made it their own, it had British origins.

first time, with the artillery that is now necessary as a deterrent and response to bombardment."[79]

Given that plans for limited NATO air strikes around Sarajevo had been in place since February 1994 and Bosnian Serb forces had consistently harassed UN troops since their initial deployment in the fall of 1992, why did the British only agree to their reinforcement following the hostage crisis? David Hannay, British ambassador to the United Nations, said to the author: "If you are thinking that they could have got to that point a bit earlier, you are not wrong in that. They could have. But there was not the will to do so."[80] Previously the government had publicly argued against consolidating troops and making them easier to protect, claiming that it would reduce their ability to deliver humanitarian aid. Neville-Jones, who coordinated Bosnian policy, disputed that justification later, saying that the force "opened up possibilities that you would not previously have had. First, we could protect our own forces much better. Secondly, the whole role you would be able to perform in relation to the civilian population was also potentially, if not transformed, greatly strengthened."[81]

In reality, the Conservative government was worried about military escalation that would lead Britain deeper into a conflict the government wanted no part of. In a striking statement, Rifkind sounded almost like a pacifist of the far left in justifying his policy as defense secretary:

> The wider reason why it did not happen earlier is the government had no desire to become a belligerent in this conflict. Inevitably if you set up a rapid reaction force, what is it going to react to? What is its role going to be? That is a step change, even if its role is just designed for protection. Whatever you say may be the rules of engagement and the purpose of an initiative, you have to see any initiative not just as you wish it to be seen, but as others will see it. What is the consequence for the relative military capabilities of forces operating in a territory? If you put a highly trained, highly professional army with sophisticated weapons in the middle of a war zone, *you* may say they are not belligerents, that they are only there for what you have laid down to be their role, but they inevitably affect the dynamics of the conflict that is taking place simply by their presence.[82]

The appeal to the spiral model was indicative of a feeling that the operation did not serve the national interest. A robustly armed force would draw

---

79. *Hansard* (31 May 1995), col. 1003 (emphasis added).
80. Interview with the author (22 June 2001).
81. Interview with the author (19 July 2001). Major used this justification as well. See *Hansard* (19 June 1995), cols. 24–25.
82. Interview with the author (19 July 2001).

Britain in further. Rifkind said: "People were worried right from the beginning that you can go in with a limited mandate, but then the force of events leads to escalation not just in your military activities, but in your commitment and the difficulty of extracting yourself from such a situation. This was a factor we always had in mind, but even if we had not, it would have been put before us by the House of Commons."[83]

By taking hostages, the Bosnian Serbs had finally made peacekeeping in Bosnia into a vital national interest. Only this allowed the British government to escalate. The Rapid Reaction Force would eventually become a key component in the August military action by NATO and the UN against the Bosnian Serbs. However, it was not initially intended as such. It was not a new sign of British resolve in favor of the Bosnian Muslims, although it involved fifty-five hundred new British troops of the 24th Air Mobile Brigade. The head of the armed services at the time, Field Marshal Peter Inge, said: "As Rupert Smith [commander of UNPROFOR in Bosnia] will tell you, he did not know what the hell he was going to do with them."[84] Political Director Neville-Jones said the brigade was put in place "for defensive purposes," as a sign "not to mess with British troops," but not as a deterrent against further Bosnian Serb aggression against the safe areas.[85] Rifkind explained: "In my capacity as defense secretary, my prime obligation was the security and well-being of the British personnel operating in Bosnia because their lives were under threat, with hostage taking. . . . Even greater than our obligation to help Bosnia was to ensure no unnecessary loss of life to our own personnel."[86]

The government was opposed enough to any peace enforcement action that ministers made their conception of the force a matter of public record, sending a clear signal of their intentions. Prime Minister Major said in the House of Commons that although "It is difficult not to give a misleading impression by saying that it is there to add muscle . . . it is emphatically not there to fight—that point should be clear. . . . The role of the rapid reaction corps is primarily to reinforce and protect."[87] The British had no plans for reprisals. Rather than use the public outcry from the hostage crisis to

83. Ibid.

84. Interview with the author (11 July 2001). See also Tim Ripley, *Operation Deliberate Force* (Lancaster, U.K.: Centre for Defence and International Security Studies, 1999), pp. 130–131.

85. Interview with the author (19 July 2001). The author asked Foreign Secretary Hurd: "Was the Rapid Reaction Force designed to make air power more effective or was this a welcome side effect only realized later in the summer when continued air strikes began?" Hurd answered: "To be honest, the second. It was the reaction to the hostage situation." Interview with the author (28 June 2001).

86. Interview with the author (19 July 2001).

87. *Hansard* (19 June 1995), col. 24. Rifkind said the same: (31 May 1995), col. 1097. He repeated those aims later in the summer: (12 July 1995), col. 958.

redouble its efforts and send signals of resolve, the government spoke increasingly of withdrawal. Rifkind, who became foreign secretary in July 1995, proclaimed: "[I]f a peacekeeping force does not receive a minimum degree of co-operation, to withdraw is in no way a humiliation."[88] British forces in Bosnia were reportedly frustrated with the government for not giving them an expanded role in peace enforcement, a feeling that persisted.[89]

The Bosnian Serbs seemed to take the government's words seriously. The British commander in Gorazde claims that British troops in the safe area were never harassed after Major announced the deployment of the air mobile brigade, an excellent war-fighting tool. But he also noted that Major simultaneously effectively declared that Britain's only national interest was the protection of its soldiers.[90] Shortly afterward, the Bosnian Serb offensive on the safe areas began. On July 12, Srebrenica fell.

Although the British government had tried to convey that British forces would not fight to defend the safe areas, officials acknowledge that their consent to the safe area plan created exaggerated expectations on the part of the civilian population in Bosnia. Neville-Jones said: "We never took the view that we were actually there to protect populations. We had taken the view that they were safe areas, which had the side effect that they were protected. This was a very equivocal position, I will grant you. You try getting that distinction across. It is not one you would be particularly proud of anyway."[91] Foreign Secretary Hurd did not believe the point had been made: "I think there may well have been people in Srebrenica who were deceived to believe it was safer than it was."[92] A Foreign Office official intimately involved with the mission said: "The defense of the safe areas was certainly implied even if not in the text. It does not make sense any way else."[93] The combination of the British conception of the UN mission as limited to peacekeeping and humanitarian aid and the international community's outrage at the plight of the Bosnian Muslims had disastrous effects, sending signals to the Bosnian Serbs that the areas would not be defended and signals to the civilians that they would.

Nevertheless, even after Srebrenica fell the British continued to argue that they did not have the ability to protect the remaining safe areas. Again the Conservatives feared military escalation and spirals. Of French plans to

---

88. Malcolm Rifkind, *Hansard* (12 July 1995), col. 965. Major was more muted, but justified the Rapid Reaction Force as potentially helpful for pulling out: (31 May 1995), col. 1005.

89. Ripley (1999), p. 118, 123, 125, 154.

90. Ibid., p. 139.

91. Interview with the author (19 July 2001).

92. Interview with the author (28 June 2001). The British ambassador to the UN said: "I think they had exaggerated expectations. They were a politico-military barrier, not a serious military barrier." Interview with the author (22 June 2001).

93. Interview with the author (6 June 2001).

reinforce the Gorazde safe haven maintained by British troops, and of American proposals to bomb artillery first, newly installed Defense Secretary Michael Portillo said: "To reinforce by helicopter carries possibly greater risks. The aircraft are vulnerable to attack unless air defences are destroyed by a massive pre-emptive attack, with all the risks of military escalation."[94] The British relented on air strikes, but restricted them to protecting Gorazde, where British troops were present, rather than all of the safe areas. This was the position that the major powers agreed to at a special conference in London in late July.[95] Only later would the British give in. After another attack on the Sarajevo marketplace in late August, the bombing began. The Cabinet was hostile to peace enforcement to the very end. "The various escalations of range and ferocity in bombing campaign were very politicized," said Political Director Neville-Jones. "We did not want to go to the most advanced stage of the air strikes."[96] The first act of the UN Bosnia Commander General Rupert Smith was to order the British forces to pull out of Gorazde. He was worried about London's resolve.[97]

Sending Signals Abroad: The Left's Critique

While the majority in the Labour and Liberal Democratic parties did not advocate the fighting of a full-scale war against the Bosnian Serbs, their reproaches against the government's behavior in regard to the hostage taking and the safe areas was inspired by the deterrence model and indicated their commitment to inclusiveness. First, the party leaderships were highly critical of the government's public discussion of withdrawal. The leader of the Labour opposition, Tony Blair, said that "talk of withdrawal in Bosnia in response to the taking of hostages is deeply unhelpful at this time. It is hardly a message of firm resolve in the face of what is effectively an act of coercive blackmail."[98] Shadow foreign secretary Robin Cook and Liberal Democratic leader Paddy Ashdown made the same plea. Both parties had the firm support of their backbenches on these points.[99] Although a few hard left, antimilitarist MPs such as Tam Dalyell feared air strikes and urged the government to "get around a table, embarrassing as it may be, and talk, talk,

---

94. Michael Portillo, *Hansard* (19 July 1995), col. 1744. On the lack of a mandate, see Malcolm Rifkind (12 July 1995), col. 965. See also Ivo H. Daalder, *Getting to Dayton* (Washington, D.C.: Brookings Institution Press, 2000), p. 72.

95. Ripley (1999), pp. 158–159; Daalder (2000), p. 77.

96. Interview with the author (19 July 2001)

97. Ripley (1999), p. 242.

98. *Hansard* (31 May 1995), col. 1007.

99. In *Hansard*, see Robin Cook (19 July 1995), cols. 1749–1752; Paddy Ashdown (31 May 1995), col. 1014. For backbencher voices, see John Gunnell (12 July 1995), col. 965; Calum MacDonald (31 May 1995), col. 1067.

talk," the overwhelming majority emphasized resolve and credible threats of force, as they had done throughout the conflict.[100]

The second focus of opposition criticism was the government's failure to live up to its commitments to the UN mission. "[T]he UN mandate should be enforced with clarity and consistency. Mixed messages on the use of force are not helpful," Blair emphasized along with other frontbenchers. When the UN does not meet its obligations, the "impact of those forces becomes significantly diminished."[101] The primary target was the safe area policy. Both Blair and Cook had made statements in support of protection of the safe areas before the events of the summer, as had Ashdown.[102] A week before the fall of Srebrenica Cook said that "having shown the necessary resolve to secure the release of the hostages, the UN must show the same resolve to protect and feed civilians in towns that the UN itself has declared safe areas."[103] Following Srebrenica's seizure, he chastised the Major government for coming up short and putting the soldiers in a situation in which they could not even defend themselves.[104]

The Loyal Opposition: The Lib-Lab Response to Conservative Failure

Despite the weakness of the Conservative government, neither the opposition's leaderships nor its backbenches ever gave any indication that they would capitalize on the Tories' troubles. Labour and the Liberal Democrats could easily have put the Conservative majority in jeopardy by calling for withdrawal from a highly ineffective military operation, thereby putting the government on the defensive against its more exclusivist backbenches. Instead, both parties supported the deployment of the Rapid Reaction Force as a way of preventing British troops from pulling out and ensuring the full implementation of UNPROFOR's mandate. Even if the force was more defensive in nature than they would have preferred, they feared that without their support, the Major government would have to pull out completely. Blair was even fending off Tory detractors in Parliament.[105] They carved out a consensus with

100. In *Hansard*, see Tam Dalyell (31 May 1995), col. 1050. Interventionists included Robin Cook (7 December 1994), col. 313; Clare Short (29 April 1993), cols. 1235–1238. Russell Johnston spoke for the Liberal Democrats: (25 September 1992), col. 148.

101. *Hansard* (31 May 1995), col. 1011. Also Robin Cook (19 July 1995), col. 1752; David Clark (12 July 1995), col. 750.

102. Tony Blair, *Hansard* (31 May 1995), col. 1011; also Paddy Ashdown (31 May 1995), col. 1015.

103. *Hansard* (5 July 1995), col. 377.

104. *Hansard* (19 July 1995), cols. 1746–1750.

105. For Ashdown, it was a "signal to the Bosnian Serbs of the seriousness of our intent." *Hansard* (31 May 1995), col. 1013. Blair said: "Anyone who, *like those Conservative Members*, doubts whether the United Nations presence has made a difference should ask those on the ground—soldiers or civilians." *Hansard* (31 May 1995), col. 1010 (emphasis added).

Tory leaders and moderates closest to them on the ideological spectrum who wanted to maintain the peacekeeping mission.

In fact, high-ranking officials in the Conservative government unanimously testify that instead of feeling that Labour was attempting to reap partisan gain from Conservative difficulties, the government considered its support critical for maintaining the British presence in Bosnia, even if Labour wanted to go further than the government. British ambassador to the UN, David Hannay, explained: "It was the government's own supporters, the back-benchers, who had their doubts, not the Labour Party. Major had a slim majority, but that is irrelevant if the official Opposition . . . was supporting the government's policy."[106] Neville-Jones expressed the same idea, adding that opposition support actually helped quell Conservative resistance: "The government held the situation together. It was never on the run in the House. However, it was able to rely on the support of the opposition, and that is something that keeps the backbenches under control. Revolting against the leadership when the opposition is supporting it is an embarrassing thing to do. . . . In a sense Ashdown's activities were a counterpoint to the doubters. I think to be frank it was quite useful for the government to have a voice from the other side saying you are not doing enough as distinct from why are you there at all."[107] This alliance is puzzling for an office-seeking approach. Indeed the government could have gone further had it so decided. An adviser to Foreign Secretary Hurd said: "You had a situation where a British Conservative government could be reasonably sure that it would not be attacked by the main opposition party for some degree of progressively ratcheted military intervention."[108] The Major government's hesitance reflected its own perception of the extent of British interest in the Balkans.

LABOURING IN OFFICE:
THE BLAIR GOVERNMENT AND THE LEFT IN KOSOVO

Whereas the Bosnian conflict had elements of an interstate conflict, Kosovo was clearly a civil war. Intervention meant a fundamentally new approach to one of the pillars of international order following the Second World War, that of noninterference in the internal affairs of states. As in Bosnia, the parties of the left and the party of the right approached the

106. Interview with the author (22 June 2001). Rifkind, when asked about staving off a hostile parliamentary party, said: "It was not as hard as that. For instance it never became a partisan matter with government vs. opposition." Interview with the author (19 July 2001).
107. Interview with the author (19 July 2001).
108. Interview with the author (26 June 2001).

situation very differently. The Labour Party again saw military action in inclusive terms as furthering the promotion of its values beyond Britain. Human rights, reasoned members, did not know borders, a particularly strong sentiment in Labour's left wing. Bill Rammell rejected the notion that military action was only justified by a threat to British lives, security, or financial interests, arguing that such an idea was "based on a view that respect for human rights, decency and civilised values is felt only within national boundaries."[109] Labour MPs connected their conception of the universality of human rights with their leftist ideology. Livingstone said: "My socialism and driving moral force are not defined or constrained by lines drawn on a map . . ."[110] To be on the left, according to Roger Casale, meant to extend domestic values: "Milosevic's actions stand in direct contradiction to the values of freedom, equality and justice that we have built into our systems of domestic legislation and into the conduct of international relations in the modern world and which have so often inspired the left."[111] Livingstone and Harry Cohen drew analogies between defending women from domestic violence and support for the action in Kosovo, demonstrating the link Labour was making to its tradition of defending the weak against the strong in domestic politics.[112]

The leadership of the party used similar arguments to justify the Kosovo intervention. "We cannot allow the values of Europe to be desecrated within one part of Europe while we live comfortably in our western corner of the continent," argued Prime Minister Blair.[113] Strong support for the Kosovo operation was the manifestation of an explicit effort to incorporate an "ethical dimension" into British foreign policy. Human rights were part of Labour's new approach to foreign policy "from day one," said Neville-Jones. The former political director had met with future Foreign Secretary Robin Cook before he took office in 1997, and Cook asked her what changes should be made at the FCO. When Neville-Jones mentioned a larger role for human rights, "Three strawberries came up" in Cook's eyes.[114] When Cook explained his initiative, he pledged to make Britain a "force for good in the world."

---

109. *Hansard* (18 May 1999), col. 957.

110. *Hansard* (25 March 1999), col. 573.

111. *Hansard* (19 April 1999), col. 637.

112. Livingstone asked why those leftists who opposed the war would intervene with force to prevent violence against women but not to protect Kosovars abroad. *Hansard* (25 March 1999), col. 573. Harry Cohen compared the sovereignty of states to the legality of spousal abuse in the past (25 March 1999), col. 609.

113. Tony Blair, "Speech at a Ceremony to Receive the Charlemagne Prize," Aachen (13 May 1999). See also Tony Blair, *Hansard* (13 April 1999), col. 32.

114. Interview with the author (19 July 2001). For a review of this effort to make foreign policy more ethical, see Nicholas J. Wheeler and Tim Dunne, "Good International Citizenship: a Third Way for British Foreign Policy," *International Affairs*, Vol. 74, No. 4 (1998), pp. 847–870.

Britain under Labour "recognized that the national interest cannot be defined only by narrow realpolitik."[115]

As in Bosnia, there was an antimilitarist opposition to the use of force against Serbia that found almost all of its support in the party's hard left. These politicians advocated the continuation of diplomacy under the stewardship of the United Nations and a pause in the bombing after the campaign began. They utilized numerous arguments against the intervention, questioning why NATO decided to intervene in the internal affairs of Serbia as opposed to other places where human rights were being violated, stressing the criminal character of the Kosovo Liberation Army so as to establish a moral equivalency, arguing that a ground offensive would be impossible as neither Greece nor Macedonia would permit Western forces to cross their territory, and objecting to the absence of a Security Council resolution authorizing the armed action.[116] Most strikingly, the opponents seemed to empathize with Milosevic's response to NATO bombing and doubted that Serb forces were engaged in ethnic cleansing.[117]

This low level of evaluative complexity was a reflection of a more fundamental antimilitarism. All considerations for the extremist left pointed to not using force. A quote from Benn, the spiritual leader of the antimilitarists, is suggestive: "NATO's threat to bomb Serbia is contrary to the charter of the United Nations which provides that only the Security Council can authorise military action . . . it would be likely to trigger a Balkan conflict, and a restart of the cold war; and it is in marked contrast with the total neglect of the plight of the Kurdish people. . . . NATO is not the international community, and [for the prime minister] to talk as if he and the United States speak for the world is to undermine the authority of the United Nations itself."[118] The lack of evaluative complexity was not unique to Benn. The general

---

115. Quoted in Louise Richardson, "A Force for Good in the World? Britain's Role in the Kosovo Crisis," in Pierre Martin and Mark R. Brawley (eds.), *Alliance Politics, Kosovo and NATO's War: Allied Force or Forced Allies* (New York: Palgrave, 2000), p. 159.

116. On the need for diplomacy, see comments in *Hansard* by Jeremy Corbyn (18 May 1999), col. 925; George Galloway (10 May 1999), cols. 27–28; Alice Mahon (13 April 1999), cols. 31–32. On the relative severity of the violations, see George Galloway (25 March 1999), col. 593. On the shadiness of the KLA, see George Galloway (25 March 1999), col. 593. On the practical difficulties, see Tam Dalyell (18 May 1999), cols. 932–933; Alice Mahon (25 March 1999), col. 577. On the operation's illegality, see Tony Benn (19 October 1998), col. 957; Jeremy Corbyn (18 May 1999), col. 924.

117. Benn said: "Whether their troops are there to repress the Kosovars or to defend their border I do not know, but if this country were threatened with a possible invasion, we would send people all over to prepare." *Hansard* (25 March 1999), col. 564. Tam Dalyell said: "If the Prime Minister were in the position of a Serbian soldier in Kosovo, knowing what was happening back at home and hearing that NATO intended to intensify the bombing, would there not be a danger that he might behave like an animal?" *Hansard* (29 March 1999), col. 742.

118. *Hansard* (19 October 1998), cols. 957–958. Ultimately Benn did not differentiate between uses of force, questioning the very possibility of using military means for inclusive purposes (25 March 1999), col. 564.

antimilitarism of intervention opponents was also evident in their pejorative references to NATO during the debates and in their view that it was intentionally usurping the role of the United Nations.[119]

This opposition, however, was marginal in comparison to the overwhelming support the government received from its backbenches, a marked contrast to its Conservative predecessor. An adviser to the prime minister said: "In terms of the Labour Party, all of this went off with no criticism at all, basically because they saw the cause as just."[120] Left-wing Labour MPs argued that Britain had a duty to prevent genocide, argued for the continuation of the air war to demonstrate NATO's resolve, rejected the argument that non-intervention in other cases of human rights abuses excused inaction in Kosovo, and openly argued for the insertion of ground forces.[121] They displayed as little evaluative complexity as their opponents. As in Bosnia, they recalled the failures of appeasement in the 1930s in justifying their support. Britain's national experience, they reasoned, had shown the need for force in particular instances in which inclusive values were at risk.[122]

Some have argued that the Blair government was able to act so decisively because of its enormous majority in parliament.[123] Office-seeking theorists might suggest that this majority provided a cushion that the Conservatives did not share. However, it was the small proportion of Labour antimilitarists relative to the party's sizable majority that made the government's position so strong. Bruce George, Labour chairman of the Defence Committee, estimated: "Within the spectrum of parliament, you had the far left of 15 maximum who were totally opposed to any action. They are semipacifists who hate NATO. We are almost 400 members so 15 is hardly worth counting. So there were more divisions in the Conservative Party than in the Labour Party."[124]

---

119. Those combining arguments in *Hansard* included Jeremy Corbyn (18 May 1999), cols. 923–925; George Galloway (25 March 1999), cols. 590–596; Alice Mahon (23 March 1999), col. 172; (25 March 1999), cols. 576–577. General antimilitarist sentiment can be found in statements by Tony Benn (25 March 1999), cols. 563–568; Jeremy Corbyn (18 May 1999), cols. 923–925; George Galloway (25 March 1999), cols. 590–596.

120. Interview with the author (2 July 2001).

121. On the importance of maintaining pressure, see comments in *Hansard* by Frank Cook (31 March 1999), col. 1216; Ken Livingstone (25 March 1999), cols. 570–575. Kingham said of the relative severity of the violations: "What are we supposed to say to people in Kosovo now? 'We are sorry, but you will have to wait and let genocide happen. We let a million die in Rwanda and we did not intervene in Bosnia, so it would not be fair.' I do not think so." Tess Kingham (19 April 1999), col. 656. On ground forces, see Tess Kingham (19 April 1999), cols. 656–657; Chris Mullin (18 May 1999), col. 907; Malcolm Wicks (19 April 1999), cols. 651–652.

122. In *Hansard*, see Ken Livingstone (18 May 1999), col. 921; Bill Rammell (18 May 1999), col. 956; Clive Soley (23 March 1999), cols. 167–168; Malcolm Wicks (29 March 1999), col. 744.

123. Ivo Daalder and Michael O'Hanlon, *Winning Ugly* (Washington, D.C.: Brookings Institution Press, 2000), p. 132.

124. Interview with the author (14 June 2001).

Matching Words with Deeds: The Blair Government

Labour's approach to the Kosovo war mirrored its policies while in the opposition. Its behavior was the essence of the compellence model. First, it was careful to restrict NATO's military objectives to those that were achievable with the means chosen. It was Britain that forced the wording of the NATO communiqué of 30 January 1999 that defined NATO's goals as "disrupting" and "degrading" Serbia's ability to repress the Albanian population.[125] British officials at the NATO Council meeting said that the United Kingdom "had great difficulty arguing that because most people said it was not a very noble objective. They said, 'You should say we are stopping it because that is what public opinion will understand.'"[126] Sensing that an air war was not capable of directly preventing a humanitarian catastrophe, the British insisted on the alternative wording.

Britain's caution did not signify that the Blair government was a weak link in the alliance. In fact, it was NATO's most strident hawk, in contrast to the Major government in Bosnia. Defense Secretary George Robertson was the first to push for planning when the situation in Kosovo deteriorated in June 1998.[127] Britain was also "on the skeptical end of NATO" when U.S. envoy Richard Holbrooke brokered a last minute agreement in October 1998 that deployed unarmed OSCE monitors to patrol a cease-fire that ultimately broke down.[128] In March 1999, the Blair government wanted to "keep all military options open in order to maintain a flexibility of response and keep Milosevic guessing as to our intentions," a Ministry of Defence (MOD) report revealed after the war. However, the need to maintain cohesion in the alliance affected Britain's behavior.[129] In public, the government backed the air war, but privately it expressed its objections. General Charles Guthrie, the head of the British armed services, described the word play: "We said we had no plan. That does not mean we did not want a plan. If we had had a ground campaign plan, and announced it, we would not have had to go on as long as we had to. We certainly were advocating that from the beginning, but we were in an alliance."[130]

Second, the Blair government highlighted the importance of demonstrating resolve in achieving NATO aims. Milosevic's response to the air strikes

125. Interview with FCO official (17 July 2001).

126. Interview with FCO official (21 June 2001).

127. Ibid.

128. Interview with Cabinet Office official (5 July 2001); Interview with FCO official (21 June 2001).

129. Ministry of Defence, *Kosovo: Lessons from the Crisis* (London: HMSO, 2000), pp. 45–46.

130. Interview with the author (16 July 2001). The air option "fell short of what we ideally would have done on our own," said an adviser to Robertson. "The UK's private view was that it was highly desirable to have a ground option to back it up, but that was as far as the coalition could be carried." Interview with the author (24 July 2001).

was to unleash a massive ethnic cleansing operation that drove millions of Kosovar refugees into neighboring Albania and Macedonia. With Milosevic absorbing the air campaign, NATO faced a choice of stepping up the pressure or conceding. A senior MOD official recalled the situation: "It is easy to get people to sign up for a bit of force that could be justified, applied to targets that are essentially military, linked to the repression and bring him to his knees. Then do you stop or do you escalate? That is the issue, isn't it?"[131] The Blair government chose the latter course as seen in its public rhetoric and behind-the-scenes behavior. One week after the bombing began, the prime minister proclaimed: "For every act of barbarity and every slaughter of the innocent, Milosevic should be made to pay a higher and higher price. . . . The proper answer to that is not weakness but strength."[132] He advocated "pounding every part of that regime day after day until it accedes to the NATO demands. That is the only thing that we can do."[133]

More importantly, the prime minister made a keynote speech on a new "doctrine of international community," making the case for a reinterpretation of the importance of sovereignty and the obligation to intervene in the internal affairs of states in cases of gross violations of human rights. Connecting this new principle of international affairs to the war in Kosovo, Blair declared that "success is the only exit strategy I am prepared to consider."[134] The prime minister was intentionally raising the stakes. In James Fearon's terminology, the Labour government sent a costly signal by raising the potential audience costs in case of failure.[135] An MOD official said of the speech: "I think that sometimes fainter hearts are made uneasy by strong language, but it may be the right thing to do in terms of getting across your message *both to your own people and the people you are facing.*"[136] The speech was the public portion of the government's strategy to build up NATO support for such an invasion.[137] The government was attempting to lead public opinion both at home and abroad. It sent its domestic press director to NATO to run the communications campaign there.[138]

131. Interview with the author (14 June 2001).

132. *Hansard* (29 March 1999), col. 731.

133. *Hansard* (26 April 1999), col. 31. See also comments by Tony Blair (23 March 1999), col. 172; Robin Cook (18 May 1999), col. 887.

134. Tony Blair, "Doctrine of the International Community," Speech to the Economic Club of Chicago (27 April 1999). On sovereignty he said: "Non-interference has long been considered an important principle of international order. And it is not one we would want to jettison too readily. . . . But the principle of non-interference must be qualified in important ways. Acts of genocide can never be a purely internal matter."

135. James Fearon, "Signaling Foreign Policy Interests: Tying Hands vs. Sinking Costs," *Journal of Conflict Resolution*, Vol. 41, No. 1 (1997), pp. 68–90.

136. Interview with the author (27 July 2001) (emphasis added).

137. Interview with FCO official (26 July 2001).

138. Vickers (2000); Richardson (2000), p. 158.

Unlike the Conservative government in Bosnia, Labour could send such signals because the parliamentary party and the government were ideologically committed to peace enforcement. Former civil servant Neville-Jones described the speech as "putting some sort of intellectual framework around the party's instincts and the ethical foreign policy Cook was starting to enunciate. It had resonance within the party."[139] Asked whether the government feared the speech would raise the stakes too high to succeed, another adviser to the defense secretary answered: "Not for us, because we were already there. We said from the beginning, 'What does it take to win?' The military said it would take a ground campaign."[140]

Privately the government began to develop plans for its own contribution to any forced ground entry into Kosovo to establish a peacekeeping presence. The Blair government was growing increasingly frustrated with NATO's inability to send resolute signals to Milosevic. "I can understand why other governments were saying, 'Oh Christ, shut up!' But you cannot coerce and influence the mind of a Milosevic if you have to pay attention all the time to the weakest link in somebody's public opinion," said a British representative at NATO.[141] Before the NATO summit in late April the prime minister convinced President Clinton to allow NATO Commander General Wesley Clark to begin informal planning. He drew heavily on existing British plans. Fearing that Clark, a ground troops advocate, was being cut out of the loop in Washington by a hesitant military establishment, Blair provided him with details of his conversations with Clinton.[142]

At a secret meeting of NATO defense ministers on 27 May 1999, Defense Secretary Robertson pledged fifty-four thousand British ground troops, and to show he was serious brought along thirty thousand letters to be sent out to reservists.[143] A senior official stressed later that "this was genuine. That was not propaganda, which is astonishing as it is half the size of our standing army."[144] Other governments were noncommittal, but the British wanted to ensure adequate time for mobilization by the fall, even if NATO had not made a decision.[145] A British official delegated to NATO at the time estimated that the government "would have been pushing very hard for a decision to initiate a ground force by the middle of June."[146] Given that Milosevic

139. Interview with the author (19 July 2001).
140. Interview with the author (24 July 2001).
141. Interview with FCO official (21 June 2001).
142. Richardson (2000), p. 154.
143. Daalder and O'Hanlon (2000), p. 158.
144. Interview with the author (3 July 2001). Richardson (2000) confirmed this commitment in her own interviews.
145. Interview with MOD official (14 June 2001).
146. Interview with FCO official (21 June 2001).

finally consented to NATO demands on June 10, the British were only days away from taking active measures to plan for ground combat. Alongside the renewed diplomatic engagement of the Russians and the maintenance of the NATO coalition during the entire course of the air campaign, the planning and increasingly public discussion of the ground campaign is regarded as one of the most important factors in NATO's victory.[147]

The Disloyal Opposition: The Conservative Response to Failures in Kosovo

NATO's victory was never assured, however, and unlike in Bosnia, the support of the main opposition party could not be taken for granted. Criticism from the Tory backbenches was virulent. Conservative opponents used arguments identical to those they put forward in Bosnia, which again overlapped significantly with those made by the extreme left of the Labour Party. They questioned why NATO was intervening in Kosovo and not in other areas where human rights were violated, accusing the government of hypocrisy.[148] They were disdainful of Labour's claims of the universality of human rights and argued that the action was illegal. Spiral model thinking was also evident. A ground invasion would prove impossible and only escalate the fighting, drawing NATO into a quagmire. Bombing Serbia would only unite the population and increase their determination.[149]

Behind these arguments, however, was a more fundamental resistance to a war that did not further British interests. The right-wing Conservative MP Peter Viggers stated this explicitly: "[T]he purpose of foreign policy is to protect and promote the interests of the United Kingdom. We should, of course, desire a peaceful and prosperous world, but we must remember that basic principle. . . . Without agreement, there would be many casualties, and for what?"[150] Evaluative complexity was also low. Those who opposed the operation on exclusivist grounds were also likely to claim it was illegal, selective, and doomed to fail.[151]

---

147. Daalder and O'Hanlon (2000) take this view. See pp. 160–161. See also Daniel L. Byman and Matthew C. Waxman, "Kosovo and the Great Air Power Debate," *International Security*, Vol. 24, No. 4 (2000), p. 7.

148. In *Hansard*, see Edward Leigh (25 March 1999), cols. 598–599. Also Christopher Gill (25 March 1999), cols. 550–551; Douglas Hogg (18 May 1999), col. 935.

149. In *Hansard*, see Alan Clark (18 May 1999), cols. 921–923; (25 March 1999), cols. 574–576; Roger Gale (13 April 1999), col. 30; Edward Leigh (25 March 1999), cols. 597–600; Peter Tapsell (23 March 1999), col. 167; (29 March 1999), col. 741.

150. *Hansard* (19 April 1999), cols. 630–632.

151. In *Hansard*, see Alan Clark (25 March 1999), cols. 574–576; Douglas Hogg (18 May 1999), col. 935; Edward Leigh (25 March 1999), cols. 598–599.

The Kosovo war put the Conservative Party in an uncomfortable position since there was intense pressure on the party, particularly as a rightist one, to back the operation after it began. As Martin O'Neill, former shadow defense secretary of the Labour Party, explained: "The Tories basically take the view, 'my country right or wrong,' and they will support our troops in war. They are a British nationalist party."[152] The most consistently supportive Tories were Conservative members of the Foreign Affairs and Defence committees and former ministers who took a more differentiated approach. They considered the operation along the hawk-dove continuum, that is, its consequences for Britain to threaten and use force in the future. They believed that once the intervention had begun, more was at stake than the fate of the Kosovars. Former defense secretary Tom King stressed the importance of seeing the operation through for credibility, a reason that Blair rejected. Foreign policy expert Sir Peter Emery pledged complete and absolute support until a solution was reached. Defense expert Julian Lewis wanted a firm statement of willingness to use ground troops, worrying about the signal NATO would send if it did not prevail.[153]

Besides these individuals, however, virtually no other Tory backbencher strongly supported the war publicly in Parliament. Even those backbenchers who did were not privately comfortable with going to war for humanitarian purposes, so their support must be considered considerably more shallow than that of their counterparts in Labour.[154] Despite this strong pressure of considerations of preserving British and NATO prestige, lone Tory interventionist Sir Patrick Cormack estimates that a third of the parliamentary party disagreed with even the frontbench's official support of the air campaign. A member of the party's shadow cabinet, he had to threaten to resign to ensure that the party leadership would come out in favor of military action, and still had to move to the backbenches in order to make speeches in favor of government policy.[155]

As it was, the party's endorsement was tepid. The leadership pledged its official support after the onset of the war, with maintaining credibility a critical part of its argumentation throughout the conflict. Conservative shadow defense secretary John Maples said: "The Government have put at stake the credibility of our armed forces and of the NATO alliance. That credibility

152. Interview with the author (27 June 2001).

153. See in *Hansard,* Tom King and Tony Blair (23 March 1999) cols. 168–169; Peter Emery (26 May 1999), col. 363 (18 May 1999), col. 886; Julian Lewis (26 April 1999), col. 34 (18 May 1999), col. 902.

154. Andrew Tyrie, for instance, stressed the need to prevail after the war began, but expressed deep reservations about the war to the author in a subsequent interview with the author. For his public statements, see *Hansard* (25 March 1999), col. 606.

155. Interview with the author (24 July 2001).

must be redeemed."[156] Yet the shadow foreign secretary, Michael Howard, made plain Tory distaste for Labour's new doctrine of intervention, declaring that "if that is the Government's view, then I can only say that the obligation has been honoured more in the breach than in the observance."[157]

In the most striking contrast to the Labour Party's behavior while in opposition, the Conservatives attempted to force the government into a definitive statement of its position on ground troops. The party itself categorically ruled out ground troops at the beginning of the operation.[158] In an effort to move the multinational coalition further, the Blair government was gradually escalating its rhetoric. At the beginning of the campaign, the prime minister said there were "difficulties" in mounting a ground operation, but one month into the operation he said that "Milosevic has no veto over NATO's actions."[159] Solidarity in NATO prevented the government from going further. While the prime minister expressed his preference that the government not divulge its thinking so as to keep Milosevic guessing, the Tories demanded that the government pin down its policy publicly even after the second day of bombing.[160] While in opposition, Labour had cautioned the Conservatives to hold their cards close to their vests. The Conservative Opposition, however, was attempting to undermine compellence, another departure from its Cold War policies.

Unlike in Bosnia, when the Conservative government expressed gratitude for Labour backing in difficult moments, ministers, Labour backbenchers, Liberal Democrats, and even civil servants all noted and criticized Tory behavior. Labour MP David Winnick said: "What was cowardly and despicable was the way in which the Tory frontbench wavered. When something went wrong like the bombing of the Chinese embassy, they exploited that. Instead of saying it was unfortunate, but in war these things happen, they said, 'Look at what has gone wrong and will it ever go right?' "[161] The more moderate Labour chairman of the Defence Committee said: "Of course they had to support the NATO line, but it was not done by the official leadership of the

156. *Hansard* (18 May 1999), col. 965. See also William Hague (29 March 1999), col. 734; John Maples (19 April 1999), col. 662;.

157. *Hansard* (25 March 1999), col. 543.

158. Conservative leader William Hague asked for an assurance that air strikes were not a prelude to a ground war and that ground forces would only be deployed to implement a diplomatic settlement. *Hansard* (23 March 1999), col. 163. Howard said the party could not support a ground war (25 March 1999), col. 543.

159. *Hansard* (23 March 1999), col. 166; (26 April 1999), col. 21.

160. Tony Blair, *Hansard* (26 April 1999), col. 25. See also comments by Conservatives William Hague (13 April 1999), col. 22; Michael Howard (18 May 1999), col. 894; John Maples (25 March 1999), col. 611.

161. Interview with the author (24 July 2001). Left-winger Clwyd made similar remarks in parliament. Anne Clwyd, *Hansard* (10 May 1999), col. 26.

party with any high enthusiasm."[162] Defense Secretary Robertson himself advised shadow defense secretary Maples: "When one's only strength is in being negative, one does not convince the country."[163] A senior bureaucrat detected a deliberate strategy to take advantage of a possible NATO failure: "All opposition parties are in difficulty when the armed forces are in action. They cannot appear to be disloyal. So there is a surface veneer of bipartisanship with a few lone voices calling for an end at all costs. But we all thought that if it had gone wrong, the opposition had positioned themselves to take the government apart on it."[164]

In contrast, the Labour Party had unswerving support from the Liberal Democratic Party throughout the campaign, suggesting that Tory criticism was not motivated by run-of-the-mill party politics, but by real ideological differences. The leftist Liberal Democratic Party backed the air strikes, proclaimed unwavering support for the government, and went so far as to criticize Tory hesitation.[165] The party's lack of evaluative complexity showed a firm ideological commitment. Foreign policy spokesperson Campbell even went as far as to defend the legal basis of the operation, one of the weakest arguments in its favor.[166] They also criticized the Conservative effort to pin Labour down as opposing a land invasion. Liberal Democratic leader Ashdown defended Blair, saying: "On the military, I agree with the Prime Minister that we ought not to be broadcasting our shots and saying in detail what we should do."[167] Only part of the opposition was loyal.

However, free from the constraints of NATO coalition-building, the Liberal Democrats complained at every opportunity that removing the ground troop option from the table sent a message to Serbia that NATO was not committed to its objectives and undermined its possible compellence effect.[168] The Liberal Democrats wanted the Labour government to go further than air strikes. Campbell elliptically stated support for a ground invasion: "Unfortunately, the troops that we now have on the ground were designed, and have a mission designed, around the Rambouillet agreement. Certain elements of that agreement have simply been overtaken by events, so we must begin to update that mission and the posture."[169] With the support of the

---

162. Interview with the author (14 June 2001). In Parliament Bruce George said: "If one criticizes almost every element of the Government's policies, it is difficult to maintain the fiction that what is upheld by those policies is worth supporting." *Hansard* (18 May 1999), col. 897.

163. *Hansard* (18 May 1999), col. 966.

164. Interview with FCO official (2 July 2001).

165. Menzies Campbell, *Hansard* (18 May 1999), col. 903.

166. *Hansard* (25 March 1999), col. 547.

167. *Hansard* (26 April 1999), col. 26.

168. In *Hansard*, see Paddy Ashdown (13 April 1999), col. 24; Menzies Campbell (25 March 1999), col. 548; (31 March 1999), col. 1209; Mike Hancock (25 March 1999), col. 582.

169. *Hansard* (26 April 1999), col. 26.

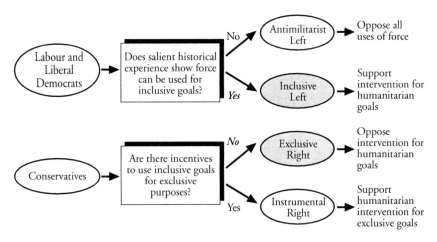

Figure 2. The British case

Liberal Democrats and his own party, Blair's case for ground troops would have had overwhelming support in Parliament.

Figure 2 provides a broad summary of the cleavage structure of British foreign policy. Cultural factors did not constrain the articulation of very different national interests by the Conservatives and Labour. National experience, however, was crucial. Britain's victory over fascism gave the left an example of how force was sometimes necessary to advance causes in line with its principles. It chose the inclusive path in the 1990s. The Conservatives, however, had a narrower conception of the national interest that did not include taking significant risks to promote human rights. They took the exclusive path. For the Tories, the Balkans were a place of little interest to Britain, another faraway place of which they knew little. Cleavages over foreign policy are not the same in all countries, however, as will be seen in the next chapter. Due to Germany's very different history, the debate was in fact originally the reverse of Britain's.

CHAPTER 4

Never Again War?
The Interparty and Intraparty Politics
of Normalization in Germany

In 1999 Germany took part in the NATO air campaign against Yugoslavia to help end the repression of the Albanian population in Kosovo. It was the first time German forces had participated in a peace enforcement mission in the 1990s. More significantly, it was the German army's first combat mission since the Second World War. The Kosovo war broke several more taboos for Germany, since it was waged without the authorization of the United Nations Security Council against a country the Nazi regime had victimized fifty years before. The change was abrupt. Germany's historical burden in the region had led the conservative Kohl government to rule out the deployment even of German peacekeeping troops to Bosnia-Herzegovina in December 1995, less than four years before NATO began its bombardment of Kosovo. Countless accounts of German foreign policy in the post–Cold War period stress the country's unique antimilitarist approach to international relations due to its tragic historical experience with militarism.[1] How did such a departure from the traditions of Germany's political culture since the Second World War come about?

Even more surprisingly, the Social Democratic (SPD) and Green parties which formed the governing coalition during the military operation had waged intense political and (in the case of the SPD) legal battles while in opposition to prevent the use of German troops "out of area"—in missions other than the defense of German or NATO territory. Germany's highest

1. The best are Thomas Berger, *Cultures of Antimilitarism: National Security in Germany and Japan* (Baltimore: Johns Hopkins University Press, 1998); John Duffield, *World Power Forsaken: Political Culture, International Institutions and German Security Policy after Unification* (Palo Alto: Stanford University Press, 1998).

court resolved the constitutional question in July 1994, but the political controversy continued into the summer of 1995 as the Bosnian war reached its peak. The SPD and the Greens had a long history of antimilitarism. The Social Democrats initially opposed rearmament in the 1950s. Significant sections of both parties protested the deployment of nuclear weapons on German soil in the 1980s. What had changed? How was a coalition of the left able to carry through such a drastic change in Germany's foreign and military policy?

Culturalists discount the significance of these events. To the extent that Kosovo stretched the boundaries of expected behavior, they stress that Germany's antimilitarism is tempered by an equally strong commitment to multilateralism. Germany strongly supports cooperation within NATO and the European Union so as to avoid falling back into the international isolation it brought upon itself during the first half of the century. Kosovo was a "perfectly normal abnormality." Germany is "still a civilian power," not a military power.[2] Nor were the partisan debates over whether the constitution allowed out-of-area deployments of the military evidence of early cracks in this consensus. Instead they are best understood as "differences of emphasis rather than of irreconcilable positions," according to John Duffield. Parties do not articulate alternative foreign policy programs as they share a "*single* German political culture that has placed distinct boundaries on the discourse employed by German political leaders and clearly proscribed some theoretically possible policy responses."[3]

This dramatically understates the intensity of the conflict and the extent of Germany's transformation. Given that military intervention became the most significant issue in international affairs after the Cold War, an understanding of these contrasting positions is critical. Contrary to cultural arguments, I contend that German participation in the air campaign against Yugoslavia was the culmination of a period of great change and partisan contestation in German foreign policy. There was never an antimilitarist consensus against intervention following reunification. Almost immediately after the end of the Cold War, the rightist Christian Democratic Union (CDU) government embarked on a deliberate strategy of pushing the boundaries of the constitution's restrictions on the use of the Bundeswehr. The goal was

2. Hanns W. Maull, "German Foreign Policy, Post-Kosovo: Still a 'Civilian Power'?" *German Politics,* Vol. 9, No. 2 (August 2000), pp. 1–24; Thomas Berger, "A Perfectly Normal Abnormality: German Foreign Policy after the Kosovo Crisis," paper presented at the meeting of the International Studies Association (16 March 2000), p. 14. On Germany's multilateralist instinct, see Thomas Banchoff, *The German Problem Transformed: Institutions, Politics and Foreign Policy, 1945–1995* (Ann Arbor: University of Michigan Press, 1999).

3. John Duffield, "Political Culture and State Behavior: Why Germany Confounds Neorealism," *International Organization,* Vol. 53, No. 4 (Autumn 1999), pp. 789–790.

to accustom the population to the use of force abroad and provoke a resolution of the issue by Germany's highest court, which the government believed
would rule in its favor. The CDU instrumentalized participation in various
humanitarian interventions to "normalize" the use of force, thereby increasing Germany's influence and regaining a certain degree of sovereignty lost
during the Cold War. Analysts have long suspected this undeclared strategy, but I provide the most solid confirmation to date.

The conservative government's strategy of normalization provoked one of
the most heated debates on foreign policy in postwar German history. The
SPD and Greens, mindful of the German past, gave an antimilitarist response
to the question whether Germany should participate in humanitarian interventions. Pacifist ideology was more powerful in Germany than the left's
inclusive inclination toward promoting human rights. To varying degrees,
the two parties held that the use of the military was inherently escalatory and
ill suited to protecting civilian populations in ethnic wars. The left determined its position with reference only to the antimilitarist continuum, focusing almost exclusively on the use of force rather than the goals sought.

Given the opposition of the SPD and Greens at the beginning of the 1990s
to out-of-area deployments of the Bundeswehr, their leading the country into
its first military intervention in over fifty years might seem to suggest that
party ideology matters very little. The left's reversal might not seem surprising to those who argue that party policy is primarily driven by the goal of
obtaining power. According to office-seeking arguments, politicians frequently
abandon their principles to win elections or discard their principles shortly
thereafter. These theorists would argue that such changes are calculated moves
to improve electoral outcomes. When parties are in opposition, they will
change course before elections. When parties are in office, they will make
such changes when they run into difficulties. The SPD, in particular, had an
incentive to move to the center to become the fulcrum for any potential coalition, a strategy it employed in 1994 and 1998. The Greens had reason to jettison antimilitarist positions to remain in power after 1998. The SPD, according
to office-seeking arguments, abandoned its antimilitarist position to attain
office, the Greens to maintain themselves in office.

In fact, however, the change in Social Democratic and Green positions
on military intervention for humanitarian purposes was the outcome of a
reflection process in which they reevaluated the internal consistency of the
inclusivist and antimilitarist elements of their ideology on the basis of
lessons drawn primarily from the failure to bring peace to Bosnia-Herzegovina. The parties increasingly engaged in differentiation, taking into
account not just their antimilitarist dispositions, but also situational factors. They began to evaluate the issue along a second, inclusivist-exclusivist

dimension, and support military intervention if undertaken for humanitarian reasons. Electoral factors only obscured the process in the case of the Green Party as it faced incentives to retain an antimilitarist profile to distinguish itself from the SPD.

Only what I term the "learning argument" can account for *who* was behind the change in policy, *why* they felt compelled to break with the parties' antimilitarist traditions and *when* decisive shifts took place.[4] Moderate party members and foreign policy experts, more predisposed toward differentiation, led the transformation process in each party. They argued that they were preserving and not giving up on leftist values. Major shifts in the positions of the parties as a whole coincided not with the timing of elections but with salient events that seemed to confirm or disprove antimilitarist ideology. As the SPD is on the whole less ideologically extreme than the Greens, its members on average differentiated more between humanitarian and strategic operations, but both parties followed the same path given their common leftist ideology. Although the beginnings of this process preceded their election, entering office reinforced it by exposing both parties not to multilateral pressures from Germany's allies, but to normative ones. The Social Democrats and Greens were now accountable for the consequences of their positions. This led the Greens in particular to give up antimilitarist rhetoric that had served them well in elections, but had not kept pace with Green thinking and voting patterns on the use of the Bundeswehr.

However, the initial failure of the Kosovo air campaign to improve the human rights situation and the increasing escalation of the hostilities led many to quickly abandon their recent embrace of military intervention. Experience can also make parties less interventionist if salient events confirm antimilitarist worries about the spirals endemic to military action. To shore up support, the SPD leadership turned to the values and ideas that had been critical for the left's initial evolution. This instrumentalization, rather than disproving the power of ideational factors, shows that ideology is often the most potent weapon that politicians have. The Green leadership, which occupied high-ranking positions in the Foreign Ministry, began a diplomatic push that pacified their party and successfully laid the groundwork for the end of the war.

Confirming the policy-seeking argument requires showing first that parties are not constrained by political culture and take very different positions on foreign policy, and second that those policies and changes to them

---

4. This also distinguishes the argument here from those made by analysts who have reached similar conclusions about the role of the Bosnian intervention as a learning process for the left and Germany as a whole but do not attempt to weigh competing arguments or test them empirically. See Adrian Hyde-Price, "Germany and the Kosovo War: Still a Civilian Power?" *German Politics,* Vol. 9, No. 2 (2000), pp. 19–34.

are not driven by office-seeking motivations. In the following sections I will first evaluate the claim of culturalists that foreign policy is uncontested *between* parties. Focusing on the out-of-area debate, I show that parties of the left and right took different positions on intervention consistent with the ideologies evident in their domestic policy stances. The public manifestations of those strategies, the various deployments of the Bundeswehr and the constitutional challenges they provoked, have been the object of extensive descriptive analysis.[5] Therefore I devote most attention to an analysis of the government's private motivations, without which the larger theoretical significance of these events is unclear. The constitutional discussion otherwise appears to be a purely technical debate between parties with conflicting legal interpretations, not a battle between parties whose jurisprudential evaluations followed their ideological goals. The deployments of the Bundeswehr seem to be purely humanitarian operations aimed at inclusivist purposes, not instrumentalizations for exclusivist aims. As Karl-Heinz Hornhues, vice president of the CDU/CSU parliamentary group, said: "The question, 'What can we or can we not do?' did not have conclusive legal answers but rather political ones."[6]

After explaining the parties' starting points, I move on to assess whether the learning or the office-seeking hypothesis best explains policy change. A lesser-known story, this requires a more painstaking review of the intraparty struggles, aided by access to records of the internal deliberations of the parties. These sources are critical as the public rhetoric sometimes obscured internal doubts. I end with some thoughts on the implication of the findings for the normalization debate.

FRAMING THE INTERPARTY DEBATE: THE DOVISH LEFT VERSUS THE HAWKISH RIGHT

Almost immediately following reunification, Christian Democratic politicians began to stress that a reunited Germany needed to be capable of acting militarily in operations other than territorial defense and the protection of NATO allies. The Christian Democrats sought to restore Germany's military sovereignty, to make the Federal Republic "normal" again. CDU foreign policy spokesperson Karl Lamers argued that Germany must "acknowledge its

---

5. The best review of the legal case is Nina Philippi, *Bundeswehr-Auslandseinsätze als außen- und sicherheitspolitisches Problem des geeinten Deutschland* (Frankfurt: Peter Lang, 1997). See also Duffield (1998), chap. 8; Andrei Markovits and Simon Reich, *The German Predicament: Memory and Power in the New Europe* (Ithaca: Cornell University Press, 1997), chap. 10.

6. Interview with the author (9 November 2000).

power" and "without forgetting its history, Germany must become as normal as possible."[7] As a rightist party, according to my conceptualization of foreign policy beliefs, the CDU should emphasize the necessity of being able to use force as a means of foreign policy. The importance of what is known as *Handlungsfähigkeit,* the capacity to act, found expression in the party's manifesto, and in statements by Lamers and by Wolfgang Schäuble, the head of its parliamentary party.[8] Normalization was of course not the only reason that the Christian Democrats wanted to participate in international peace operations. Alliance solidarity and an interest in promoting international security were surely present. Normalization was what distinguished the right from the left, however. Nor did this policy goal signal a return to power politics. It did, however, signify going beyond being a mere "civilian power."

The Gulf War had shown the political consequences of not embarking on such a course for Germany's narrower, more exclusivist interests. Although the Germans had paid for over half of the total costs of the military operation, this "checkbook diplomacy" gave it very little control of events. The defense minister's chief of staff, Hans-Joachim Falenski, recalled bitterly: "The Belgians sent a ship and they had more influence than us."[9] Defense Minister Volker Rühe also put it bluntly: "Only those who act have international influence; those who watch don't."[10] The Christian Democratic government quickly devised strategies for circumventing the two largest obstacles—a reluctant public and a constitution that placed numerous but often ambiguous restrictions on the use of force.

Ideology and Interpretation: The Constitutional Positions of the CDU, FDP, and CSU

All parties had agreed during the Cold War that the constitution forbade any deployment out of area other than for self-defense or the defense of NATO allies. After reunification, however, the CDU and its sister party, the Christian Social Union (CSU), revised their interpretation. They now argued that the constitution allowed not only German contributions to UN

---

7. Quoted in Philip H. Gordon, "The Normalization of German Foreign Policy," *Orbis,* Vol. 38, No. 2 (Spring 1994), p. 234. See other comments by Lamers in Philippi (1997), p. 87.

8. See CDU, *Freiheit in Verantwortung: Grundsatzprogramm der Christlichen Demokratischen Union Deutschlands* (1994), pp. 92–94; Karl Lamers, "Von deutscher Drückebergerei," *Der Spiegel* (16 March 1992); Wolfgang Schäuble, "Wir brauchen klare Zielvorstellung," *Nordsee Zeitung* (18 July 1992).

9. Interview with the author (2 February 2001).

10. Quoted in Maja Zehfuss, *Constructivism in International Relations: The Politics of Reality* (Cambridge: Cambridge University Press, 2002), p. 185. See other comments by the defense minister in Duffield (1998), p. 183.

peacekeeping and peace enforcement missions, but also to out-of-area missions undertaken without a UN mandate by regional military organizations such as the Western European Union (WEU) and NATO. The CDU maintained that these qualified as collective security structures, as part of which the Bundeswehr could serve according to the constitution's Article 24. The party held that only a "clarification" of the constitution was legally necessary, not an amendment.[11]

According to leading CDU figures, the new jurisprudential evaluation had political motivations. The geopolitical environment had changed, and with it the political utility of the earlier restrictions. When asked about the reversal, Falenski said that from the beginning, the CDU's position was based on political, not legal considerations: "A reflection process began that eventually led to us saying that although we had interpreted the constitution this way until now, political facts had been created. When Germany was divided, the worst of all possible situations would have been for West German and East German troops to be on opposite sides. Therefore we said that in order to avoid this, we will stand back on the sidelines. So [SPD Chancellor] Helmut Schmidt created this rule that the constitution would not allow the Bundeswehr to be deployed outside of the NATO area. This danger disappeared after reunification."[12] The party's defense policy spokesperson, Paul Breuer, described the process almost identically: "As long as Germany was divided, participating in out-of-area missions posed a great problem. After reunification and Europe got a new face, we had to change the reality of the constitution, not the constitution itself."[13]

The CDU faced pressures from its left and its right. It was forced to take into account the views of its coalition partner, the Free Democratic Party (FDP). Parts of the FDP also embraced these calls for an active German role, although less fervently.[14] However, the centrist FDP favored more restrictions on the use of force than its rightist partners, as the party ideology argument would expect. A sizable minority even argued that any use of German troops should be made contingent on placing them under UN command so as prevent their misuse for exclusivist purposes. Ultimately, the party settled on the condition that any use of the Bundeswehr would require a UN mandate and the approval of not just a majority of the parliamentarians present, but a majority of the Bundestag's members. The FDP took a more centrist legal position as well, criticizing the abrupt volte-face of the CDU and arguing

---

11. Philippi (1997), pp. 82–101; Duffield (1998), p. 183; Zehfuss (2002), p. 160.
12. Interview with the author (2 February 2001).
13. Interview with the author (12 February 2001).
14. Klaus Kinkel, "Verantwortung, Realismus, Zukunftssicherung," *Frankfurter Allgemeine Zeitung* (19 March 1993). See also comments by the foreign minister in Gordon (1994), p. 234.

that an amendment was absolutely necessary.[15] Since this required the approval of two-thirds of the parliament and therefore the support of the Social Democrats, the CDU needed to seek a compromise with the SPD so as to avoid a coalitional fight with the FDP, even though it believed that no constitutional change was legally necessary. The FDP repeatedly stressed the need to "build bridges" to the SPD.[16] In an attempt to address FDP concerns, Defense Minister Rühe went so far as to offer an amendment that would allow German participation in combat operations provided that two-thirds of the parliament approved, thereby granting the SPD a de facto veto. The foreign minister, FDP head Klaus Kinkel, representing his more moderate and therefore antimilitarist party, proposed a two-thirds requirement for all deployments of German armed forces.[17]

With less need to take the FDP's wishes into account, the parliamentary party was more strident than CDU politicians in the government. Karl Lamers, the foreign policy spokesperson of the CDU caucus, signaled the CDU's outright opposition to any constitutional amendment requiring a UN mandate for the use of force. The more right-wing CSU was even more insistent on a free hand, as the party ideology argument would expect. Some Christian Democrats were prepared to make concessions to the FDP and SPD, authorizing out-of-area operations without a UN mandate only under the leadership of the WEU and NATO. However, the CSU's parliamentary president, Wolfgang Bötsch, proposed only that the use of the military not be unilateral, without having to be bound to any international organization. Lamers and Bötsch succeeded in shooting down Rühe's constitutional amendment offer to the SPD of a two-thirds requirement for combat missions.[18]

---

15. FDP, "Freiheit und Verantwortung gehören zusammen" (unpublished document, 25 May 1991). For the FDP's position, see *Liberal denken. Leistung wählen* (1994 election manifesto), p. 121; FDP, "Für ein europäisches Deutschland: Leitsätze der FDP zur Europawahl" (unpublished document, 22 January 1994), p. 16; Philippi (1997), p. 102. For a critique of the CDU, see Ulrich Irmer, "SPD darf sich nicht länger verweigern," *Pressedienst der FDP Bundestagsfraktion*, No. 16 (11 January 1992).

16. Werner Hoyer, "Ohne Tabus sachlich diskutieren," *Pressedienst der FDP Bundestagsfraktion*, No. 762 (22 July 1992); Werner Hoyer, "Grundkonsenz erforderlich," *Pressedienst der FDP Bundestagsfraktion*, No. 871 (6 September 1992); Werner Hoyer, "Nicht in den Gräben verschanzen," *Pressedienst der FDP Bundestagsfraktion*, No. 35 (15 January 1993); Otto Solms, "SPD ist gescheitert," *Pressedienst der FDP Bundestagsfraktion*, No. 575 (24 June 1993).

17. For Rühe's proposals, see *Bundestag Drucksache* 12/4107 (13 January 1993). Philippi (1997), p. 89; Duffield (1998), p. 204. For Kinkel's proposals see Philippi (1997), p. 95; Duffield (1998), pp. 206–207.

18. Lamers (1992). For compromise proposals, see Karl-Heinz Hornhues, "Beteiligung der Bundeswehr an Friedensmissionen: SPD Vorschläge machen Deutschland europaunfähig," *Deutschland-Union Dienst* (16 June 1992). On the CSU position, see "Union uneins über internationale Aufgabe der Bundeswehr," *Süddeutsche Zeitung* (15 March 1991).

Instrumentalizing Interventions: The Right's Secretive Strategy

Despite these public disputes, however, the CDU government and parliamentary party were privately united on a strategy to instrumentalize humanitarian interventions so as to lay the political foundations for a more assertive German military role. Defense Minister Rühe recognized that due to Germany's historical experience, the country had a "culture of restraint" that needed time to change before it could behave like other powers its size,[19] But this did not prevent the CDU government from hastening that process. With the complete backing of the parliamentary party, the government deliberately set out to change the German public's approach to the use of force by gradually escalating the scale of participation. The plan would also create legal precedents that would expand the radius of intervention for the Bundeswehr and surely provoke a constitutional challenge by the left, which would force the Constitutional Court to make a ruling that the right figured would go in its favor.[20]

This plan is described by CDU politicians as a "strategy of habituation."[21] CDU foreign policy expert Andreas Schockenhoff said: "The first intervention was in Cambodia and was humanitarian. Then there was Somalia where we delivered supplies and we widened the geographical scope of intervention. In Bosnia we had ground troops, but it was peacekeeping and not peace enforcement. It was a systematic expansion of German participation. We had broad agreement for every intervention from the public that we would not have had if we had started with peace enforcement."[22] The former Yugoslavia was the primary field of action. The government sent ships to the Adriatic to monitor the embargo against Serbia and aircraft to detect violations of the no-fly zone over Bosnia. The defense minister's chief of staff admitted: "That was a strategy. One has to say that honestly. The SPD did not want to make a deal. Therefore we had to create facts on the ground. So we participated in the embargo in the Adriatic."[23] The government engaged in some political manipulation to make the Adriatic deployment easier to accept. The government argued that it was not an out-of-area intervention because Italian waters were part of NATO's defense perimeter. "We made great efforts to make sure that it was not portrayed as an intervention. That was rhetorical and political trickery. Of course it was an intervention."[24]

19. Quoted in Philippi (1997), p. 87.
20. Duffield (1998), p. 193.
21. Interview with Andreas Schockenhoff, CDU member of the Foreign Policy Committee (October 2000); interview with Hans-Joachim Falenski (2 February 2001). Both used the same phrase: "Strategie der Gewöhnung."
22. Interview with the author (October 2000).
23. Interview with the author (2 February 2001).
24. Ibid.

The rightist government was using these interventions as an instrument to regain German military sovereignty, using inclusivist purposes for exclusivist and hawkish goals. The delivery of humanitarian aid had large-scale public support.[25] Germany sent over fifteen hundred soldiers to Somalia in 1993 for the purpose of distributing food and relief supplies to pacified areas of the country. However, only seven hundred soldiers were even indirectly involved with helping the Somalians, leading Zehfuss to wonder what the point of the operation was.[26] Falenski provided the answer. It was part of the domestic strategy. "We would otherwise never have gone to Somalia because we knew from the beginning that the operation would fail. Rühe wanted it purely from the point of view of creating facts on the ground. In the end the strategy was successful."[27]

Although there were undoubtedly Christian Democratic politicians who favored intervention in Yugoslavia for humanitarian reasons, the rightist government turned down requests by the UN to intervene in other crisis areas beyond Europe if they did not aid in this strategy. There were exclusivist limits to the strategy. Defense Minister Rühe justified the German refusal to send peacekeeping forces to Haiti and Rwanda on the grounds that Germany's interests lay in Europe and its periphery. His chief of staff said: "We have to make it clear that we cannot be a part of all of these operations. We were asked to send a ship for the Haiti operation. Rühe said certainly not. As we see it our interests are security in and for Europe—and we interpret the 'for' as going beyond Europe to include the Middle East and northern Africa." The CDU does not support worldwide military interventions unless more narrow exclusivist interests are at stake. "Naturally we can expand this security conception when a concrete economic and strategic threat presents itself as justifying a military intervention," Falenski added.[28]

Christian Democrats stress that apart from the habituation strategy, it was Germany's strategic position that made them more interventionist in the Balkans than the British Conservatives. Schockenhoff, when asked how to explain the difference between the willingness of both parties to intervene in Bosnia, argued: "Due to our geostrategic position we are more affected by instability in the Balkans and its consequences. We took in more refugees than any other country by far. We cannot say it is merely a humanitarian intervention that does not concern our strategic goals because instability in southern

---

25. For a review of public opinion data, see Philippi (1997), pp. 163–175.

26. Zehfuss (2002), pp. 80–82.

27. Interview with the author (2 February 2001).

28. Ibid. For the defense minister's comments, see "Rühe: UNO-Mandat Voraussetzung für Auslandseinsatz," *Süddeutsche Zeitung* (25 November 1995).

Europe is a strategic threat for Germany."[29] The vice president of the CDU's parliamentary party, Hornhues, said the same: "We have to be concerned. It is in our interests in so far as our new strategic interest is not to be overwhelmed with refugees. In this way our strategic interests are different from those of the British, who took in a hundred times fewer refugees than us."[30]

Contesting Christian Democratic Policy: The Left in Opposition

The opposition SPD and Greens described the CDU's strategy as "salami tactics" aimed at the "militarization" of German foreign policy.[31] SPD party chairman Bjorn Engholm wrote: "[I]t is clear what the government wants: a blank check that allows the Bundeswehr to intervene without restrictions in all parts of the world."[32] The SPD party conference in 1991 voted to limit the use of the military to peacekeeping missions, and only then with significant restrictions.[33] Its 1994 electoral program refused the transformation of the military into an "intervention army," and rejected its use in any war-fighting activities regardless whether commanded by the UN, NATO, or the WEU. The Greens opposed even peacekeeping.[34]

The disputes between the CDU and the SPD-Green opposition were more than differences in emphasis. They involved the difference between policing and war-fighting. Unlike in other countries, the controversy over participation in humanitarian interventions was not over how engaged

29. Interview with the author (October 2000).

30. Interview with the author (9 November 2000).

31. This is a colloquial metaphorical phrase to describe a strategy that is put into place piecemeal to achieve a goal unattainable in one rapid step. Ludger Volmer, *Gewaltfreiheit und Menschenrechte—Friedenspolitische Grundlinien von Bündnis 90/Die Grünen*, Resolution A-2, Extraordinary Party Conference, Bonn (9 October 1993); Jürgen Trittin and Kerstin Müller, "Sieben Gründe warum es in Deutschland weiterhin Parteien geben sollte: Germans to the front?" (unpublished document, 12 July 1995). See comments made in the Bundestag *Plenarprotokoll,* the record of parliamentary debates, on the left's suspicion of rightist motives. Gila Altmann, 13/76 (6 December 1995), Anlage 7; Norbert Gansel, 13/48 (30 June 1995), pp. 3985–3987; Winfried Nachtwei, 13/48 (30 June 1995), pp. 3991–3993; Konrad Kunick, 13/76 (6 December 1995), pp. 6696–6697; Gila Altmann, 13/76 (6 December 1995), pp. 6694–6695.

32. Bjorn Engholm, "Mitteilung für die Presse," *Presseservice der SPD,* No. 20 (13 January 1993).

33. These conditions included a resolution from the UN Security Council, the consent of the conflicting parties, control of the operation by the UN secretary general, limitation of the use of force to self-defense, and the prior approval of the Bundestag. Even so, Bjorn Engholm, the SPD party chairman, only succeeded by tying approval to a vote of confidence in his leadership. See Philippi (1997), p. 116; Duffield (1998), p. 185. For the 1994 electoral program, see "Regierungsprogramm" in *Protokoll,* SPD Party Conference, Halle (22 June 1994). Although the SPD's position had moderated since 1991, foreseeing peacekeeping operations upon official request by the secretary general even if not under his control, it still refused any combat operations. For its formal offer to the coalition on an amendment, see *Bundestag Drucksache* 12/2895 (23 June 1992).

34. For Green Party policy, see Volmer (1993).

Germany would be in the internal affairs of other countries. It was framed along a hawk-dove foreign policy continuum. Three times the SPD appealed to the Constitutional Court to prevent the deployment of German troops in out-of-area missions. It rejected all offers from government officials for constitutional amendments, even ones that would grant the party a de facto veto on any use of the military, since the proposals did not include enough statutory limitations on the types of missions the Bundeswehr could conduct. The interparty conflict would continue even after the Constitutional Court rejected the SPD's case, showing that the debate was political, not legal. For the SPD and the Greens, the controversy over out-of-area missions was "a debate over whether Germany will remain a civilian trading power or should become a military power," according to Heidemarie Wieczorek-Zeul, one of the SPD's most powerful figures.[35]

Why was this the case? The Social Democrats and Greens emphasize equality in their programs and policies, which should lead them to support uses of force with inclusivist purposes, as was true in Britain. A 1997 party resolution of the SPD read: "Social Democrats know: things cannot be going well if they are getting progressively better for a few and progressively worse for many."[36] The two parties distinguish themselves from the CDU in this regard. The Greens 1998 election manifesto criticized the Kohl government for its divisive policies that privileged the many over the few: "Instead of democratically involving all those concerned, the government aims at division: the employed versus the unemployed, the west against the east, the healthy against the sick, the young against the old, men against women, Germans against foreigners, singles against families."[37] This stress on equality is coupled with a more inclusive conception of the national interest. The parties of the German left call for the extension of democratic and human rights to other countries. Both the SPD and the Greens explicitly reject the principle of noninterference in the internal affairs of other states, while the CDU makes no mention of noninterference in its major policy documents.[38] Leftist parties seek to abolish hierarchies in both domestic and international affairs.

---

35. Heidemarie Wieczorek-Zeul, "Zivile Handels- oder Militärmacht," *Sozialdemokratischer Pressedienst,* Vol. 48, No. 69 (13 April 1993), p. 1.

36. "Beschlußübersicht: Außen-, Sicherheits- und Entwicklungspolitik," *Presseservice der SPD* (3 December 1997).

37. Bündnis 90/Die Grünen, *Grün ist der Wechsel: Programm zur Bundestagswahl '98* (1998).

38. SPD Parteivorstand, "Perspektive einer neuen Außen- und Sicherheitspolitik," in *Protokoll,* SPD Party Conference, Antrag 1, Wiesbaden (16–19 November 1993), p. 990. Green policy was as follows: "When it comes to human rights, the principle of nonintervention in internal matters should not apply. Human rights are universal and indivisible." Volmer (1993). On the CDU's foreign policy orientation, see *Freiheit in Verantwortung: Das Grundsatzprogramm der CDU* (1994).

At the beginning of the 1990s, however, the overwhelming majority of party members at all levels thought an inclusive conception of the national interest was perfectly consistent with antimilitarism. This was more the case in Germany than in other countries because of its past. For the left, according to Green parliamentarian and foreign policy expert Ludger Volmer, "[A] positive description of military intervention was unimaginable—a mentality that in view of the historic crimes of German militarism objectively signified civilized progress." Militarism was inextricably intertwined with an exclusivist conception of the national interest. Volmer continues: "Any consideration of a concrete military intervention by Germany renewed the association with offensive, chauvinistic, great power politics."[39] The Greens cited history as the source of their pacifism.[40] The SPD saw its mission as eradicating the use of coercion from international relations: "The commanding principle of German foreign policy should be replacing the power of the strong, which still predominates on our globe, with the power of law. The power of law as the highest principle—that is the lesson to draw from German history."[41]

Therefore, as the issue of participation in United Nations peace missions emerged in the waning days of the Cold War and took on growing importance as ethnic conflicts attracted increasing international attention, the German left responded negatively. History was an ubiquitous reference in justifying the antimilitarist position in parliament and elsewhere. The SPD's vice president, Günther Verheugen, declared that any change in the constitution threatened a "slippery slope," a "break with our previously shared conviction which we have learnt from Germany history: that war must not be a means of policy any more."[42] Politicians still stress history's importance in the debate. For the German left, military force meant destruction, both at home and abroad. SPD parliamentarian Werner Schulz said later: "The ideal view of 1945, 'never again war,' was largely a product of our emotions. . . . It was the shame and despair about what had happened. We saw that our country was destroyed."[43] SPD deputy Peter Zumkley agreed: "We fought wars everywhere and brought misery everywhere, not least in the Balkans. This feeling had to be overcome."[44]

---

39. Ludger Volmer, *Die Grünen und die Außenpolitik: Ein schwieriges Verhältnis* (Münster: Westfalisches Dampfboot, 1998), p. 493.

40. Volmer (1993).

41. SPD Parteivorstand (1993), p. 989.

42. Günther Verheugen, *Plenarprotokoll* 12/132 (15 January 1993), p. 11479. For other examples, see Peter Glotz, 12/151 (21 April 1993), p. 12968; Rudolf Scharping, 12/240 (22 July 1994), p. 21174.

43. Interview with the author (24 November 2000).

44. Interview with the author (4 December 2000).

FRAMING THE INTRAPARTY DEBATE:
THE IDEOLOGICAL LEFT VERSUS THE PRAGMATIC RIGHT

Antimilitarism as Ideological End: The Left Wings of the SPD and the Greens

Although the SPD was united on the need for significant restrictions on military deployment out of area, differences quickly emerged as to the extent of these restrictions—divisions that were intensified by the growing intraparty debate over how to respond to the war in Bosnia. In the SPD, opposition to any military intervention clustered around the Frankfurt Circle, an informal grouping of left-wing party members that met primarily to discuss domestic issues. There was no such organization in the Greens, but the left wing of the party carried the torch for the antimilitarists since the party's so-called fundamentalist wing had largely departed following the 1990 election.[45] The left wings of both parties differentiated little among possible uses of the Bundeswehr. They both questioned the humanitarian characterization of these operations in general. Katrin Fuchs of the SPD summarized the position: "Military interventions are not humanitarian actions."[46] Wieczorek-Zeul said that "semantics" should be done away with: "Peace enforcement means fighting wars."[47] The left wings avoided weighing humanitarian against antimilitarist considerations as German history showed they were mutually dependent. "The only lesson to draw from German history is that German soldiers can never again be deployed anywhere. . . . Whoever claims that military engagement is a precondition for humanitarian aid and describes NATO battle missions as peace missions has learned nothing from all of the wars of this world," said Green Gila Altmann.[48]

The left wing in each party confirmed its antimilitarist disposition in other ways. Although the official policy of both parties was that the UN should enjoy a monopoly on the use of force, thereby making it impossible for nation-

---

45. The so-called *Fundis* wanted the Greens to remain a party of "fundamental opposition" that did not seek to govern at the national level. The *Realos,* or realists, argued that the implementation of Green ideas required holding office.

46. Katrin Fuchs, "Militäreinsätze sind keine 'humanitäre Aktion,'" *Sozialdemokratischer Pressedienst,* Vol. 48, No. 115 (21 June 1993), pp. 1–3.

47. "Das Nein war deutlich," *Der Spiegel* (7 March 1994), p. 22.

48. *Plenarprotokoll* 13/76 (6 December 1995), p. 6695. The same argumentation was used behind closed doors by the SPD. At a meeting of the parliamentary party on 27 April 1993, Rudolf Bindig argued that the military was not an appropriate provider of humanitarian help, and Katrin Fuchs claimed the military could not restore peace. Parliamentary group's internal minutes (27 April 1993), provided by the Archive of Social Democracy at the Friedrich Ebert Foundation in Bonn, Germany. See also comments by Green parliamentarians. Christina Nickels, *Plenarprotokoll* 13/76 (6 December 1995), pp. 6663–6665; Elisabeth Altmann, 13/76 (6 December 1995), pp. 6670–6671.

states to use military means to advance their own exclusivist interests, the left wings even condemned efforts by the UN to go beyond peacekeeping and apply enforcement measures authorized by the UN Charter under Chapter VII. SPD leftist Gernot Erler derided the UN for its forceful actions in Somalia as the situation deteriorated. In a resolution passed by the Green party conference, the left-winger Ludger Volmer advocated demilitarizing the UN itself, calling for the removal of Chapter VII from the UN Charter.[49] As NATO became more deeply militarily involved in Bosnia, the left wings of both parties opposed this tendency, arguing that military interventions would give the military alliance a new raison d'être. The growing influence of the alliance threatened to make the UN into a NATO "subcontractor," according to Wieczorek-Zeul and others.[50] NATO was an organization ill-suited for humanitarian purposes, based on a "deterrence philosophy"[51] that had nothing in common with the UN.

As the UN and NATO contemplated increasingly strong measures in Bosnia and the mission began to creep from peacekeeping to peace enforcement, the left wings of both parties argued that military force would be ineffective and would lead to an escalation of the hostilities. As in the Cold War, the use or threat of force was thought to increase rather than deter conflict. Hostilities would spiral. In response to NATO's threat of air strikes, which seemed to succeed in breaking the siege of Sarajevo in February 1994, Wieczorek-Zeul wrote: "The situation in the former Yugoslavia cannot be changed or improved through war, but rather only through diplomacy. . . . Luckily we were spared the proof of whether bombing would have calmed the situation or, *as we all fear, widened the war.*"[52] They made the same argument at other crucial points in the conflict.[53] A resolution by the Greens' federal council that expressed generic support for the

49. Gernot Erler, "Mogadischu: Idee der Blauhelme zerstört," *Sozialdemokratischer Pressedienst,* Vol. 48, No. 111 (15 June 1993), p. 1; Volmer (1993).

50. Wieczorek-Zeul (1993). See, among dozens of comments in the *Plenarprotokoll,* those by left-wing Green parliamentarians. Winfried Nachtwei, 13/76 (6 December 1995), pp. 6671–6672; Angelika Beer, 13/76 (6 December 1995), p. 6672.

51. Gernot Erler, *Plenarprotokoll* 13/48 (30 June 1995), p. 4002; Angelika Beer, "Keine Deutsche Beteiligung an Schneller Eingreiftruppe," *Bundestagfraktion Pressemitteilung,* No. 390 (5 June 1995). Most Green documents cited in this chapter were found at the Heinrich Böll Foundation archive in Berlin.

52. "Das Nein war deutlich," *Der Spiegel* (7 March 1994), p. 24 (emphasis added). The same argumentation was used at parliamentary party meetings, according to internal minutes. Left-winger Horst Kubatschka criticized NATO strikes against Bosnian Serb tanks in Gorazde, arguing that "no conflict is solved through bombs." If the Serbs had not pulled back, then NATO would have had begun bombing, he feared. Wieczorek-Zeul made the same point. Parliamentary party's internal minutes (26 April 1994).

53. Margitta Terborg, *Plenarprotokoll* 13/48 (30 June 1995), pp. 4015–4016; Heidemarie Wieczorek-Zeul, 13/48 (30 June 1995), pp. 4037–4038.

right of UNPROFOR to protect aid convoys from harassment generated a huge outcry and provoked a special party conference.[54] Green left-wingers also feared escalation dynamics: "How far does one escalate to ensure victory when the criminal is matching your strength? And how will one avoid the accusation of standing by helplessly while murders are being committed when the readiness to take the next step is not there?"[55] Instead, the left wings stressed civilian means of conflict resolution. Volmer wrote for his pacifist faction in the Greens: "Economic sanctions are for us the ultima ratio of international peace enforcement."[56]

The Military as Means: The Interventionists in the SPD and the Greens

The left wings could count on the support of the overwhelming majority of their parties at all levels. SPD Chairman Engholm's proposal to allow German participation in robust peacekeeping under UN command failed at the party conference even though it was contingent on the (rather unrealistic) condition of reforming the UN so as to give it a monopoly on the use of force.[57] Nevertheless, in response to the new crises of the post–Cold War period, the right wing of each party combined with a growing number of foreign and defense policy experts to agitate for a change in the constitution that would allow a German role in UN peace enforcement operations. Citing the growing catastrophe in Bosnia, the interventionists began to question the consistency and coherence of antimilitarism and an inclusive conception of the national interest. The Bosnian war provoked more conflict within the parties than any other foreign policy issue. Walter Kolbow, defense spokesperson for the SPD, said: "The events in Bosnia changed the quality of opposing further military involvement. It became increasingly difficult to stand by and watch murders take place. It placed those opposed to German involvement in an

---

54. Helmut Lippelt, "Resolutionsentwurf für den Länderrat vom 12.6.93." (unpublished document).

55. Kerstin Müller, Claudia Roth, Jürgen Trittin, and Ludger Volmer, "Wohin führt die Forderung nach einer militärischen Interventionspflicht gegen Völkermord? Ein offener Brief an die Mitglieder von Bündnis 90/Die Grünen" (unpublished document, 31 October 1995). For other worries about escalation among left-wing Greens, see Beer (1995); Volmer (1993); Barbara Höhn, *Frieden, Entwicklung und ökologischer Umbau—Positionbestimmung von Bündnis 90/Die Grünen zur Internationalen Politik,* Antrag A-4, Extraordinary Party Conference, Bonn (9 October 1993). Escalation was also a concern of the right wing of the Greens. See Hubert Kleinert, *Für eine gewaltfreie Politik in einer gewalttätigen Zeit,* Antrag A-21, Extraordinary Party Conference, Bonn (9 October 1993), a resolution signed by Joschka Fischer.

56. Ludger Volmer, *Aktive Friedens- und Menschenrechtspolitik statt militärischer Kampfeinsätze: Leitgedanken für eine Zivilisierung der Außenpolitik,* Antrag A-1, Green Party Conference, Bremen (1–3 December 1995). Volmer (1993) is the most extensive statement of Green thinking. See also Kleinert (1993).

57. Philippi (1997), p. 120; Duffield (1998), pp. 202–203.

inhumane situation. We came increasingly to the realization that if we did not intervene, we would bear the guilt for failing to protect people."[58]

The interventionists would increasingly apply the deterrence model to Bosnia. "We learned that there are situations even today after the experience of two world wars in which prevention and diplomatic and political efforts do not suffice. The military option has to be available as a last resort to prevent genocide and mass expulsions and also to show dictators that this will be done with determination in the future," said Kolbow.[59] In contrast to Wieczorek-Zeul, Hans-Ulrich Klose, the moderate head of the parliamentary party, greeted the Sarajevo ultimatum, the first threat of significant force by NATO in the Bosnian war, as an example of "credible deterrence."[60] Members of the Greens also disputed the applicability of the spiral model to the conflict. Helmut Lippelt, a foreign policy expert for the Greens, argued that military intervention did not always widen wars. Force was necessary to open the concentration camps in Bosnia, as it had been in the Second World War. Gerd Poppe, foreign policy spokesperson for the Green Party in the Bundestag, advocated the strengthening of the peacekeepers' mandate to allow the firepower needed to force through humanitarian aid convoys.[61] Support for a German role in enforcement actions was strongest in the right wing, which was disposed toward differentiation. In a position paper of the Seeheim Circle, an informal grouping of moderate SPD members, Dieter Schloten labeled the party's left wing "isolationists" and argued that German participation in the UN operation in Bosnia was necessary.[62]

The interventionists were not trying to position the party in the center, but instead claimed that they were the true representatives of leftist values, a label they would have avoided if their position had been electorally motivated. The differences between the left wing and the interventionists on foreign policy did not reflect broader substantive ideological disagreements, but rather different levels of differentiation. Norbert Gansel, a defense expert and long-time advocate of disarmament, predicted: "Time will prove that [our position] is no departure from the common path of social democracy. . . .

---

58. Interview with the author (25 January 2001).

59. Ibid.

60. "Das Nein war deutlich," *Der Spiegel* (7 March 1994), p. 24. Scharping welcomed the ultimatum as well. See Hans-Ulrich Klose, *Plenarprotokoll* 12/219 (14 April 1994), pp. 18910–18911.

61. "Suche nach Nischen," *Der Spiegel* (24 August 1992); Helmut Lippelt, "Intervenieren in Jugoslawien?" in Katrin Fuchs, Peter von Örtzen, and Ludger Volmer (eds.), *Zieht die Linke in den Krieg? Beiträge zur Debatte um Kampfeinsätze aus rot-grüner Sicht* (Cologne: spw-Verlag, 1993), p 130; Gerd Poppe, "Keine Veränderung der Appeasement-Politik der UNO gegen Bosnien," *Pressemitteilung*, No. 47 (5 March 1993); Gerd Poppe, "Verweigerung militärischen Schutzes bedeutet das Ende des bosnischen Volkes," *Pressemitteilung*, No. 162 (21 July 1993).

62. "Dokumentation eines Entwurfs für den Seeheim-Kreis zur Außen-, Europa-, und Sicherheitspolitik der SPD," *tageszeitung* (19 January 1995).

Like pacifism, this conviction also belongs to humanistic internationalism, to the tradition of the German left, to the legacy of liberal socialism. . . . After blockades, threats, shelling, murder and hostage-taking, our duty to help and to militarily protect the peacekeepers now weighs more heavily than any history that forbids us from forcing others to their knees."[63] Joschka Fischer, the leader of the moderate *Realo* wing of the Green Party, also noted the similarities between exclusivist right-wing and antimilitarist left-wing argumentation, arguing that "Left means solidarity with the weak, the defenseless, and the victims. Whoever abandons these fundamental values abandons the values of the universalistic and internationalist left and ends up with isolationism."[64] Although the left wing of the Green Party accused Fischer of being a "witness for the conservative prosecution," the interventionists were trying to reframe the debate in inclusive terms.[65] Christian Zöpel, who would later become a deputy foreign minister, argued at a meeting of the SPD parliamentary party that this was not a traditional intraparty left-right debate between hawks and doves, but rather a historically new problem that could not be judged by the same standards as the Cold War.[66]

Those SPD and Green politicians favoring a German role in peace enforcement missions and a more forceful strategy in Bosnia still favored restrictions on the use of the Bundeswehr. Unlike the CDU, their point was not to make the use of force normal again. Gansel still stressed the differences between the SPD and the CDU, declaring that Germany should only participate in those missions managed or mandated by the UN.[67] Karsten Voigt, foreign policy spokesperson for the SPD, favored German participation in peace enforcement and concluded that his party would lose its suit before the Constitutional Court. Rather than simply allowing this, however, he advised the parliamentary party privately that it should agree with the CDU on a constitutional amendment that would entail some limitations on the use of the Bundeswehr. At closed-door parliamentary party meetings he opposed CDU proposals that would allow the military to intervene under NATO or the WEU without a UN mandate. Nor did the interventionists believe that force was a panacea. Voigt did not see air strikes resolving the Bosnian conflict completely, but thought they might lead to a decrease in violence and provide pressure to return to the negotiating table. Every application of force had to be evaluated individually so as to ascertain whether it would improve

---

63. *Plenarprotokoll* 13/48 (30 June 1995), pp. 4011–4012.

64. Joschka Fischer, "Auf der Flucht vor der Wirklichkeit: Eine öffentliche Antwort auf den offenen Brief von Kerstin Müller, Claudia Roth, Jürgen Trittin, und Ludger Volmer an unsere Partei" (unpublished document, 27 November 1995).

65. Müller et al. (1995).

66. Parliamentary party's internal minutes (17 January 1995).

67. *Plenarprotokoll* 13/48 (30 June 1995), pp. 4011–4012.

or worsen the situation, he cautioned, even behind closed doors. This of course is the essence of differentiation.[68]

Interventionist Incentives? The 1994 Election

Despite their efforts, these more interventionist SPD politicians could not initiate major changes in their party's position. When Rudolf Scharping was selected as party chairman in the spring of 1993, he announced that the SPD had to reconsider its policy restricting German involvement to peacekeeping or "blue helmet" missions. Scharping appointed the moderate Ulrich Klose to gauge support for a constitutional amendment that would allow Bundeswehr involvement in all types of interventions provided there was two-thirds support in the Bundestag. When the overwhelming majority of the party opposed this compromise, Scharping dropped his support for Klose's proposal, voting against it at the party conference and opting to consolidate his authority rather than revisit the policy and risk a fight.[69] Office-seeking theorists can make a plausible case that Scharping was driven by electoral considerations. The party was moderating its stance on several issues, including economic policy and civil liberties, in an attempt to win back centrist voters in the October 1994 election.[70] However, even if Scharping's initial efforts are best explained by the office-seeking argument (and this is doubtful given his centrist history and later testimony), the outcome is not. The leadership could not change party policy unless it could persuade at least part of the left wing. That required changing minds, not winning elections.

The Greens faced very different electoral incentives. With the SPD moving to the center on domestic policy, the Greens could capture abandoned left-wing voters. Any incentives to move to the center themselves were offset by the growing strength of the Party of Democratic Socialism (PDS) on their left. The Greens also had a core group of pacifist voters formerly active in the peace movements of the 1980s. Seemingly in keeping with the office-seeking argument, the Greens stressed the differences between themselves and the SPD, opposing involvement even in peacekeeping operations.[71]

---

68. Parliamentary party's internal minutes (14 January 1993, 15 June 1993, 26 April 1994).

69. Andrew Denison, "The European Dilemmas of the German Left: the Social Democratic Party and West European Security Cooperation" (Ph.D. diss., Johns Hopkins University, 1996), p. 495.

70. "SPD will sich in der Blauhelme-Frage bewegen," *Parlamentarisches Presse-Protokoll* (30 June 1993), p. 4. For an overview of the election and the SPD's strategy, see Gerard Braunthal, "The Social Democrats: From Offense to Defense," in Russell Dalton (ed.), *Germans Divided* (Oxford: Berg, 1996), pp. 43–60; Alison Roberts, "German SPD moves right," *New Statesman and Society,* Vol. 6, No. 280 (26 November 1993), p. 10.

The moderate wing of the party noted the contradictions between the goals of human rights and antimilitarism, but did not call for a revision of policy.[72] The campaign platform belied the changes that were taking place under the surface, however. Volmer, the leading left-wing figure in foreign policy who drafted most of the party's resolutions, later claimed that he felt under increasing pressure to respond to the accusation that pacifism was synonymous with the inability to respond to human rights violations, and as a result he was gradually making the Green position more interventionist.[73] The party's rhetoric was not keeping pace with the changes in its thinking. The disjuncture would increase.

That the SPD and the Greens were both becoming gradually more interventionist despite their very different competitive situations and rhetoric suggests that the reversal of the German left's position was a learning process, rather than an opportunistic electoral strategy. The timing is more consistent with the policy-seeking argument. Major changes would come about not before elections but following events with major implications for the coherence of leftist ideology.

FROM *GERMAN* LEFT TO GERMAN *LEFT:* BOSNIA, THE DETERRENCE MODEL, AND THE DEPAROCHIALIZATION OF RED-GREEN POLICY

The situation in Bosnia deteriorated significantly during the spring of 1995. In response to the hostage crisis, several contributors to UNPROFOR decided to deploy a Rapid Reaction Force tasked with protecting the UN troops, thereby allowing them to carry out their mission more effectively. The CDU/FDP cabinet agreed to provide transport aircraft for shuttling UN troops, first aid workers for a German-French hospital in Croatia, and additional personnel for the international headquarters of UNPROFOR. The operation posed no problems for the coalition. It was sanctioned by a UN mandate, furthered the government's interest in habituating the country to overseas deployments, and involved a region important for Germany's strategic interests.

---

71. Volmer (1993). On the Greens' incentives, see E. Gene Frankland, "Greens' Comeback in 1994: The Third Party of Germany," in Dalton (1996), pp. 85–108. The PDS was the successor party to the East German Communist party and had embraced a postmaterialist and libertarian agenda similar to the Greens.

72. Kleinert (1993).

73. In 1993, the party endorsed Volmer's proposal to support specially trained units for enforcing embargoes, although they would be placed under the UN. See Volmer (1993). In 1995, the party endorsed his proposal to support German blue helmets that the Foreign Ministry, rather than the Defense Ministry, could place at the service of the UN. See Volmer (1995).

No ground troops would be stationed in Bosnia itself. At this point, the CDU government still believed that the presence of German troops in a region they had occupied during the Second World War would be dangerous. This had become known as the "Kohl doctrine." Germany would, however, send Tornado aircraft that could detect and locate Bosnian Serb air defenses to be destroyed in cases of aggression against the peacekeepers. The Social Democratic and Green parliamentary parties argued that this crossed the line into peace enforcement and opposed it in parliament, where majority approval by the Bundestag for deployment was necessary according to the ruling of the Constitutional Court in July 1994.[74]

The debate in late June 1995 exposed as many intraparty as interparty divisions, however. SPD party leader Scharping tried again to formulate a compromise that would unite the party, but his left-wing rival, Oskar Lafontaine, forced the introduction of a clause into the party board's statement that expressly prohibited the use of Tornados.[75] When this sentence found its way into the resolution of the parliamentary party, foreign policy spokesperson Voigt organized a revolt of 45 of the 252 members to vote with the government and against their own party's resolution. This group included 12 of the 13 members of the SPD foreign policy working group, a majority of the members of the defense working group, and the vast majority of the moderate Seeheim Circle. Support for the interventionist position was even stronger in the parliamentary party's closed meeting before the vote, where 69 favored a motion to eliminate the restriction on the Tornados.[76]

Voigt thought it would be the end of his political career. He had consistently called for party unity so as not to distract attention from the differences between the CDU and FDP over the out-of-area question, but he now believed confrontation was the only way of forcing change within the party. The leadership agreed substantively, but favoring a more gradual strategy, they tried to suppress his efforts. Voigt gathered the support of four Green members of parliament as well, all foreign policy specialists, and later said that he needed to avoid the impression that he was opportunistically seeking to move his party toward the right and a grand coalition with the

---

74. "Entschließungsantrag der Fraktion der SPD zum Antrag der Bundesregierung," *Bundestag Drucksache* 13/1835 (28 June 1995); "Entschließungsantrag der Fraktion Bündnis 90/Die Grünen," *Bundestag Drucksache* 13/1828 (28 June 1995). The government's proposal was "Antrag der Bundesregierung: Deutsche Beteiligung an den Maßnahmen zum Schutz und zur Unterstützung des schnellen Einsatzverbands im früheren Jugoslawien einschließlich der Unterstützung eines eventuellen Abzugs der VN-Friedenstruppen," *Bundestag Drucksache* 13/1802 (26 June 1995).

75. "Scharping: SPD nicht isoliert," *Frankfurter Allgemeine Zeitung* (28 June 1995).

76. "Bosnien-Abstimmung wird zur Zerreißprobe für die SPD," *Frankfurter Allgemeine Zeitung* (26 June 1995); interview with Karsten Voigt (20 February 2001); parliamentary party's internal minutes (27 June 1995).

CDU.[77] Among the Greens, Gerd Poppe stressed the need to use force to deter Bosnian Serb aggression. A fifth Green member of parliament, Angelika Köster-Lossack, abstained in the deployment vote, arguing that the Rapid Reaction Force and the measures provided for in the CDU's resolution would ultimately not be enough to protect the UN safe areas from Serbian aggression.[78]

Learning by Force: The Failure to Deter at Srebrenica

Köster-Lossack was proved right. In July 1995 Bosnian Serb forces took over the UN-declared safe area of Srebrenica and killed over seven thousand people, mostly young men of fighting age. The massacre was the single most important event for the reorientation of the German left's position on the use of force. The failure of the UN mission induced a period of serious introspection for both the Greens and the SPD. It posed a serious challenge to the view that the German left could simultaneously demand the protection of human rights and the resolution of conflicts through nonmilitary means. So, too, did the sustained NATO bombing campaign of Bosnian Serb positions in late August and September 1995, widely thought to have contributed to the establishment of a cease-fire and the signing of the Dayton peace accords.

The debate was most public among the Greens. Fischer, then a co-leader of the party, wrote in an open letter: "The only conclusion to draw from the massacre [in Srebrenica] that the left can support is that the UN, in accordance with the duty that it had accepted, should have intervened militarily earlier to protect the civilians from mass murder and the death march."[79] Fischer had noted contradictions in leftist party ideology in a previous resolution, but it was only after Srebrenica that he came down on a particular side. The left in Germany had always said: "Never again war," but also "Never again Auschwitz."[80] The issue of peace enforcement forced a choice. For the moderate wing of the party, Germany's responsibility now weighed more heavily than its historical burden.

77. Interview with the author (20 February 2001). For his previous comments, see parliamentary party's internal minutes (23 November 1992 and 24 June 1993). This group of Greens was comprised of Gerd Poppe, Marieluise Beck, Helmut Lippelt, and Waltraud Schoppe, all of whom had previously spoken out for a more forceful posture vis-à-vis the Bosnian Serbs.

78. Gerd Poppe, *Plenarprotokoll* 13/48 (30 June 1995), p. 4003; Angelika Köster-Lossack, 13/48 (30 June 1995), p. 4022. Köster-Lossack had previously argued along with Gerd Poppe for the expansion of the UN mandate to defend not only UN troops but also the Bosnian safe areas themselves. Gerd Poppe and Angelika Köster-Lossack, "UNPROFOR-Mandat für Bosnien muß erweitert werden" (unpublished document, 31 May 1995).

79. Joschka Fischer, "Die Katastrophe in Bosnien und die Konsequenzen für unsere Partei," *Blätter für deutsche und internationale Politik,* Vol. 40, No. 9 (1995), p. 1148.

80. Kleinert (1993).

Differentiation was increasing as a growing number of Greens took situational factors into account and saw antimilitarism as less an end than a means. Fischer wrote that the left would never resolve this value conflict, but instead must decide anew in every circumstance. Gerd Poppe wrote: "The Greens do not have to betray their principles to save human lives, because their preservation is itself the principle. Nonviolence is not an end in itself."[81] A resolution based on this position won the support of almost 40 percent of the delegates at the Green party conference in December 1995, and a majority of the parliamentary group signaled its intent to vote for the deployment of German forces to the former Yugoslavia to secure the peace, despite the conference's opposition. In the end four members abstained to ensure that the number of yes and no votes would be equal.[82]

The left wing responded to Fischer's open letter with its own that stressed the militarist domestic consequences of peace enforcement actions abroad.[83] Like the extreme pacifists in Britain, they utilized a number of other arguments as well. Intervention, they claimed, was unlikely to be effective given that political will was hard to mobilize in the most serious cases. Peace enforcement was impractical. Peace enforcement was also too selective. There was no way of deciding where it should be employed among the many places where human rights violations were taking place. Also as in Britain, these latter arguments overlapped with rightist objections. Fischer pointed out the similarity of these statements to those of "conservative realists" who argue "against leftist idealists and their illusions of a principled foreign policy."[84]

Despite their opposition to intervention, however, almost all of the authors of the open letter agreed that the previous Green position, permitting German participation only in customs units to monitor embargoes, was no longer sufficient.[85] The Greens did not really think like the exclusivist right.

---

81. Gerd Poppe, "Bosnischer und Bonner Sommer," *Kommune*, No. 9 (1995); p. 20; Fischer (27 November 1995.) Others were calling for robust action. Cem Özdemir, " 'Ausbluten' lassen oder eingreifen?'" *Kommune*, No. 9 (1995).

82. For the resolution, see Hubert Kleinert, *Menschenrechte, Gewaltfreiheit und die Zivilisierung der internationalen Politik—Aufgabe und Verantwortung der Bündnisgrünen*, Antrag 8, Green Party Conference, Bremen (1–3 December 1995). "Wieviel Pazifismus darf's noch sein?" *Süddeutsche Zeitung* (4 December 1995); "Zerreißprobe der Bündnisgrünen, *tageszeitung* (7 December 1995).

83. Müller et al. (1995).

84. Fischer (27 November 1995).

85. Trittin admitted that the refusal by the Greens of German participation in peacekeeping deployments had been "overtaken" and took up the previous position of Bündnis 90 that German peacekeeping forces could be placed under direct control of the United Nations. See "Frau Sager für 'Friedenserzwingung,'" *Frankfurter Allgemeine Zeitung* (14 September 1995). Volmer concurred that the "grounds for rejecting peacekeeping support were no longer convincing." See "Eine ernsthafte Zerreißprobe für Bündnis 90/Die Grünen," *Frankfurter Allgemeine Zeitung* (15 September 1995). Müller was more reserved, admitting to "holes" in their position. See "Der Chor der Empörten bleibt merkwürdig dünn," *Frankfurter Allgemeine Zeitung* (3 August 1995).

Privately the Greens were expressing more serious doubts. In a discussion paper circulated within the party, the left-wing defense expert Winfried Nachtwei identified questions for which the party had no answer, such as how to stop the Serbs, how to protect the civilian population, and how to prevent the complete withdrawal of the blue helmets. In the end, he wrote, it was still unclear whether the Greens could maintain a "good conscience" regarding their programmatic position, or whether a more fundamental reevaluation was necessary.

The ramifications of the events in Bosnia in 1995 were clearer for the SPD, although not as publicly voiced. "Srebrenica was interpreted as a capitulation of the international community," said one member of the defense committee. "I will say it somewhat polemically. We said, 'All those in need, come to us and you will be protected in the enclaves.' And what happened was that not all could be protected on account of the legal and political situation. That led ultimately to a new assessment. We began to see what type of conflict this was."[86] Although the contribution proposed by the Kohl government to IFOR, the robust peacekeeping force in Bosnia, resembled that made to the Rapid Reaction Force and again included the use of Tornado aircraft, the SPD parliamentary party decided this time to support the government.[87]

The vote on IFOR in December 1995 contrasted sharply with the June 1995 experience. At that time the more moderate party chairman Scharping acquiesced to pressure by the left-wing leader Lafontaine to add a ban on the use of Tornados in the resolution introduced by the SPD parliamentary party. After Srebrenica and the air operation in August 1995, the parliamentary party rejected a proposal containing a similar clause added by Lafontaine, now even more powerful as the newly elected party chairman. The overwhelming majority of the caucus (187 yes votes, 55 no votes, one abstention) voted with the government on the IFOR deployment, almost the mirror image of the previous vote in June. Those in favor even included a number of left-wing members according to Erler, himself a leading member of the faction.[88] Shortly afterwards this became the party's official position.[89] Scharping, still the head

86. Interview with the author (7 November 2000).

87. "Antrag der Bundesregierung: Deutsche Beteiligung an den militärischen Maßnahmen zur Absicherung des Friedensvertrages für Bosnien-Herzegowina," *Bundestag Drucksache* 13/3122 (28 November 1995).

88. Interview with the author (7 February 2001). For the vote against Lafontaine's proposal, see the parliamentary party's internal minutes (5 December 1995). See also "Rede des stellvertretenden SPD-Vorsitzenden zur Außen- und Wirtschaftspolitik," *Süddeutsche Zeitung* (16 November 1995); "In Mannheim Jubel und eine Unterschriftensammlung für Lafontaine," *Frankfurter Allgemeine Zeitung* (16 November 1995).

89. Schwerpunktkommission Außen- und Sicherheitspolitik, "Sozialdemokratische Außenpolitik im Übergang zum 21. Jahrhundert" (unpublished document, 2 May 1997); "Beschlußbericht A1: Außen-, Sicherheits- und Entwicklungspolitik," *Presseservice der SPD* (3 December 1997).

of the parliamentary party but now free of the need to reconcile conflicting positions as head of the entire party, argued that the lesson of the war was "brutally clear"—that humanitarian help was not enough. "The Bosnian war is an example that aggression and genocide can only be ended through determined action by the civilized world."[90] The party was now in line with other social democratic parties in Europe, a point made by Scharping in the Bundestag and by Günther Verheugen during the parliamentary party's private meeting as well.[91] The SPD's position on intervention was becoming less parochial. It was normalizing.

Learning from Peace: The Success of IFOR

The same was true for the Greens. Although all but two voted against the government's proposed contribution to SFOR, the successor to the IFOR peacekeeping force, the party's counterproposal was the first explicit statement of support for a German contribution to a peacekeeping mission. Even the left-winger Angelika Beer was careful in her speech to stress that the party wanted the Bundeswehr to remain.[92] Volmer later said that the Greens would have lent their support had they been needed for a majority. He feared that although he personally accepted the use of force as a last resort, his party's support would make it easier for the government to neglect the development of civilian means of conflict resolution and prevention.[93] Nachtwei noted this concern, but felt that adhering to such a position betrayed leftist goals. "Of course Rühe had a strategy of taking small steps and getting the public accustomed to military intervention. The efforts to find nonmilitary solutions were also insufficient. However, this does not change the fact that there was no alternative to using military force." Maintaining a superficial opposition to intervention also had a more cynical purpose. Criticizing the government was also a way to distinguish the party from the CDU and the SPD. "We continued a critique, for domestic political reasons, that was not right in view of what was necessary for the Balkans."[94] Electoral considerations obscured the extent of the evolution in Green thinking.

---

90. *Plenarprotokoll* 13/76 (6 December 1995), p. 6635. Scharping would admit that he had previously represented positions he had not advocated personally. "Lafontaine bringt Antrag gegen Tornado-Einsatz ein," *Süddeutsche Zeitung* (16 November 1995).

91. *Plenarprotokoll* 13/76, pp. 6634–6638; Parliamentary party's internal minutes (24 October 1995).

92. *Plenarprotokoll* 13/149 (13 December 1996), p. 13508. For the party's counterproposal, see "Entschließungsantrag der Fraktion Bündnis 90/Die Grünen," *Bundestag Drucksache* 13/6501 (11 December 1996).

93. Interview with the author (18 May 2001).

94. Interview with the author (15 February 2001).

Under the government's proposal, German ground troops would be placed for the first time on the soil of Bosnia, a region where the Reichswehr had committed serious atrocities during the Second World War.[95] Most striking about the debate was that no speaker objected to this particular step forward. For the SPD, the number opposed to the mission actually declined from 55 to 41 with a few abstentions. Crucial for a more positive evaluation of the SFOR mission was the fact that there had been no military escalation within the region. Fears that German participation would endanger the process in view of Germany's past crimes in the region had not proved true. Nachtwei put it plainly: "These are facts, even when they irritate us due to our fundamentally critical position concerning the military."[96] Wieczorek-Zeul, perhaps the most powerful foreign policy figure on the SPD's left, made the same admission and voted for the operation.[97] Volker Beck and Andrea Fischer, two Green members of parliament who had feared escalation, wrote: "Today, two years later, we ask ourselves if our decision then was wrong. Soldiers have not been rejected but instead are respected. The troops have shown they can keep the peace."[98] Although IFOR went much farther than the official party position endorsed three months before, 33 of 47 Greens voted for SFOR's maintenance only months before the election.[99]

For other members of the Green left wing, however, Defense Minister Rühe's newly published remarks that a UN mandate would not be necessary in case of an attack on Yugoslavia to punish it for its repression of the Albanian minority in Kosovo rekindled fears about conservative intentions to militarize German foreign policy. Milosevic had cracked down on the civilian population to quell the independence movement and create a more ethnically pure Serbian province. Volmer and Beer among others wrote: "As we cannot judge the government's resolution on the participation in the SFOR successor operation without taking into account the comments of the defense minister on the Kosovo question that reveal his more far-reaching intentions, we cannot agree to the government's resolution. . . . Even in the case of the worst of all thinkable human rights violations, genocide . . . no departure from the necessity of an authorizing resolution of the Security

95. "Antrag der Bundesregierung: Deutsche Beteiligung an der von der NATO geplanten Operation zur weiteren militärischen Absicherung des Friedensprozesses im früheren Jugoslawien," *Bundestag Drucksache* 13/6500 (11 December 1996).

96. Winfried Nachtwei, "Bosnien-Reise der Vorstände von Bundestagsfraktion und Partei von Bündnis 90/Die Grünen: Wesentliche Eindrücke und erste Schlußfolgerungen" (unpublished document, 4 November 1996).

97. *Plenarprotokoll* 13/149 (13 December 1996), pp. 13526–13527.

98. *Plenarprotokoll* 13/242 (19 June 1998), p. 22479. For other expressions of self-doubt, see Christina Nickels, 13/76 (6 December 1995), pp. 6663–6665, Franziska Eichstädt-Bohlig, 13/76 (6 December 1995), pp. 6695–6696; Winfried Nachtwei, 13/242 (19 June 1998), p. 22482–22483.

99. For the official party position, see Bündnis 90/Die Grünen (1998).

Council would be possible."[100] Part of the left wing was still applying simple evaluative rules. Their words would soon be tested when they found themselves in a very different vantage point—the government benches.

FROM OPPOSITION INTO OFFICE: KOSOVO, THE SPIRAL MODEL, AND THE RESPONSIBILITIES OF GOVERNING

Following their election, but before entering office, the SPD and Greens voted overwhelmingly on 16 October 1998 in favor of German participation in the use of NATO air power against Yugoslavia in order to avert a humanitarian catastrophe in Kosovo, despite the lack of a UN mandate. The evolution of the left's policy on the use of force seemed complete. As I indicated earlier, there are competing explanations of how the SPD and Greens were able to approve this mission. CDU critics and office-seeking theorists argue that the Greens in particular were opportunists, trading their political principles for power. Those who make this argument believe that the government could not have lasted unless it participated in the air war because any German government needed international legitimacy to survive. Culturalists and critics from the far left wing of the Greens and the SPD also claim that the government had to demonstrate its loyalty to NATO. However, they believe it was pressure from the United States that forced German participation in the air war.[101]

Neither account squares well with the evidence, however. Following the election, a delegation including chancellor-designate Gerhard Schröder, probable foreign minister Fischer, Verheugen, and Volmer traveled to Washington to ask President Clinton for his understanding if Germany chose not to participate in the air war immediately or even at all. Any deployment of the Bundeswehr required parliamentary approval, but the Bundestag was out of session and no longer had a popular mandate since a new government had just been elected.[102] The leadership therefore did not appear to feel that participation was a defining test of NATO solidarity. Clinton initially expressed

---

100. *Plenarprotokoll* 13/242 (19 June 1998), p. 22483.

101. Hornhues made the accusation of opportunism: "For years the thought of being in power had buzzed around Fischer's head. How does a Green politician gain power? He has to formulate positions that are acceptable to a coalition partner. That began the process of change that was partly a confrontation with reality but insofar as it concerned the leadership was more a case of simple opportunism. It was a radical change that took place due to the spell Fischer was under of being foreign minister." Interview with the former vice president of the CDU parliamentary group and chair of the Foreign Policy Committee (9 November 2000). Multilateral pressure theories came out in interviews with Hans-Christian Ströbele (26 February 2001) and Konrad Gilges (17 May 2001), respectively Green and SPD Bundestag deputies.

102. Interview with Ludger Volmer (18 May 2001).

understanding and agreed that Germany should postpone its decision until the new government was sworn in.[103]

Just a few days later, however, the Americans reversed their position and, according to Fischer, gave the party leaders fifteen minutes to decide if they would be on board in case of war.[104] If the two leaders concluded that participation was necessary to gain the international legitimacy necessary to govern, it was based on only a hunch of two individuals and not reflective of the overall positions of their parties. (The coalition's behavior several years later in the Iraq crisis also seems to suggest that the Greens and Social Democrats are not afraid to oppose the Americans when they disagree with them.) Participation would just as likely break up the coalition as keep it together, and therefore was quite risky from an office-seeking point of view. Schröder and Fischer did not yet know which would happen. Volmer recalled the context of the moment: "The coalition negotiations were still taking place. The new government had not been constructed. It was not yet clear if we could agree."[105] The decision to go along was obviously not made with a firm knowledge of party sentiment since there was no time for consultation.

Accountability and the Albanians

Schröder and Fischer had less reason to be concerned than they might have thought. The October Bundestag debate on participation in the air war was quite uneventful in comparison to previous debates. The Green Party had evolved more than its electoral rhetoric let on, as was evident in the voting patterns on earlier deployments, so its position seemed more opportunistic than it was. Volmer, now a deputy foreign minister, would concede afterward that the position on intervention before the election was a "halfway" measure to develop a distinctive electoral profile.[106] Politicians approached the issue differently when in power, not due to the pressures of allies but because of the responsibility for making decisions directly affecting the Albanian minority in Kosovo. In opposition the lack of a feasible alternative might not have been as problematic, but in office it posed a serious problem. Defense policy expert Nachtwei described the different vantage point: "[In the opposition] the domestic consequences of policy are the most important. We noticed that in an extreme way with the responsibility of governing. What is crucial is what one does in a particular situation under the given conditions

103. Ibid. "Wie Deutschland in den Krieg geriet," *Die Zeit* (12 May 1999).
104. Ibid.
105. Ibid.
106. Ludger Volmer, "Krieg in Jugoslawien: Hintergrund einer grünen Entscheidung" (unpublished document, 26 March 1999).

of international politics. To a certain degree we avoided this central question. One can do that in the opposition. When one is a little self-critical, one notices that one is avoiding this question."[107]

Accountability exposed the two parties to human rights norms from which they were largely insulated while in opposition. This forced them to differentiate between humanitarian and strategic military operations. Several leftists including Christian Sterzing and Kerstin Müller wrote: "Above all [in government] one has to act . . . because one is now *responsible* for human lives and for war and peace. In addition to the questions of our political values and the goals of our policy we cannot avoid the question of their consequences. When we bear responsibility for others, we cannot be conscientious objectors." Others in the party echoed those beliefs.[108] Sentiments were similar on the left wing of the SPD. A member of the Foreign Policy Committee said: "I think that many of those who could be classified as being on the left of the party went through the same process I did. There is a large difference between the ideals that one has and the real world, and in particular situations one has to create policies on the basis of how they correspond to the real world. This was about aircraft and people being murdered. That is real. A lot of us were convinced that our responsibility was not to let that happen."[109] SPD and Green policies were therefore becoming less parochial in a second sense. They were focused less on the consequences of out-of-area missions for Germany itself and the "militarization" of German foreign policy, and more on the implications for those on whose behalf NATO would intervene.

Pressure to support NATO was also present, but the pressure came from within and was linked to its specific goal, not to an instinctive multilateralism. The goal was inclusive. Rudolf Scharping, former head of the SPD and now defense minister, asked: "What sense does it make to praise our liberal constitution . . . and limit the application of the first article of our constitution, our duty to protect the dignity of humanity, to ourselves, those with a German passport?"[110] If the left supported the goal, it could no longer

107. Interview with the author (15 February 2001). Beer agreed. In a letter to the members of her own party, she stated, "I hope that those who label us or me personally a warmonger will finally answer my question, what the alternative to this difficult decision would have been." Angelika Beer, "Offener Brief an die Mitglieder der Partei Bündnis 90/Die Grünen: Krieg im Kosovo,"(unpublished document, 31 March 1999).

108. Winfried Nachtwei, Kerstin Müller, Winfried Hermann, Volker Beck, Hans-Josef Fell, Klaus Müller, and Christian Sterzing, "Kosovo-Einsatz der Bundeswehr: Notwendige Friedenstruppe oder Interventionstruppe gegen Serbien?" (unpublished document, 1 March 1999). In a letter to her party, Beer wrote, "I ask you not to begin this discussion with the expectation of a solution to our problems. The issue is above all the problems of the Kosovar Albanians." Beer (31 March 1999); Volmer (26 March 1999).

109. Interview with the author (7 November 2000).

110. *Plenarprotokoll* 14/31 (26 March 1999), p. 2609.

refuse the means to attain it. An SPD member said: "As a foreign policy specialist I had to explain to a Danish or an American or a French mother why she had to send her son into a dangerous mission and why a German mother was not affected by this. This argumentation is hard to sustain."[111] A member of the party's right wing was more blunt, criticizing the party's "mentality of exceptionalism," or *Sondermentalität.* "Let others die and we'll pay for it. That cannot be sustained for long. We cannot say to the Americans, the British, and the French: 'Please do our dirty work for us. We will sit elegantly on the sidelines. Excuse our history. Check our pocketbooks. We'll pay for those who stick their necks out for *things that we also think are good and important.*'"[112]

Multilateralism and responsibility would not have been enough to bring the majority of both parties behind the air war in Kosovo, however, without the learning process that they had previously undergone as a result of Bosnia. Uta Zapf, a defense committee member on the left of the party, said: "Having the responsibility of governing, to be in an alliance that demands solidarity, that helped a lot. But that would not have been so easy if there had not already been this developmental process."[113] Eberhard Brecht, member of the Foreign Policy Committee, recounted: "A lot had happened in people's heads. We knew what had happened in Srebrenica."[114] Green deputy Nachtwei feared a "second Bosnia."[115] Especially critical for the support of the left wing of the Green Party was the relative absence of any clear exclusivist Western interests in the Balkans. NATO's aims were consistent with inclusivist Green concerns. "The NATO military action is not about territorial conquest or oil," wrote Nachtwei.[116] This was not an easy admission. "That the primary goal of the NATO threat is unequivocally humanitarian and that it seeks the implementation of UN Security Council Resolution 1199 as a precondition for a peace process in Kosovo cannot simply be wished away," wrote Müller and Nachtwei.[117] Asked why such a realization had been painful for the left-wing Greens, Nachtwei answered: "Because the dominant view for us for a long time had been that NATO was not capable of acting for humanitarian purposes, but rather that it was only driven by power considerations."[118]

111. Interview with the author (27 November 2000).
112. Interview with the author (16 November 2000) (emphasis added).
113. Interview with the author (22 January 2001).
114. Interview with the author (27 November 2000).
115. Winfried Nachtwei, "NATO-Luftangriffe: Antiserbische Aggression oder einzige Rettungschance für den Kosovo" (unpublished document, 26 March 1999).
116. Ibid. The same point is found in Angelika Beer, Helmut Lippelt, and Christian Sterzing, "Erklärung zum Kosovo-Krieg," *In der Debatte,* No. 18 (22 April 1999).
117. *Plenarprotokoll* 13/248 (16 October 1998), p. 23167.
118. Interview with the author (15 February 2001).

Unlearning the Lessons of Deterrence: The Spiraling Kosovo Conflict

The German left, a more recent convert to just wars, responded differently than their British counterparts when the air campaign initially showed no signs of hindering Milosevic's ethnic cleansing operation, however. Following the beginning of the air strikes in late March 1999, Milosevic's security forces stepped up a systematic ethnic cleansing operation against which the air war was initially powerless. Thousands were killed and more than a million were displaced internally and in neighboring countries. Military force was not only proving ineffective, it was escalating. NATO responded by increasing the number of sorties and eventually broadening the scope of strikes to include targets whose destruction had negative consequences for the civilian population, such as electricity plants. The spiral model of conflict seemed to be playing itself out.

The left wings of both parties were the first to raise doubts about the operation—the same politicians who had never questioned their own antimilitarist positions during the Bosnian conflict or had done so most reluctantly or belatedly. The Frankfurt Circle, in a resolution drawn up by Herman Scheer, demanded that the government immediately end the bombing and begin a process of political dialogue. A halt in the bombing would break the escalatory "logic of war," argued left-winger Detlev von Larcher, spokesperson for the Frankfurt Circle, at the SPD party conference.[119] More critically, almost every single discussion paper written during the war by left-wing members of the Green parliamentary party, even those who had come out originally in support of the operation, raised the prospect of an "escalation spiral."[120] Beer argued: "NATO is acting as inflexibly as Milosevic. The options are military escalation on both sides or political de-escalation."[121]

This was a notable departure from the statements made by the same politicians at the beginning of the war, which stressed the need for forceful action against Milosevic to deter aggression against the Kosovar Albanians and made little mention of spirals.[122] That had been the powerful effect of the Bosnian experience.[123] Kosovo proved very different, however. Claiming that the air strikes

---

119. SPD, *Verantwortung,* SPD Party Conference, Bonn (12 April 1999), pp. 94–96.

120. Christian Sterzing, Winfried Hermann, Winfried Nachtwei, Claudia Roth, Hans-Josef Fell, and Klaus Müller, "Zurück zur Politik!" (unpublished document, 13 April 1999); Angelika Beer, "Grüne fordern Bundesregierung zu diplomatischer Initiative im Kosovo-Konflikt auf" (unpublished document, 2 April 1999)

121. Angelika Beer, "Krieg im Kosovo—und kein Ende?" (unpublished document, 11 April 1999).

122. "Not to intervene with military force would mean allowing Milosevic free rein and permit a second Bosnia. At the same time it would destroy the credibility of the international community . . ." Nachtwei (26 March 1999). "Ask yourself what the consequence would be of an end to the NATO action if Milosevic had a free hand to murder." Beer (11 April 1999).

123. At the beginning of the war the Green party board stressed that limited military action by NATO had forced a return to diplomacy in other cases. See Bündnis 90/Die Grünen Bundesvorstand, "Zu den Lufteinsätzen der NATO in Jugoslawien," *Pressedienst,* No. 39 (25 March 1999).

had not proven effective, the party board and prominent Greens began to advocate a temporary unilateral bombing pause to allow heads to cool and negotiations to recommence. The other option was ground troops, which every Green politician rejected.[124] This provides further evidence for the argument above. If policy change reflects the interaction between ideology and conclusions drawn from experience, then lessons learned can be unlearned when more recent events contradict earlier inferences. Nevertheless, prominent Greens from both the right and the left wings of the party made sure to point out that an unconditional end to the air campaign would send the signal to Milosevic that he had won.[125] The party was fluctuating between spiral and deterrence logic.

Instrumentalizing Ideas: Shoring up SPD Support

Fearing a loss of parliamentary backing, the SPD leadership turned to the human rights norms that had been so critical for bringing the party around to embracing military intervention in the first place. This had been true for politicians from all wings of the party. Now that the leadership was under tremendous pressure to maintain the coalition or risk its collapse, however, those same norms became its weapons.[126] Like Blair, Defense Minister Scharping was trying to lead his party and public opinion as well, although his task was harder. The government used references to genocide and comparisons to the Holocaust to maintain not only public backing, but also internal party support. Scharping was charged with keeping the parliamentary party on board through both public statements and private meetings. All of his speeches in the Bundestag recited a litany of abuses by the Milosevic government. Defense Ministry briefing sheets featured drawings by children in refugee camps of the tragedies they had experienced. Most controversially, Scharping made frequent mention of Operation Horseshoe, reportedly the calculated and systematic ethnic cleansing plan of the Yugoslavian government whose authenticity was always shrouded in doubt.[127]

124. Sterzing et al. (13 April 1999); Bündnis 90/Die Grünen Bundesvorstand, "Kein Einsatz von Bodentrupen," *Pressedienst*, No. 53 (19 April 1999).

125. Beer et al. (22 April 1999).

126. It should be made clear that utilizing and even exaggerating arguments does not necessarily imply that they are not genuinely felt. In private, senior government officials always related their personal experiences with the tragedies in Kosovo.

127. Scharping spoke at the party convention of "dark clouds of genocide." See SPD (1999), *Verantwortung*, p. 60. Also see his comments in *Plenarprotokoll* 14/31 (26 March 1999), pp. 2607–2610; 14/32 (15 April 1999), pp. 2645–2649; 14/40 (7 May 1999), pp. 3392–3395. The drawings are included in Bundesministerium für Verteidigung, *Der Kosovo-Konflikt* (1999). Most controversial about Operation Horseshoe was the fact that the plan had a title in a different dialect of Serbo-Croatian than would be expected. Scharping also claimed to have had knowledge of the plan before the air campaign began, exposing himself to criticism for NATO's being caught by surprise by the ethnic cleansing that followed the beginning of the bombing.

Some parliamentary members wonder if this moral rhetoric was necessary. One said: "Of course it was important that so many Kosovars were driven out and that genocide was a tool of Milosevic's. We could not sit by and watch . . . but I do not know if Scharping could not have argued that it was necessary for reasons of regional stability. If Milosevic had not been stopped in Kosovo, then Montenegro was next."[128] Scharping was using the most effective means for convincing his own party, however—a type of argumentation that was not necessary in the CDU. Although many SPD members later privately said they were uncomfortable with how Scharping justified the war, they did not doubt the short-term effectiveness of the strategy. "I find it problematic when one discovers new facts and only knows after the fact the true character of Operation Horseshoe," said Erler. "It is especially problematic when one knows what role it played in the discussion."[129] Brecht accused Scharping of "emotionalizing and moralizing the debate. He wanted to bring the parliamentary party behind him. It worked."[130] The experience in Kosovo provides further evidence for the argument about ideological change. Although the leaderships of both parties might either have been driven by the desire to stay in power or been genuinely convinced of their cause, it was ideas and values that moved the parliamentary parties as a whole.

Opportunism or Lack of Options? The Green Party Conference

This strategy was less effective against the more antimilitarist Green Party. Indeed the increasingly emotional rhetoric made the Greens even wearier as it was indicative of a spiraling conflict and of a hardening of positions that made a resolution of the conflict impossible. The party called the government's language a "moral armament."[131] Pressure from the party contributed to Foreign Minister Fischer's efforts to find some room for negotiation. Germany presented a peace plan to the European Union in mid-April. It incorporated NATO's five demands—an end to Serbian repression, withdrawal of Yugoslav forces, return of refugees, deployment of a peacekeeping force, and commitment to negotiate an agreement on the status of Kosovo—but also suggested that NATO agree to a twenty-four-hour bombing pause as soon as Serb forces began to withdraw from Kosovo.[132] The Allied precondition had been a full pullout of the police and military. German resolve was weakening. The Americans, sensing a climbdown, were wary of the proposal.

128. Interview with SPD deputy (17 November 2000).
129. Interview with the author (7 February 2001).
130. Interview with the author (27 November 2001).
131. Bündnis 90/Die Grünen Vorstand, "Eckpunkte für einen Leitantrag des Bundesvorstandes zur Sonder-BDK," *Pressedienst*, No. 54 (27 April 1999).
132. On the Fischer plan, see Daalder and O'Hanlon (2000), p. 166.

The question for Germany was whether the initiative would be enough to keep the coalition together. As the war wore on, a special Green Party conference was held in Bielefeld in May 1999. At stake was the future of the coalition. Two competing resolutions were on the table. Both demanded some degree of de-escalation on the part of NATO because the air strikes had proven ineffective, inflaming rather than resolving the situation. Both resolutions expressed fears that if unilateral measures were not taken to step back from the spiral of war, a ground war would result, an outcome that all condemned. At this point the resolutions parted ways. The party board's resolution called for an unconditional pause in the bombing, after which Milosevic should remove his forces from Kosovo. The cease-fire would be extended as long as Yugoslav forces were beginning to exit the province. The authors justified their position as seeking to reconcile the value conflict within the Greens.[133]

The other resolution, written by a group of hard-core antimilitarists from the Bundestag who called themselves the "Upright Seven," demanded an outright end to the air campaign. According to Hans-Christian Ströbele, one of the group's members, it was drawn from the far left of the party. As the majority of both parties had done in the early 1990s, the group denied any conflict between leftist goals, evaluating intervention solely from an antimilitarist viewpoint: "Human rights and peace cannot be separated. . . . Our shared principles of renouncing force and human rights cannot be allowed to be played against each other." "War," they reminded the Greens, "is also a human rights violation."[134] Like the pure antimilitarists in France and Britain, the group also noted the part played in the civil war by the armed Albanian independence organization, the Kosovo Liberation Army (KLA), and hypothesized that NATO's intention in the war was to undermine the UN. Their initiative was widely believed to mean an end to the red-green coalition. However, following a raucous caucus during which Foreign Minister Fischer suffered a burst eardrum after he was struck by a balloon full of paint, 60 percent of the party delegates voted instead for the leadership's recommendation.

Whether the events of the party conference were indicative of office or policy-seeking motivation is not immediately evident from the behavior of the delegates. Although most Green politicians acknowledge that there are opportunists in their party as Downs might expect, I would argue that the

---

133. Bündnis 90/Die Grünen Vorstand, *Frieden und Menschenrechte vereinbaren! Für einen Frieden im Kosovo, der seinen Namen zu Recht trägt*, Antrag 1, 2nd Extraordinary Party Conference, Bielefeld (13 May 1999).

134. The antimilitarist resolution is Claudia Roth and Hans-Christian Ströbele, *Die Luftangriffe sofort beenden und mit der Logik der Kriegsführung brechen*, Antrag 74, 2nd Extraordinary Party Conference, Bielefeld (13 May 1999). Christian Simmert, Annelie Buntenbach, Monika Knoche, Steffi Lemke, Irmingard Schewe-Gerigk, Christian Ströbele and Sylvia Voss, "Luftangriffe sofort beenden—zurück an den Verhandlungstisch" (unpublished document, 20 April 1999).

outcome in Bielefeld was more than a party clinging to power. The rationale of key ministers was that only by remaining in the government could the Green Party, through its foreign minister, make sure that diplomacy was not swallowed up by the logic of war. This was the reasoning behind the resolution that passed. If the party left the coalition, German efforts at diplomacy might end. Deputy Foreign Minister Volmer later said: "The decision of the party conference was necessary in order for it to be possible to continue with the Fischer peace plan. If the other resolution had passed . . . the coalition would have ended. A grand coalition between the SPD and the CDU would have probably formed, and it is doubtful whether they would have continued with this. At this time there was already planning for a ground invasion. Therefore the resolution that seemingly supported the war was the one that in the end provided a way out of the war. The resolution that seemingly rejected the war would have escalated and prolonged the war."[135] It was a policy-seeking strategy of "voice" that only the most antimilitarist party in Germany could carry out.

There is reason to believe Volmer was right. The Fischer peace initiative did have an important successful element that sowed the seeds of peace. It suggested that a final settlement could be negotiated by the G-8 countries, a move that was meant to include Russia. Volmer explained: "Milosevic was trying to rekindle Cold War rivalries between Russia and the West. This could be countered by offering Russia another alternative than unconditional solidarity with Belgrade. Our peace plan accepted the Russians as an important European power and argued that a final solution to the Balkan problems without Russia was unthinkable."[136] The Fischer plan marked the beginning of a renewed Russian engagement that would ultimately isolate Milosevic entirely. Yeltsin expressed an immediate interest, and a special G-8 meeting later endorsed a peace plan based on Fischer's that formed the basis for the final negotiations with Milosevic.

There was a genuine belief on the part of most Greens, even those in the left wing of the party, that simply ending a military campaign was not a viable option. This was not an endorsement intended merely to enable the party to remain in the coalition. The Greens argued that the bombing would have to continue if Yugoslavia made no overtures. Experience with Milosevic in Bosnia, they argued, had shown that he only negotiated under pressure. This position was part of the resolution passed at the party conference.[137] Credibility and resolve, the hallmarks of the deterrence model, were still present in Green thinking. Diplomacy did need to be backed by force. Volmer explained the

---

135. Interview with the author (18 May 2001).
136. Ibid.
137. Bündnis 90/Die Grünen Vorstand (13 May 1999); Beer (11 April 1999).

position of the Green-led foreign ministry: "In opposition to an escalation strategy of ground troops we wanted to *use the military pressure that had already been built up to open up negotiating possibilities.*"[138] No Green could have said this five years earlier.

A viable policy was critical for a governing party, and most of the Greens believed that a unilateral end to air strikes was not credible. Greater accountability made for different policies. "Building models of how the world can think better" was the job of the opposition, argued Volmer during the party conference. He knew this personally. "I belong to the best of the model builders," he said. Now a deputy foreign minister, Volmer said of his "old friends": "They want to hold on to their vision of the world."[139] When asked what vision that was, Volmer described the pure spiral model: "During the Cold War, the problem was how to mutually reduce nuclear capabilities. We demanded unilateral reductions by NATO. This model of unilateral disarmament, which made sense during the 1980s, was applied to a situation where it did not apply."[140]

Unlike the party conference in December 1995, the resolution seemed to reflect the parliamentary party's position as well. That the parliamentarians this time drafted their own resolution with the same demands indicates that they genuinely supported the policy.[141] Even those Greens who would be most likely to make accusations of opportunism, the radical pacifists who never supported an out-of-area mission for the Bundeswehr, including the author of the antimilitarist resolution, agreed that the majority of the delegates were genuinely convinced of the morality of the bombing campaign.[142]

The maintenance of the coalition was in its own right a tremendous relief to the SPD and ultimately to NATO. Solidarity was an important factor in NATO's ultimate victory. In personal conversations, Milosevic had set his sights on Germany from the beginning as a potential weak link, claiming that he, unlike the Germans, could "step over corpses."[143] Beyond Germany's usual contribution of aircraft to suppress air defenses, it had made a contribution to offensive military operations as well. Although culturalists have

---

138. Interview with the author (18 May 2001) (emphasis added).

139. "Bangen vor dem Himmelfahrtstag," *Süddeutsche Zeitung* (10 May 1999).

140. Interview with the author (18 May 2001).

141. "Beschluß der Fraktion Bündnis 90/Die Grünen zum Kosovo-Krieg," *In der Debatte,* No. 23 (31 May 1995).

142. Annelle Buntenbach said: "Many were shocked and thought that [the moral justification] went too far, but many allowed themselves to be swept away by this emotional argumentation." Interview with the author (10 May 2001). Hans-Christian Ströbele said: "Most of them were convinced that war was necessary to protect the Albanians from expulsion and murder. That was the propaganda." Interview with the author (26 February 2001).

143. Volmer (26 March 1999).

downplayed the extent of its contribution, the limits had more to do with the outdated munitions of its fighter planes than with a persistent pacifism.[144]

Nevertheless, there is every indication that if the Social Democrats had decided to participate in a ground war, they would have done so with a new coalition partner. The Greens would not have gone this far. There were ideological limits to the "voice" option. Beer noted in an internal party document that 100 percent of the party voted for resolutions that took issue with the existing NATO strategy. The issue was how to make the Social Democrats hear them.[145] The chancellor seemed to respond, making extremely blunt statements against a NATO invasion just a few days later. Unlike in France and Britain, countries with more positive military histories, the left did not choose to escalate dramatically in the face of failure. A land invasion was a bridge too far.

The Reluctant Right: The CDU in Opposition

It is hardly clear whether the CDU would have gone along with a ground war either. Despite the left's weaknesses, the right was no more determined to escalate the fighting. The kind of argumentation used by Defense Minister Scharping to bring his party into line was not necessary in the CDU, since its members believed Germany's strategic interests were at stake as well. "The red-green government needed moral justification, which was necessary due to the history of both parties. Fundamentally we do not need this moral rhetoric like the Greens and the SPD because of another factor—the refugees," said Falenski, still adviser to the former CDU defense minister.[146] Germany, by virtue of its geographic position, was likely to be more tangibly affected by the conflict, and this exclusivist argument separated the left from the right.

Despite this, however, neither the centrist FDP nor the rightist CDU was willing to grant that the interests at stake were significant enough to justify a ground war. Schäuble, the head of the parliamentary party, stated that the CDU was the party most convinced of the need to resort to force in extreme cases, but his public statements showed no more determination than those of the leftist coalition partners. He also criticized the government for its moralizing rhetoric in spiral terms, claiming that emotionalism increased the possibility of military escalation.[147] In an oblique reference to ground troops, the

---

144. See Duffield (1999). Germany contributed thirty-three aircraft. Even opposition politicians admit: "That was simply all we had for an air war. And all we still have." Interview with Hans-Joachim Falenski (2 February 2001).

145. Angelika Beer, "Vorlage für AK IV am 17.05.99" (unpublished document, 16 May 1999).

146. Interview with the author (2 February 2001).

147. "Die neue Ernsthaftigkeit," *Die Zeit* (22 April 1999). See also Wolfgang Schäuble, *Plenarprotokoll* 14/32 (15 April 1999), p. 2626.

CDU foreign policy spokesperson Lamers said: "No one's responsibility reaches further than his abilities. No one has to do more than he can."[148] The defense policy spokesperson Breuer was more direct, asserting flatly that "There will be no intervention with ground troops, definitely not German soldiers."[149] Both the CDU and the FDP party conferences passed resolutions ruling out an invasion. No major figure in either party came out in favor of a ground war.

This was a striking departure for a party that had based much of its argument for participating in out-of-area missions on the need for alliance solidarity. Indeed, former Defense Minister Rühe took pride in the fact that it was his party and its leaders Schäuble and Edmund Stoiber who had first ruled out ground troops.[150] Former foreign minister Kinkel complained that the red-green coalition's endorsement of NATO's policy was "overtaking" the opposition "on the right."[151]

THE DUAL NORMALIZATION PROCESS

Kinkel's quote implies that the traditional understanding of left and right in Germany as doves and hawks respectively is changing. Germany is normalizing, but in a very different way than that foreseen by those who predicted that with the strictures on its sovereignty removed, Germany would seek its rightful place at the table of the world powers.[152] Instead it is becoming more like other countries in the sense that leftist parties are defined by their more inclusive conception of the national interest and less by their antimilitarism. Figure 3 displays the partisan cleavage over humanitarian intervention in the early 1990s. The rightist CDU, eager to break free of the restrictions on the use of force placed on Germany by its historical burden, used humanitarian interventions as a way to make Germany "normal" again. It took the instrumental path. The leftist Social Democratic and Green parties opposed this effort, resolving the value conflict very differently than in Britain, taking the antimilitarist path instead.

---

148. Karl Lamers, *Plenarprotokoll* 14/32 (15 April 1999), p. 2649.

149. "Unzufriedenheit mit Nato-Strategie nimmt zu," *Associated Press* (11 April 1999).

150. "Überanpassung der Bundesregierung," *Süddeutsche Zeitung* (28 April 1999).

151. " 'Rot-Grün überholt uns heute rechts,' " *tageszeitung* (30 May 1999). "CDU lehnt Einsatz von Bodentruppen ab," *Süddeutsche Zeitung* (27 April 1999).

152. For the realist view, see Kenneth Waltz, "The Emerging Structure of International Politics," *International Security*, Vol. 18, No. 2 (1993), pp. 44–79. For Mearsheimer this even meant the acquisition of nuclear weapons. John Mearsheimer, "Back to the Future: Instability in Europe after the Cold War," *International Security*, Vol. 15, No. 1 (1990), pp. 5–56.

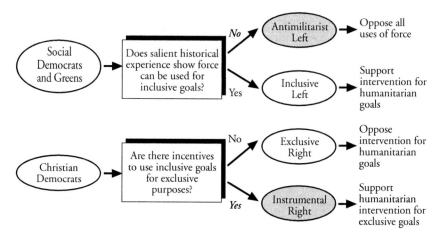

Figure 3. The German case

The experience of Bosnia exposed an ideological contradiction, however, and led to an incredible evolution in leftist foreign policy. That a similar process is occurring in the Party for Democratic Socialism suggests again that change is motivated primarily by policy-seeking and not by office-seeking concerns. The successor to the East German Communists and the most extreme leftist party in Germany, the PDS utilized all of the arguments that the far left in other nations had marshaled against humanitarian interventions.[153] Despite this pacifist policy, however, the head of the party, Gregor Gysi, triggered an intense intraparty debate by suggesting soon after Kosovo that the party evaluate each possible military intervention individually, rather than apply a simple and antimilitarist evaluative rule. His suggestion of differentiation found its way into resolutions passed by both the party executive and the parliamentary party.[154] Although the party leadership lost this battle at the party conference, which endorsed a stricter antimilitarist document composed by Sylvia-Yvonne Kaufmann, it was not a victory of ideologically pure fundamentalists over an office-seeking leadership. In fact it was the left wing of the party that stressed the electoral benefits of a strict pacifist "profile" due to the recent policy changes of the Green Party.[155]

---

153. See PDS Parteivorstand, "Resolution on the War against Yugoslavia" (unpublished document, April 1999). Also comments by Gregor Gysi in *Plenarprotokoll* 13/248 (16 October 1998) and 14/32 (15 April 1999).

154. Gregor Gysi, "Zum Verhältnis der PDS und ihrer Bundestagsfraktion zum Einsatz von VN-Truppen in Krisenregionen," *Arbeitsunterlagen,* No. 1 (9 November 1999), pp. 1–4. For the final resolution, see the same volume.

155. Sylvia-Yvonne Kaufmann, "Zum Verhältnis der PDS und ihrer Bundestagsfraktion zum Einsatz von VN-Truppen in Krisenregionen," *Arbeitsunterlagen,* No. 1 (9 November 1999), pp. 5–8.

Germany is becoming more like other countries in a second way. As the left increasingly stresses inclusivist over antimilitarist concerns, it has begun to differentiate itself from the right in a way that resembles partisan cleavages in Britain and the United States. During the debate over the East Timor deployment proposed by the red-green government, the CDU expressed private displeasure about the limited extent to which national interests were at stake. Hornhues said: "There was an intense discussion. We did not want to embarrass ourselves, but under our breath we said, 'Enough of this nonsense.'"[156] Former defense minister Rühe was also opposed, according to his chief of staff. "The parliamentary party voted for it, even though we were against it. There was no real need for medical support by German soldiers. That could have been done by German medical and civilian organizations. Sometimes we have to say no."[157] Again the CDU stressed the importance of Germany's strategic interests in determining the use of its armed forces. Hornhues said: "The question was posed very clearly. Where do we intervene for humanitarian reasons? All around the world? Above all we should intervene in cases of strategic interest that we define as in Europe, very close to us, limited to our neighborhood."[158]

The left opposed this narrow definition of German interests based on its less instrumental concern for humanitarian causes. Poppe, the longtime Green interventionist who has since become the government's spokesperson on human rights, said of East Timor: "A part of the opposition asked why we were doing this as others could do it better, but I agreed with Fischer's argumentation that we could not intervene in Kosovo where there was no UN mandate and reject an operation when there was a clear mandate and we were requested to help."[159] Therefore, by the end of the 1990s, the partisan pattern looked very similar to Britain's. With Germany's military sovereignty fully restored, the CDU felt little need to embark on operations that did not serve Germany's fundamental interests, while the Greens and SPD, with a broader conception of those interests, looked increasingly like leftist parties in other countries. The motto "Never again war" is steadily fading.

---

156. Interview with the author (9 November 2000).
157. Interview with the author (2 February 2001).
158. Interview with the author (9 November 2000).
159. Interview with the author (13 February 2001).

CHAPTER 5

The French Exception?
Presidential Prerogatives and the
Public and Private Politics of Intervention

A re there limits to the partisan argument? Is France, which prides itself on its unique qualities, also exceptional when it comes to the domestic politics of humanitarian intervention in the post–Cold War period? After all, it was the Gaullist president, Jacques Chirac, who dealt most forcefully with the Bosnian Serbs and led his country into the war against Yugoslavia. His predecessor, the Socialist François Mitterrand, resisted such action for years, a policy for which he was chided not only by his own party but also by the right. In addition, the Socialists, who occupied the key posts of prime, foreign, and defense minister during Kosovo, were much more muted than the British left.

France exemplifies two factors that logically circumscribe the articulation of clear partisan alternatives on international issues. First, partisanship in foreign policy decreases when parties are guided by unique ideologies that blend rightist and leftist positions in both domestic and foreign affairs. In France, that particular ideology is Gaullism, which defines as its goal the enhancement of France's international stature. It is commonly maintained that the kind of isolationism (perhaps better conceived of as exclusiveness) seen in the United States or Britain, where the right argues that crises that do not clearly affect vital interests are unimportant, does not exist in France.[1] In the most recent formulation of Gaullism, its adherents see participation in United Nations missions as consistent with France's exceptional role in foreign affairs, since humanitarian interventions serve their

1. Adrian Treacher, "A Case of Reinvention: France and Military Intervention in the 1990s," *International Peacekeeping*, Vol. 7, No. 2 (2000), p. 27.

particular definition of France's exclusive national interest—promoting French influence abroad. Second, partisan ideology is less decisive when institutional parameters restrict the influence of parties in the policy-making process. Foreign policy is naturally less partisan when parties are precluded from involvement in its formulation. Of particular importance is the distinction between presidential and parliamentary governments. As was demonstrated earlier, the executive branch was compelled to take into account the preferences of governing parties in the parliamentary systems of Great Britain and Germany. As will be shown here, French presidents were able to ignore these pressures.

Nevertheless, the French exception has its limits. First, when humanitarian interventions present Gaullists with foreign policy challenges that entail significant costs, they begin to lose the qualities that distinguish them from their rightist counterparts abroad. As their interest in peacekeeping and peace enforcement missions arises from a more self-interested conception of the national interest, their support for such missions is shallower than the left's. Gaullism is unique but not completely distinct from the more commonplace right. Second, dynamics similar to those found in Britain and Germany occur in France in periods of "cohabitation," when power is shared between political parties and the parliamentary majority becomes a more significant player in foreign policy–making. The unique cultural and institutional features of France's foreign policy obscure public party differences, so my investigation must go below the surface.

THE EXCEPTIONS

The Ideological Exception? The Left, the Right, and Gaullism

Gaullism's primary interest is the promotion of French national glory. It is considered by most to be first and foremost a foreign, and not a domestic, policy approach with the aim of promoting France's *rang* (rank) and *grandeur*.[2] These concepts were central to de Gaulle's personal strategy of restoring France's self-confidence following its humiliating defeat and occupation

---

2. The importance of these concepts is best captured in de Gaulle's famous statement that "France is not really herself unless she is in the first rank. . . . France cannot be France without grandeur." Charles de Gaulle, *Mémoires de guerre, Vol. 1* (Paris: Plon, 1954), p. 5. On the fundamental nationalist basis of Gaullism, see Robert Aron, *An Explanation of de Gaulle* (New York: Harper and Row, 1966), p. 188; Anthony Hartley, *Gaullism: The Rise and Fall of a Political Movement* (New York: Outerbridge and Dienstfrey, 1971), p. 17; Stanley Hoffmann, *Decline or Renewal? France since the 1930s* (New York: Viking Press, 1974), p. 283; Frank L. Wilson, *French Political Parties under the Fifth Republic* (New York: Praeger, 1982), p. 131.

during the Second World War. Scholars who point to the crucial role played by Gaullism in French foreign policy are less self-consciously theoretical than those who examine German antimilitarism, but their argument is almost identical. They point to the importance of the "Gaullist model," a "world-view" or set of "ideas" and "rules" that is "translated into a coherent overall policy," extends across the political spectrum, and persists today.[3] They argue that de Gaulle's particular response to France's military failure in the Second World War has provided a stable set of guidelines for postwar French foreign policy. These guidelines have manifested themselves most clearly in France's development of an independent nuclear arsenal and its departure from NATO's integrated military command structure, both meant to show that France is still a great power that cannot be taken for granted. *Grandeur* and *rang* still find expression in the manifestos of the Gaullist party. The Rally for the Republic's (RPR) 1993 electoral program lamented that France had become an "average country," claimed that "the glory of France is above all the will of the nation to affirm its genius," and promised to help the country redis-cover the "French exception."[4]

Gaullist international objectives are served by a complementary domestic program. Restoring France's greatness requires national cohesion and a strong state capable of directing the country's renewal. In practical terms this means an extensive social welfare system so as to ameliorate class conflict, differen-tiating de Gaulle's rightist ideology from that of the traditional and more exclusive French right, although for very different purposes than the left envis-ages. Gaullism combines this social agenda with a more traditional rightist approach toward political authority. Institutionally, playing an influential role in international affairs requires a strong presidency and state to repre-sent the entire nation's interests, rather than the narrower, sectional goals pro-moted by political parties.[5] For this reason, de Gaulle's political apparatus, even after its recent merger with the Union for French Democracy (UDF), is called a "rally" or movement. The emphasis on a strong executive branch

---

3. Philip H. Gordon, *A Certain Idea of France: French Security Policy and the Gaullist Legacy* (Princeton: Princeton University Press, 1993), pp. 3–5.

4. Rassemblement pour la Republique, *Avec le RPR* (1993 election manifesto).

5. On the subordination of domestic politics to international politics, see Hoffmann (1974), p. 191; Edward A. Kolodziej, *French International Policy under de Gaulle and Pompidou: The Politics of Grandeur* (Ithaca: Cornell University Press, 1974), p. 28. On Gaullist social welfare policies, see Alistair Cole, *French Political Parties in Transition* (Aldershot: Dartmouth, 1990), p. 140; John Frears, *Parties and Voters in France* (New York: St. Martin's Press, 1991), p. 47; Hartley (1971), pp. 18, 24; Hoffmann (1974), pp. 9, 12, 291; Kolodziej (1974), p. 29; Wilson (1982), p. 129. On Gaullist atti-tudes toward parties, see Aron (1966), p. 184; David S. Bell, *Parties and Democracy in France: Par-ties under Presidentialism* (London: Ashgate, 2000), p. 63; Cole (1990), p. 172; Frears (1991) p. 47; Hoffmann (1974), p. 194; Kolodziej, pp. 33, 37; Wilson (1982), p. 127.

and national cohesion were still part of the RPR's electoral appeals throughout the 1990s.[6]

In international politics, de Gaulle also drew from Republican traditions generally associated with the left, stressing that France is the birthplace of democratic values and therefore has a special mission in world politics. Gaullism rejects the distinction between an inclusive and exclusive conception of the national interest, and uses the former to justify the latter. De Gaulle declared that France's "greatness is the condition sine qua non of world peace."[7] Hoffmann writes of the Gaullist perspective: "Its self-interest and universal mission were one. Assisting France's quest for *grandeur* was in the interest of other states too."[8] The RPR still proclaims that de Gaulle's "certain idea of France" is "an idea for all peoples of the earth" and that France has to "rediscover its role for peace and liberty that it incarnated close to three centuries ago."[9]

De Gaulle's ideology is powerful, and culturalists stress how his personal success saw the gradual acceptance of *grandeur* and *rang* as central concepts by all political parties. Even the presidential policies of his most powerful domestic adversary on the left, François Mitterrand, were "Gaullism by any other name."[10] Scholars talk of a "national defense consensus" and a doctrine "accepted by such a large majority" that it would be "a gamble for a politician on either the Left or the Right to tamper with [it]."[11] As applied to the contemporary issue of military intervention for humanitarian purposes, the Gaullist consensus manifests itself in the propensity for French governments of all political stripes to play a leading role on the ground in order to influence major events and demonstrate France's great power status. In the post–Cold War world, the prestige of France's nuclear deterrent faded, forcing its leaders to search for other ways to maintain its global stature. The UN provided a "privileged means of exercising influence on the

6. The 1993 electoral program claims that the "national question" of promoting France's grandeur abroad cannot be disassociated from the "social question" of greater equality at home, and laments a "two-speed France" while claiming as part of de Gaulle's legacy one of the best social security systems in the world. The document also states that "nothing can be done without a respected state" and expresses disgust that the justice system is "ridiculed." RPR (1993). Chirac's 2002 electoral platform claims that economic decline "menaces our cohesion" and consequently "our capacity to influence world affairs." He also favors a strong state that acts against every infraction so as to deter crime. Jacques Chirac, *Mon engagement pour la France* (2002 presidential election manifesto).

7. Quoted in Hartley (1971), p. 14. See also Gordon (1993), p. 16.

8. Hoffmann (1974), p. 46. See also Michael Harrison, *The Reluctant Ally: France and Atlantic Security* (Baltimore: Johns Hopkins University Press, 1981), p. 53.

9. RPR (1993).

10. Stanley Hoffmann, "Mitterrand's Foreign Policy, or Gaullism by Any Other Name," in George Ross, Stanley Hoffmann, and Sylvia Malzacher (eds.), *The Mitterrand Experiment: Continuity and Change in Modern France* (Cambridge: Polity Press, 1987), pp. 294–305.

11. Gordon (1993), pp. xv, 108; Harrison (1981), p. 2.

international scene."[12] Already by 1992, France was providing ten thousand of the sixty thousand UN troops stationed around the world in peace-keeping and humanitarian operations. The pursuit of *grandeur* and *rang* led directly to its leadership role in Bosnia and Kosovo.[13] These culturalist scholars regard both the left and right as Gaullist.

Although Gaullist ideology is crucial for understanding the dynamics of political debate on military intervention in France, I take issue with the culturalist assertion that Gaullist ideology provides a set of principles that guide all political parties in the post–Cold War period. Rather than constraining partisan debate, Gaullist ideas have different effects on the right and the left. As in Britain and Germany, historical experience, or at least de Gaulle's unique interpretation of it, is important for French positions today, but not in the stifling way that culturalists claim. Gaullism creates a particular language that all parties utilize. However, on the left, Gaullist justifications are heard most when they resonate with concerns typical of socialist, green, and communist parties cross-nationally due to their antimilitarism, such as the preeminent role of NATO in European security affairs, and with the inclusiveness of such parties, such as France's special vocation in promoting human rights. Indeed, the Gaullists appropriated these concerns from the left in the first place. Gaullist political culture might increase the sensitivity of leftist parties to issues of NATO influence compared with that of leftist parties in other countries, making these concerns more mainstream and widespread in the moderate leftist factions in France. This does not mark a real departure from leftist principles, however.

On the right, the effect of Gaullism is more pronounced. Due to the Gaullist emphasis on playing a prominent role on the world stage, the pedestrian exclusivist ideology found among rightist parties in other countries is not as evident at first glance. This gives the appearance of a left-right consensus, but the internationalism of each side rests on different fundamentals. For the Gaullists, an inclusive foreign policy aids in the pursuit of France's more exclusive national interests. While German conservatives instrumentalized humanitarian interventions for the narrower purpose of normalizing the use of force, French conservatives did the same to promote French

    12. Thierry Tardy, "French Policy towards Peace Support Operations," *International Peacekeeping*, Vol. 6, No. 1 (1999), p. 61. Also Alex Macleod, "French Policy toward the War in the Former Yugoslavia: A Bid for International Leadership," *International Journal*, Vol. 52, No. 2 (1997), pp. 243–264; Treacher (2000), p. 25.
    13. On France's participation see Jolyon Howorth, "Debate in France over Military Intervention in Europe," in Lawrence Freedman (ed.), *Military Intervention in European Conflicts* (Oxford: Blackwell, 1994), p. 110. On Bosnia see Macleod (1997), p. 254. On Kosovo, see Alex Macleod, "Competing for Leadership in West European Defense: French and British Strategies in Kosovo," paper presented at the International Studies Association Conference (2000).

standing abroad. Significant resistance to intervention in Bosnia and Kosovo was at least initially confined to the extreme right of the RPR and of the French political spectrum as a whole.

However, even for the RPR, Gaullist doctrine is not all-encompassing. Although sharing a unique combination of ideas that differentiate their party from others, Gaullists are still a rightist party with a more exclusive conception of the national interest than their competitors on the left who stress a more egalitarian approach both at home and abroad.[14] The desire for influence is somewhat shallow when it involves substantial costs on issues to which the right cross-nationally is less committed. Under duress, Gaullism gives way to a more commonplace rightist approach. The tension between Gaullism's unique quest for influence and its affinity with more general rightist ideology helps explain the inconsistencies and contradictions in the behavior of the Balladur government during the Bosnian war.

The Institutional Exception: Electoral Insulation or Lack of Voice?

While de Gaulle's legacy might not be a consensus on the national interest, he did leave behind a new set of institutions. If his intention was to create a strong executive branch under the leadership of a president who would represent France's interests unhampered by political parties, did he succeed? In his study of military intervention, David Auerswald argues that without the possibility of parliamentary sanction and consequent fear of losing office in case of failure, presidents do indeed have wide latitude to pursue their chosen policies. As a result France will be consistently more interventionist than other countries.[15] I maintain, however, that although presidential systems do offer room for maneuver for heads of state by limiting the influence of political parties, they may or may not make use of these opportunities. This was de Gaulle's explicit intent in framing the constitution of the Fifth Republic.[16] As will be seen, this helps account for the inconsistency that France displayed over the course of the conflicts in Bosnia and Kosovo—more inclined to use force than Britain in the former, but less assertive in the latter.

Nor is presidential authority absolute. The Fifth Republic's constitution also confers some power over foreign policy on the parliamentary government as well. The president is the head of the armed services but the prime

14. As in Britain and Germany, the Socialist Party calls for the creation of a right of intervention in cases where human rights are violated. Parti socialiste, *Le contrat pour la France 1993/1998* (1993 election manifesto). On their inclusive domestic agenda, see also Lionel Jospin, *Changeons d'avenir* (1995 presidential election manifesto).

15. David P. Auerswald, *Disarmed Democracies* (Ann Arbor: University of Michigan Press, 2000).

16. Anand Menon, "Domestic Constraints on French NATO Policy," *French Politics, Culture and Society*, Vol. 18, No. 2 (2000), p. 50.

minister is given the authority to organize them. Presidential prerogatives are
partly institutional and partly deferential. In periods of single-party rule, the
parliamentary Cabinet has historically deferred to the president in matters
of high politics. During cohabitation, in which power is shared between right
and left, this has not been the case.[17] Contrary to the expectations developed
by Auerswald, the president only has complete control over foreign policy
when his party also maintains a parliamentary majority. When power is shared,
decision-making authority is shared, although the president has a degree of
veto power. This insight allows for comparisons within France, in particular of the positions on intervention taken by the prime minister and the president. If Auerswald's argument is correct, the president will be consistently
more inclined to use force than the heads of the parliamentary coalition, since
the latter are ultimately accountable to their majority and fear failure. If the
partisan argument is more powerful, the position of the parliamentary majority will depend on the ideological approach of the larger party toward
intervention, which may be more or less hawkish than that of the chief executive. These preferences must be taken into account.

    In the sections that follow, I will review the evidence from the four suc-
cessive French governments that managed the crises in Bosnia and Kosovo.
The Socialists held a monopoly on executive and legislative power from the
beginning of the crises in Yugoslavia until spring 1993, when the Socialist
president Mitterrand was forced into cohabitation with a rightist parliamentary majority of the RPR and the Union for French Democracy (UDF).
In spring 1995, the conservative coalition partners consolidated their power
with the election of the Gaullist president Jacques Chirac. By the time of
the Kosovo war, another cohabitation was in place, between Chirac and a
parliamentary majority of the "plural left" including the Socialists, Greens,
and Communists.

    I will demonstrate that France's Bosnia policy under Mitterrand was activist,
but limited to the delivery of humanitarian aid, consequently provoking criticism from the whole spectrum of the Socialist Party and part of the right for
not being forceful enough. Mitterrand was able to ignore this criticism until
the rightist coalition entered office. The RPR-UDF government pursued a
highly contradictory policy. It advocated forceful action that enhanced France's
role in the resolution of the conflict. This required the twisting of President
Mitterrand's arm, evidence that that the president is not necessarily more
interventionist than the parliamentary majority. Simultaneously, however,
the Gaullist prime minister, Edouard Balladur, quickly began reducing the
French presence in Bosnia, reflecting his party's more exclusive approach to

17. Ibid., p. 51.

foreign policy. As in Britain, this drew the ire of left-wing parties for indicating a lack of resolve. Aided by the public humiliation of the UN and French troops in summer 1995, President Chirac ended this ambivalence through strong leadership that key decision-makers say reflected his own personal approach to foreign affairs.

In Kosovo, Chirac was more publicly interventionist than the Socialist prime minister, Lionel Jospin, because the latter's party was constrained by its extreme leftist coalition partners, particularly the Communists. These anti-militarist voices in the coalition, as well as the backlash created by the initial failure of the air strikes, prevented the French Socialists from publicly—though not privately—taking the strident stand on ground troops proposed by the British Labour Party. It was the more inclusive Green Party that advocated an invasion. Due to France's history, the Greens took a more differentiated position than their German counterparts.

THE *DOMAINE RÉSERVÉ:*
PRESIDENT MITTERRAND AND THE IMPOTENT SOCIALIST PARTY

As had been the case in the Gulf War and before, the president controlled foreign and defense policy during the Bosnian conflict. Given the length of Mitterrand's presidency, his monopoly over matters of high politics, the *domaine réservé* (reserved domain), had even increased.[18] He chaired weekly meetings of senior officials on foreign policy. His former diplomatic adviser, Hubert Védrine, estimates that only a dozen people followed the situation in Bosnia.[19] Under Mitterrand's leadership, France played an active role in the initial decisions, taken over British objections, to move elements of the UN force from Croatia into Bosnia so as to protect the delivery of humanitarian aid. France initially pledged eleven hundred troops toward this end. By February 1993, there were over forty-six hundred French peacekeeping soldiers in the former Yugoslavia, more than from any other country. President Mitterrand justified their presence by invoking France's vocation, claiming that France should be everywhere where human rights are under threat.[20]

---

18. Jolyon Howorth, "François Mitterrand and the *Domaine Réservé:* From Cohabitation to the Gulf War," *French Politics and Society,* Vol. 10, No. 1 (1992), pp. 43–58. Gordon says the Socialist Party "played no role at all" in defense policy during Mitterrand's presidency. Gordon (1993), p. 113. Also, Howorth (1994), p. 112; Tierry Tardy, *La France et la gestion des conflits yougoslaves (1991–1995)* (Brussels: Etablissements Emile Bruylant, 1999), p. 205.

19. Tardy (1999), *La France,* p. 207.

20. Ibid., p. 212. On this period, see Ministry of Foreign Affairs Press Service, *Speeches and Statements,* No. 33 (11 March 1993); Pia Christian Wood, "France and the Post Cold War Order: The Case of Yugoslavia," *European Security,* Vol. 3, No. 1 (1994); Tardy (1999), *La France,* p. 166.

The president categorically ruled out peace enforcement, however. Both those close to Mitterrand and his domestic adversaries attributed his reluctance to an instinctive and highly personal approach, inspired by history, that prevented him from advocating tougher measures against the Serbs, France's allies against the Germans in two world wars. The French ambassador to the UN during the Bosnian conflict, Jean-Bernard Merimée, remembers that Mitterrand's pro-Serb leanings made it difficult to establish sanctions against Serbia.[21] It was a not uncommon bias in the Ministry of Foreign Affairs. A senior diplomat recalled: "Mitterrand said we will never make war against the Serbs. That's difficult for outsiders to understand. For France, Serbia was a heroic country. Even for me, Serbia was good. For us the Croats are fascists. This was particularly true of Mitterrand's generation. He was born in 1916."[22] His adviser's attempted defense of Mitterrand on this issue actually served as an acknowledgment of the president's bias. Védrine complained that "The simple fact of recalling those episodes where the Serbs were not at fault, but victims of Ustasha Croats or Nazis" was "suspect" to the interventionists.[23] References to the historical amity with Serbia came under suspicion, however, because they were used as justification not to intervene militarily in Bosnia by morally equating the warring factions. Most famously, Mitterrand raised fears about military ineffectiveness and cycles of violence. He invoked the spiral model, cautioning not to "add war to war."[24]

Védrine claims that Mitterrand made these statements even though he knew how they would be interpreted by the leadership in Belgrade and the damage they would do to efforts to deter aggression. It was necessary to quiet interventionist domestic opinion.[25] In contrast to the rightist British Conservatives, who needed to send reassuring signals to exclusivist backbenchers who opposed intervention, the Socialist president had to stifle hawkish opinion in his own leftist party. Calls for military action became particularly intense following the revelation in July 1992 of detention camps run by Bosnian Serbs. The head of the party, Laurent Fabius, called for European countries to intervene, claiming that air strikes were "perfectly possible" and thereby directly contradicting the president.[26] Together with Gérard Fuchs, a foreign

21. Interview with the author (25 April 2001).
22. Interview with the author (13 March 2001).
23. Hubert Védrine, *Les mondes de François Mitterrand* (Paris: Fayard, 1996), p. 629.
24. Howorth (1994), p. 115; Tardy (1999), *La France*, p. 215.
25. Védrine (1996), p. 638.
26. "Le president Mitterrand exclut toute intervention autre que strictement humanitaire," *Agence France Presse* (13 August 1992); See also "A l'exception des communistes les partis politiques français jugent insuffisante une action humanitaire en Bosnie-Herzegovine," *Le Monde* (13 August 1992); "Tollé de l'opposition contre la 'non-intervention' française et silence du Parti socialiste," *Agence France Presse* (14 August 1992).

policy expert in the party, he stated that the UN should "impose" its resolutions, forbidding modifications to borders by force and gaining entry into the camps. Fuchs later advocated compelling a cease-fire by sanctioning air strikes against any violators with a Chapter VII resolution. The deterrence logic was clear. Only "determination" and "dissuasion" by the UN would stop Milosevic and lead him to call off Bosnian Serb forces.[27]

The idea of military intervention also found a great deal of support in France's "Second Left," a faction of the Socialist Party that had long taken issue with the lack of moral principle in Mitterrand's foreign policy. The movement was critical of past Socialist government policy in Algeria as well as of Mitterrand's abandonment of pledges to restrict arms sales to dictators and to take a tougher line with corrupt African regimes. The Second Left was also the intellectual home of the followers of *tiers-mondisme* ("Third-Worldism"), the extension of the left's battle for equality to less developed countries.[28] A component of this struggle was the idea of the *droit d'ingérence,* the right or duty to intervene or interfere in the internal affairs of other states when grave human rights violations take place. This new doctrine's most famous champion was Bernard Kouchner, founder of Doctors Without Borders. The Second Left was primarily responsible for defining humanitarian intervention as an issue for the left, not only in France but internationally. The movement's leader and likely Socialist presidential candidate, Michel Rocard, and its strong social Catholic base favored military action by the UN against Belgrade if it failed to remove its irregular troops from Bosnia.[29]

Calls for military action extended into the outer reaches of the Socialist Party. Julien Dray, a leader of the left wing, expressed his support for air strikes to neutralize artillery batteries and create security zones around besieged Bosnian cities, as well as to liberate the camps, claiming that conferences, embargoes and other "half-measures" were no longer enough.[30] The Green Party passed a resolution in favor of an armed intervention in Bosnia. Noel Mamère and Brice Lalonde, leading figures in the other green party, the Ecological

27. On the camps, see "Le PS estime qu'en cas d'échec des negocations l'ONU devra 'imposer le droit,'" *Le Monde* (26 August 1992). On the cease-fire, see Gérard Fuchs, "Pour une intervention en Bosnie-Herzegovine," *Le Monde* (23 November 1992).

28. On the *deuxième gauche,* see Jonah Levy, *Tocqueville's Revenge: State, Society and Economy in Contemporary France* (Cambridge: Harvard University Press, 1999), pp. 72–78. On Mitterrand's broken promises, see Hoffmann (1987). On *tiers-mondisme,* see Philippe Guillot, "France, Peacekeeping and Humanitarian Intervention," *International Peacekeeping,* Vol. 1, No. 1 (1994), pp. 34–36.

29. "Les réactions en France; M. Rocard: l'action humanitaire ne suffit pas," *Le Monde* (29 August 1992). See also "M. Michel Rocard marque sa différence sur la Yougoslavie," *Agence France Presse* (27 August 1992); Michel Rocard, "Donnons-nous les moyens," *Le Monde* (25 December 1992).

30. Julien Dray and Charles Millon, "Non à l'abandon!" *Le Monde* (22 December 1992); "Lettre ouverte a M. Mitterrand pour réclamer un ultimatum à la Serbie," *Agence France Presse* (22 December 1992).

Generation, also expressed their support for the use of force.[31] As in Britain, elements of the far left distinguished support for such an operation from a more exclusivist pursuit like the Gulf War, and questioned why France could summon the strength to intervene in the Middle East but was unable to do so three hundred kilometers from the Italian coast.[32] On the left, only the extremist Communist Party came out openly in support of Mitterrand's position, saying it "could only approve."[33] The Socialist Party organization itself expressed no official support for its own government's position, remaining conspicuously silent.[34]

Mitterrand was encountering resistance within his Cabinet as well, most notably from Kouchner, now the minister for health and humanitarian affairs. Arguing that his right of intervention needed a courageous spokesperson, Kouchner urged Mitterrand to take up this role, a natural for France with its "humanist traditions." The president replied curtly that the right of intervention did not exist.[35] Others were also failing to have an effect on Mitterrand in face-to-face meetings. The Socialist head of the parliamentary Defense Committee, Jean-Michel Boucheron, received no reply to his private notes urging military action in Bosnia despite his strong friendship with Mitterrand, and his requests were denied when he met with the president. Boucheron's only alternative was to author a newspaper article urging air strikes against Belgrade, which he hoped would send a signal of resolve.[36] The party organization and the parliament were equally impotent. The executive office of the Socialist Party demanded that the foreign and defense ministers explain their positions. The Socialist president of the National Assembly wrote to the prime minister claiming that a majority of deputies supported stronger action. Without a change-of-heart by the president, these efforts were futile. When Foreign Minister Roland Dumas made comments that France might consider

31. "Le débat en France sur une eventuelle intervention en Bosnie-Herzegovine," *Le Monde* (18 August 1992); "Lettre ouverte à M. Mitterrand pour réclamer un ultimatum à la Serbie," *Agence France Presse* (22 December 1992); "Les réactions après les declarations du ministre des affaires étrangères sur la libération des camps en Bosnie: Les Verts français favorables à une intervention militaire," *Le Monde* (13 January 1993).

32. Julien Dray and Charles Millon, "Non à l'abandon!" *Le Monde* (22 December 1992); "Les réactions après les declarations du ministre des affaires étrangères sur la libération des camps en Bosnie: Les Verts français favorables à une intervention militaire," *Le Monde* (13 January 1993).

33. "La guerre civile en Bosnie-Herzegovine et ses repercutions internationales: M. Chirac juge M. Mitterrand 'objectivement complice' de la poursuite de la guerre," *Le Monde* (15 August 1992).

34. "Tollé de l'opposition contre la 'non-intervention' française et silence du Parti socialiste," *Agence France Presse* (14 August 1992).

35. Bernard Kouchner, *Ce que je crois* (Paris: Grasset, 1995). Quoted in Védrine (1996), pp. 641–643.

36. Interview with the author (24 April 2001). For the article, see "Boucheron: Il faut intervenir en Bosnie," *Ouest-France* (19 January 1993).

unilateral military action in Bosnia, he was rebuked by the Elysée, which stressed its "permanent position."[37]

The Opposition: The Hawkish Right versus the Exclusive Right

Unlike in Britain, however, support for more robust action also found strong backing from the center-right Gaullists, then in opposition. Most vocal was the head of the party and mayor of Paris, Jacques Chirac, who promoted the use of air strikes on the infrastructure of the Serb army and the use of ground troops to gain entry into the internment camps. He argued that a credible threat would prove effective, saying he was "convinced that the national-communist Serbian leaders would think twice before continuing their war of aggression if it is going to cost them their air bases, munitions dumps, and main logistical positions." Not to intervene was to "render one-self complicit" in the atrocities. Chirac focused his criticism particularly on Mitterrand's Serbian allegiance, alleging that the president's approach reverted to the "dusty pages of the First World War."[38] His demands grew increasingly strident. While initially he protested that the blue helmets did not have adequate armaments for protecting civilian populations, by the beginning of 1993 he demanded the withdrawal of UN troops to allow the use of air power.[39] Other leading figures supported him. Alain Juppé, the RPR's general secretary, complained that France was not identifying the true aggressor, thereby encouraging the Serbs, and favored the graduated use of force. Michèle Alliot-Marie, in charge of foreign affairs, Nicolas Sarkozy, the party's vice chair, and Edouard Balladur repeated this reproach.[40]

Resistance to a military intervention on exclusivist grounds existed, but due to the unique ideology of Gaullism was much weaker than in Britain.

---

37. "Le débat sur une intervention française," *Le Figaro* (13 January 1993). On the Socialist Party's efforts, see "M. Emmanuelli assure qu'une majorité de députés souhaite 'un engagement plus ferme,'" *Le Monde* (25 December 1992).

38. "Refuser d'intervenir, c'est se rendre complice," *Le Figaro* (14 August 1992). It was an accusation Chirac made against Germany as well, arguing that both countries had reverted to the "reflexes of 1920." See Jacques Chirac, "Devant le massacre: La démission de l'Europe," *Le Figaro* (1 June 1992).

39. Chirac (1992); "M. Chirac réclame une intervention aérienne en Bosnie," *Agence France Presse* (17 January 1993).

40. On Juppé's position, see "'La France a fait tout ce qu'elle devait faire' déclare M. Roland Dumans devant la commission des affaires étrangères de l'Assemblée nationale," *Le Monde* (20 August 1992); "La position française pour une action militaire en Bosnie répond à une pression interieure croissante," *Agence France Presse* (30 December 1992). For the views of the others, see "La guerre civile en Bosnie-Herzegovine et ses repercutions internationales: M. Chirac juge M. Mitterrand 'objectivement complice' de la poursuite de la guerre," *Le Monde* (15 August 1992); "La plupart des responsables politiques envisagent favorablement une intervention militaire," *Le Monde* (12 January 1993).

As expected by the partisan argument, it initially found its most pronounced expression in the RPR's right wing and its extremist competitor, the National Front. Charles Pasqua, head of the more extreme faction of the Gaullists, used the spiral model, arguing that no military solution existed and that using force would worsen the situation.[41] Jean-Marie Le Pen, leader of the National Front, was more direct, deploring the fact that France was losing sight of the true function of the military by making legionnaires and parachutists into "nannies." For Le Pen, the "law of the strong" governed foreign policy, and helping victims prolonged their misery. He called for the withdrawal of the French contingent and opposed any escalation in the use of force for fear of drawing France in further. Like rightist opponents in Britain, he then speciously questioned why Bosnia was a more pressing human rights concern than other areas of the globe.[42] Orignally low, the more general rightist resistance to intervention on exclusivist grounds would grow as the crisis became more acute.

THE FIRST COHABITATION: PUBLIC RESOLVE, PRIVATE DOUBTS

The RPR's words were tested when it entered office in a coalition with the rightist Union for French Democracy (UDF) following their crushing defeat of the Socialists in parliamentary elections in April 1993. Bosnia was high on the agenda. In contrast to the firm control over foreign and defense policy Mitterrand exercised under a Socialist majority, the new government shared equally in decision-making, and the influence of the Gaullists grew as Mitterrand's health deteriorated.[43] According to the president's adviser Védrine, a rigorous method of consultation was put into place in which all received the same information. The president, Prime Minister Edouard Balladur, Minister of Foreign Affairs Alain Juppé, and Minister of Defense François Léotard met weekly to direct policy.[44] The conservative government

---

41. "M. Emmanuelli assure qu'une majorité de députés souhaite 'un engagement plus ferme,'" *Le Monde* (25 December 1992); "Le débat sur une intervention française," *Le Figaro* (13 January 1993).

42. "M. Le Pen accuse le premier ministre de 'contrefaçon,'" *Le Monde* (13 January 1994); "Jean-Marie Le Pen: 'Le Front National est la seule ésperance des exclus,'" *Agence France Presse* (6 February 1994); "Après ses rencontres avec les dirigeants des partis: M. Balladur se félicite de la cohésion des français," *Le Monde* (23 February 1994); "M. Balladur: Le probleme du retrait est posé," *Le Monde* (19 April 1995); "Jean-Marie Le Pen: 'quitter le plus rapidement possible' la Bosnie," *Agence France Presse* (13 July 1995).

43. Tardy (1999), *La France*, p. 216.

44. Ibid., p. 216; Védrine (1996). Balladur and Juppé both confirmed this arrangement. Ministry of Foreign Affairs Press Service, *Speeches and Statements*, No. 57 (29 April 1993); Ministry of Foreign Affairs Press Service, *Statements*, No. 209 (8 December 1994).

acted quickly to counter criticism that France favored the Serbs, pushing through what they called the toughest sanctions ever passed by the UN Security Council over the initial objections of the president.[45] Juppé stressed repeatedly that the Bosnian Muslims were the victims and the Bosnian Serbs the aggressors in the conflict, and considered France's tougher attitude toward the latter as one of the achievements of his administration.[46]

The Public Strategy: An Active Diplomacy

The conservative government combined this less evenhanded approach with an activist foreign policy in the Gaullist tradition of influencing world events. Foreign Minister Juppé was behind two of the most significant Western initiatives during the Bosnian conflict: the creation of the safe areas and the Sarajevo ultimatum. Shortly after taking power, he submitted a memorandum to the UN Security Council on 19 May 1993 outlining options for the creation of security zones. While some have argued that the French, like the British, never saw their role as protecting the civilian populations, it is clear that Paris did indeed envision a more robust mandate.[47] In his memorandum, Juppé defined a safe area as "a zone encircled, defined by a precise perimeter, placed under protection of the UN where humanitarian aid is assured and where all aggression is prohibited."[48] He was also careful to distinguish this new task, which would require a peace enforcement mandate under Chapter VII, from UNPROFOR's previous peacekeeping and humanitarian functions. "It's no longer a matter of protecting humanitarian convoys, but of protecting people in the safe areas," he stressed.[49]

According to the prime minister, the Gaullists pursued a deliberate strategy of capitalizing on international support following particularly egregious acts by the Bosnian Serbs.[50] Foreign Minister Juppé spearheaded the international community's response to the shelling of the Sarajevo marketplace in early February 1994, which left approximately seventy civilians dead. He called for the withdrawal of heavy weaponry from an exclusion zone of thirty kilometers around the besieged city or its collection and oversight at

45. Interview with the French ambassador to the UN, Jean-Bernard Merimée (25 April 2001).

46. Alain Juppé, "Sarajevo: What I Believe," *Le Monde* (21 May 1994). He claimed that when he took office, "French policy was generally considered as extremely indulgent toward Belgrade and the Serbs." Quoted in Macleod (1997), p. 244.

47. Jan Willem Honig and Norbert Both, *Srebrenica: Record of a War Crime* (New York: Penguin Books, 1997), chap. 5. In interviews British officials confirmed that the French were more forceful on this issue.

48. Quoted in Tardy (1999), *La France*, p. 221.

49. Ministry of Foreign Affairs Press Service, *Speeches and Statements*, No. 72 (3 June 1993); Tardy (1999), *La France*, p. 222.

50. Edouard Balladur, *Deux ans à Matignon* (Paris: Plon, 1995), p. 113.

UN posts within that perimeter. A communiqué from the Ministry for Foreign Affairs asked the UN to consult with NATO on the use of air power to enforce the establishment of this demilitarized area should the Bosnian Serbs not surrender their armaments or pull back. The North Atlantic Council consented to this role, approving an unprecedented Franco-American joint proposal the next day over British objections.[51] The Bosnian Serbs complied with the ultimatum, the first victory of the UN and NATO during the entire Bosnian conflict. Steeled by the foreign minister's determination to "learn the lessons" of Sarajevo and "not give in," the French tried to extend the ultimatum formula to the other safe areas, most notably Gorazde, which came under attack in April 1994.[52] These efforts were much less successful. The international community was not able to gain momentum from the response to the Sarajevo shelling.

Although the office-seeking argument expects the French president to be more inclined to support the use of force than the parliamentary government because of his insulation from sanctions in case of failure, it was only following intensive lobbying of Mitterrand by Foreign Minister Juppé that the president consented to the ultimatum. A senior French diplomat recalled, "It was really Juppé convincing Mitterrand that enough was enough and to use that outrage to fight the Serbs. Unless you teach the Serbs a lesson, there would be a credibility problem."[53] The head of state's autonomy under the presidential system did not make him more interventionist, only less attentive to his party's voice.

Why was the French right different from the British Conservatives who resisted military engagement in Bosnia? Only the National Front openly condemned the ultimatum policy. Its leader Le Pen claimed that France did not always have to be the "Christ of nations," and demanded the retreat of French forces.[54] The evidence suggests that for the Gaullists the Bosnian mission was a means by which France could heighten its international profile. Ministers continually repeated that France was the largest contributor not only to the operation in the former Yugoslavia, but also to peacekeeping operations more generally. "That is our vocation," said the prime minister of France's "ambition . . . in the service of peace."[55] France was the "homeland of human rights"

51. Ministry of Foreign Affairs Press Service, *Speeches and Statements,* Nos. 21, 22 (8 February 1994); Tardy (1999), *La France,* p. 246.

52. Alain Juppé, *Journal officiel* (12 April 1994), pp. 681–686; Ministry of Foreign Affairs Press Service, *Speeches and Statements,* No. 64 (20 April 1994), No. 76 (27 April 1994).

53. Interview with the author (4 April 2001).

54. "Prudente satisfaction à Paris," *Les Echos* (22 February 1994).

55. Edouard Balladur, *Journal officiel* (11 May 1994), p. 1682. Ministry of Foreign Affairs Press Service, *Speeches and Statements,* No. 57 (29 April 1993), No. 1 (12 January 1994), No. 25 (10 February 1994), No. 72 (12 April 1994); Ministry of Foreign Affairs Press Service, *Statements,* No. 85 (4 May 1995).

and the "bearer of ideals of liberty and solidarity" and would lose its *rang* if it compromised on those principles, he wrote.[56] This was the Gaullist line in parliament as well. Richard Cazenave stressed that French soldiers were "defending the values of our civilization," and also noted that France had suffered the most casualties of any country contributing troops in Bosnia.[57] This is a point also made privately. Defense Minister Léotard persistently noted in an interview with the author that France was the "premier contributor," that it "served as an example for the international community in offering troops."[58] The right was instrumentalizing the mission in Bosnia to promote French status internationally. At the height of the Bosnian crisis in 1994, France had almost seven thousand troops in Yugoslavia, the most of any country.

The Private Strategy: A Quiet Withdrawal

Gaullist exceptionalism should not be overstated, however. Despite their warm words before their election, immediately upon entering office the rightists began to put an end to the increase of the French contingent in Bosnia and consistently raised the specter of the complete withdrawal of French forces.[59] French ministers threatened to pull out their soldiers in April 1993; in January, February, March, May, November, and December 1994; and in April and May 1995.[60] Most observers have correctly interpreted these threats as bluffs serving ulterior motives. An adviser to Prime Minister Balladur said: "The message was not to take for granted that we will be there forever."[61] The French made their continued presence dependent on NATO issuing the Sarajevo ultimatum, improving the UN chain of command, or on the dispatch of American ground forces. Other mentions of retreat coincided with the deterioration of peace talks or the death of French soldiers.

The French threats were not empty, however. Despite its diplomatic activism, the Gaullist government was more willing than even the British Conservatives to pull out its forces. In fact, it began actively doing so. Védrine remembers

---

56. Edouard Balladur, "Une attitude exemplaire dans l'avenir," *Le Monde* (7 April 1995).
57. *Journal officiel* (12 April 1994), p. 692.
58. Interview with the author (24 April 2001).
59. Balladur (1995), p. 112.
60. "France Threatens to Withdraw Troops from Bosnia," *UPI* (28 April 1993); "France Seeks Right to Shoot Back at Bosnia Aggressors," *The Times* (6 January 1994); "France Ready to Withdraw Troops from Bosnia if NATO Fails to Act," *UPI* (8 February 1994); "France, after Attack, Warns about Its Part in UN Force in Bosnia," *Agence France Presse* (17 March 1994); "France Hints at Withdrawal from Bosnia," *UPI* (11 May 1994); "Juppé Says France Might Pull Out of Bosnia," *Deutsche Presse Agentur* (18 April 1995); Ministry of Foreign Affairs Press Service, *Statements*, No. 198 (21 November 1994), No. 209 (8 December 1994), No. 76 (16 April 1995), No. 83 (1 May 1995), No. 85 (4 May 1995), No. 86 (5 May 1995).
61. Interview with the author (23 April 2001). Treacher (2000) interprets the French threats as bluffs.

that Prime Minister Balladur and Defense Minister Léotard were actively pushing for a reduction in the French presence. In May 1994 roughly fifteen hundred troops left the enclave of Bihac—a third of the French forces in Bosnia. The remaining forces collected around Sarajevo in order to better defend themselves and, according to the prime minister, to prepare for their eventual departure.[62] An adviser to Léotard explained: "From the beginning, there was the feeling in the right-wing government, especially on the part of the prime minister and minister of defense, that UNPROFOR was really a trap, and the way to get out of the trap was to reduce the size of the contingent. If you follow the size of the contingent, you'll see there was a steady decline. It was a deliberate policy first to reduce the size of the contingent and second to reduce the dispersion of the contingent. That is the reason that we left Bihac and that we refused requests by the UN Command to send small contingents to some parts of Bosnia."[63]

This policy interfered with other French initiatives. Although the chief of the French armed forces, Admiral Jacques Lanxade, wanted the prime minister to deploy five thousand additional troops so that there would be sufficient UN forces to protect the safe areas, Balladur refused to countenance any additional contribution.[64] The combination of lack of forces and British and UN reluctance to add to the mandate of UNPROFOR led to the peculiar wording of the UN resolution in which UN troops would "deter" attacks by their presence but not "defend" the enclaves.[65] Lanxade said it was "politically difficult for the French government to be very active in promoting the safe areas and at the same time reduce its involvement," but the government pushed ahead anyway.[66] Its exclusive conception of the national interest was winning out over its desire for international influence.[67]

---

62. Balladur (1995), p. 112. Also Ministry of Foreign Affairs Press Service, *Speeches and Statements*, No. 93 (17 May 1994); Védrine (1996), p. 666; Tardy (1999), *La France*, p. 257.

63. Interview with the author (13 March 2001).

64. Balladur (1995), p. 112.

65. Interview with senior French diplomat at NATO (4 April 2001).

66. Interview with the author (18 April 2001).

67. This same disjuncture between trumpeting France's commitment to humanitarianism and pursuing a more calculated strategy on the ground was also evident in the Gaullist government's Rwanda policy. France made much of its role in leading Operation Turquoise when in fact it only intervened several months after most of the killing had ended and in the view of most, primarily with the purpose of protecting the Hutu government that had committed most of the atrocities and against which the military tide had turned. France had provided arms to the Rwandan government for years to fight Tutsi rebels, and reports indicate that this favoritism continued even during the genocide. France, it was said, helped leading officials and even war criminals escape and continued to provide the Rwandan government with military aid, accusations that prompted a parliamentary inquiry. For a partially firsthand account, see Gérard Prunier, *The Rwanda Crisis: History of a Genocide* (New York: Columbia University Press, 1995). The most comprehensive account is Alison Des Forges, *Leave None to Tell the Story* (New York: Human Rights Watch), pp. 654–692.

Gaullists outside the government exhibited the same contradictions on Bosnian intervention. Pierre Lellouche, a Gaullist deputy and defense adviser to Jacques Chirac, was the first backbencher in the RPR to openly call for the withdrawal of the blue helmets if the belligerents did not want to make peace. He couched his position in exclusivist terms, saying: "Three years and 200,000 dead after the start of this war and with massacres continuing, I think it's important to ask why we are still there. Why are young Frenchmen being killed or wounded today?"[68] Yet Lellouche also argued for military action following a withdrawal. Chirac himself said, "We must withdraw and strike, or the inverse."[69] Gaullism led to a schizophrenic Bosnian policy.

The Opposition: Inclusive Socialists and Greens versus Antimilitarist Communists

President Mitterrand's position did not reflect sentiment in his party as a whole, which welcomed the threat of force against Bosnian Serbs in Sarajevo. So did leading Green politician Brice Lalonde. Former Socialist Party head Fabius and Lalonde both expressed support for applying the threat of air strikes to other safe areas. Jean-Yves Le Deaut, speaking for the Socialists in parliament, advanced the same line. Rocard, now head of the Socialist Party, went even further, advocating reinforcements that would allow UN troops to force through aid over land into Sarajevo.[70] He also created a controversy by endorsing the platform of an alternative list for elections to the European Parliament organized by leading intellectuals that was dedicated solely to raising awareness of the Bosnian issue. Mitterrand loyalists, including former foreign minister Dumas, called for his censure, but the national party office rejected the motion.[71] The left wing of the Socialist Party insisted on a more forceful approach. Julien Dray initially criticized the safe area plan for not offering enough protection for Bosnian Muslims, and feared there "would not be any Bosniaks left" by the time a diplomatic solution was reached.[72] Without a direct say in policy, however, the Socialists had very little influence over events.

68. "Dissonances en France sur le rôle de l'ONU et le maintien des Casques blues," *Agence France Presse* (26 January 1994); "France Calls for Air Strikes in Bosnia," *Independent* (27 January 1994).

69. "Tandis que le débat sur la Bosnie s'envenime au sein de la majorité M. Mitterrand et M. Balladur lancent un appel conjoint à la communaute internationale," *Le Monde* (28 January 1994); 'Les réactions en France après le massacre de Sarajevo,' *Le Monde* (9 February 1994).

70. "Les réactions en France après le massacre de Sarajevo," *Le Monde* (9 February 1994); "Après l'ultimatum de l'OTAN aux Serbes de Bosnie: Soulagement et prudence chez les responsables politiques français," *Le Monde* (11 February 1994); "Après ses rencontres avec les dirigeants des partis M. Balladur se félicite de la cohésion des français," *Le Monde* (23 February 1994); Jean-Yves Le Deaut, *Journal officiel* (20 April 1994), p. 987.

71. "Les débats parmi les socialistes," *Le Monde* (3 June 1994).

72. *Journal officiel* (26 May 1993), p. 671; (20 April 1994), p. 989.

As in Britain, the only leftist opposition came from the extreme end of the spectrum, from the Communist Party. More ideological than the other parties, it was unable to differentiate between uses of force. Its parliamentary leader, Georges Hage, denied that the Sarajevo ultimatum had improved the situation in the city. Evoking the spiral model, he declared that "War only creates more war" and "feeds the nationalist cancer" in the region, a constant refrain in Communist statements.[73] France should instead promote the political resolution of conflicts through negotiation. The arguments used by the Communists showed little evaluative complexity. The party's intense opposition to a military action led it to marshal numerous arguments. The Western powers involved were not driven by inclusive concerns, but were instead seeking zones of influence. France was demonstrating moral inconsistency by its different handling of the Kurdish question in Turkey, it claimed.

The party's more fundamental antimilitarist objections shone through in their fears of NATO becoming an instrument of domination by the United States. It could be argued that this reflected a particularly French sentiment, but Communist parliamentary leader Hage rejected any permanent intervention capacity for the UN as well, echoing left-wing German Green positions seen earlier. So too did his statement that war serves no one but arms producers.[74] At no time, however, did the Communists call for a withdrawal of French forces. Instead, the party insisted on limiting their mandate to peacekeeping and the delivery of humanitarian aid.[75] Its quarrel was with the military means and not the aim of the operation. The party could support a peacekeeping mission in line with leftist inclusivist and antimilitarist principles, but could not make the value trade-off necessary to support enforcement.

As in Great Britain, the Socialists responded sharply to any threat of withdrawal. Party head Rocard and right of intervention advocate Kouchner derided Gaullist tactics as "blackmail" and favored enforcing resolutions with the necessary military means.[76] Successful deterrence required a credible commitment to restoring peace in Bosnia. In parliament, Socialist deputy Le Deaut criticized Lellouche and other Gaullists who were expressing doubts about remaining in Bosnia, saying that such sentiments did not send a

---

73. *Journal officiel* (12 April 1994), p. 693. For spiral thinking, see also Alain Bocquet (31 May 1995), p. 380. Hage referred to an "infernal dialectic between provocation and retaliation," (6 June 1995), p. 431.

74. For all of these arguments, see Georges Hage, *Journal officiel* (12 April 1994), pp. 693–695; (6 June 1995), p. 431.

75. In *Journal officiel,* see Alain Bocquet (31 May 1995), pp. 380–381; Georges Hage (6 June 1995), pp. 431–432.

76. Quoted in Guillot (1994), p. 39.

message of determination and found no adherents in the Socialist Party. Henri Emmanuelli, leader of the Socialist parliamentary group, repeated that critique, and sensed that threats of withdrawal were not always being used purely as levers of negotiation.[77] He was extremely perceptive. According to Lanxade, the head of the armed forces, the Gaullist government had made a decision in principle in spring 1995 to withdraw French forces from Bosnia.[78] The Gaullists, although eager to leave France's mark on the international community's response to the Bosnian war, were not as committed as the parties of the center-left to the continued presence of French forces in the Balkans.

THE CHIRAC PRESIDENCY: HUMILIATION AND *HONNEUR*

The government's plans were put on hold with the election of the Gaullist Jacques Chirac in May 1995 and the decisive events in Bosnia that quickly followed. Decision-making on foreign and defense policy returned to the Elysée. The new foreign minister, Hervé de Charette, did not play the same role that Juppé had played under Mitterrand, and Juppé, now prime minister, also found his role in foreign policy diminished.[79] Almost immediately after entering office, Chirac was confronted with the hostage crisis in which the Bosnian Serbs seized ninety-two French soldiers among others in response to NATO air strikes that were themselves triggered by Serb violation of the terms of the Sarajevo ultimatum.

President Chirac's answer was robust. In the first offensive action by the UN in Bosnia, he circumvented the UN chain of command and ordered French soldiers to retake the Vrbanja bridge outside of Sarajevo on May 27. Two soldiers died as a result but the mission, which went far beyond UNPROFOR's mandate, was ultimately successful. The president also seized on the British idea for a Rapid Reaction Force, making it his own and summoning the defense ministers of the NATO countries to Paris for a conference to discuss its creation. France would contribute four thousand troops to the new contingent. At French insistence, these soldiers would not wear blue helmets or paint their vehicles white.[80]

Chirac's actions did not have the complete support of the larger government, however. His order to retake the Vrbanja bridge sparked a bitter row with the French head of the armed services, who threatened to resign.

77. In *Journal officiel* see Jean-Yves Le Deaut (12 April 1994), p. 699; Henri Emmanuelli (6 June 1995), p. 433.
78. Interview with the author (18 April 2001).
79. Tardy (1999), *La France,* p. 269.
80. Ibid., pp. 274–276.

Prime Minister Juppé and Defense Minister Charles Millon backed Admiral Lanxade, who recalled the military and political situation: "We had a group of twenty or thirty men surrounded by tanks and guns and the first impulse by the president was to order these people to resist but without the means. I refused. I told the president they had no chance to be successful and a lot of soldiers could die. What happened after that? Two died. The president thought the honor of the French army was involved in this affair. That was not my position. I had the support of the prime minister and the defense minister, but he overruled them."[81] Unlike in Germany or Britain, those closely involved unanimously attribute the strong French response to the leadership and personality of their head of state rather than to a general party tendency. A senior diplomat noted the contrast with the Gaullist Balladur government and said: "You have to realize these are the same people. Chirac made the difference and it has to do with how he himself was formed."[82] Even former defense minister Léotard, who had just been replaced, agreed: "It was the arrival of Chirac that provoked this. I do not know if Mitterrand would have had the same attitude."[83] A French diplomat reverently summarized these analyses: "A great man is the meeting of a moment with a person."[84]

The French response did not reflect a general *chiraquien* approach to peace enforcement, but rather Chirac's reaction to a particular set of circumstances. That he was not a crusader for human rights became clear when he proclaimed that France would withdraw if UNPROFOR were not strengthened.[85] The president was deeply embarrassed by the hostage-taking, and humiliation featured in every explanation of his response.[86] Said one diplomat: "He is a military-minded man in the sense that you do not trample the flag. There are things you accept, and things you do not accept. You cannot have soldiers tied to tanks."[87] An adviser to the defense minister agreed, recalling Chirac's personal fury and adding: "It was a personal reaction of Chirac to seeing unarmed soldiers in this situation. To see hostages—for him that was unacceptable."[88] The president

81. Interview with the author (18 April 2001).
82. Interview with the author (4 April 2001).
83. Interview with the author (24 April 2001).
84. Interview with the author (23 April 2001).
85. Ministry of Foreign Affairs, *Statements*, No. 98 (28 May 1995), No. 101 (30 May 1995).
86. An adviser to the defense minister said: "The new president was very keen on avoiding the humiliation of the French military. The man had served in Algeria, while Mitterrand had been the man who had sent the conscripts to Algeria. So their viewpoints were very different." Interview with the author (19 March 2001).
87. Interview with the author (4 April 2001).
88. Interview with the author (5 June 2001).

was exasperated. He reportedly said that the killing of French soldiers was acceptable, but not their humiliation.[89]

For a party whose somewhat unique ideology was based on French prestige and status, humiliation served as a potent tool for assembling parliamentary support—an instrument that did not exist to the same degree in Britain. The Socialist defense policy expert Michel Boucheron welcomed the introduction of the Rapid Reaction Force in parliament on behalf of his party as a way of maintaining the French presence in Bosnia, but later opined that the Gaullists needed something more for motivation: "There was a difference in the response to the hostage situation. The parties on the right were very sensitive to the humiliation that the soldiers suffered."[90] Unlike in Britain, this was a constant justification for the dispatch of the additional troops in the Rapid Reaction Force in statements by the ministers and the president. In addition to the three Rs of the force's mission—reinforcing, repositioning, and riposte—a fourth element was added: earning respect.[91] This resonated with parliamentarians. The three RPR deputies who spoke in the National Assembly in the debates following the hostage crisis all stressed the humiliation suffered by the French armed forces and the honor they had won by retaking the Vrbanja bridge. So, too, did former defense minister Léotard, when asked about the major shift between the policy of the government of which he had been a member and that of Chirac as president.[92]

Nevertheless, as in Britain, the French right expressed skepticism about any peace enforcement role for UNPROFOR. Unsurprisingly, the National Front called for a retreat as soon as possible.[93] Even in the Gaullist party, this sentiment was rising. As costs increased, exclusivist concerns common to rightist parties emerged. Two of the three RPR speakers in the hostage crisis debate showed their disquiet. While criticizing the errors of the past that had weakened the UN's credibility and capacity for deterrence, François Guillaume simultaneously evoked the prospect of falling into a guerilla war. Imposing peace in Yugoslavia was impossible as the Wehrmacht had learned. Jacques Boyon, the Gaullist head of the Defense Committee, was more circumspect,

89. David Halberstam, *War in a Time of Peace: Bush, Clinton, and the Generals* (New York: Simon and Schuster, 2001), p. 305.

90. Interview with the author (24 April 2001). *Journal officiel* (31 May 1995), p. 380.

91. Ministry of Foreign Affairs Press Service, *Statements,* No. 98 (28 May 1995), No. 102 (31 May 1995), No. 110 (7 June 1995), No. 128 (26 June 1995). On the four elements of the mission see Charles Millon, *Journal officiel* (6 June 1995), p. 424.

92. In the *Journal officiel,* see Christian Vaneste (31 May 1995), p. 379; François Guillaume (6 June 1995), p. 429; Jacques Boyon (6 June 1995), pp. 435–436. Léotard said, "For us, it was the exasperation and the humiliation." Interview with the author (24 April 2001).

93. "Jean-Marie Le Pen: 'Quitter le plus rapidement possible' la Bosnie," *Agence France Presse* (13 July 1995).

but pointed out the very small margin of maneuver. There were calls for withdrawal from RPR members of the Foreign Affairs Committee as well.[94] Their uneasiness was mirrored in statements in parliament by the prime minister and the foreign minister, both of whom stressed that the Rapid Reaction Force was not designed for war. Since they had to take into account exclusivist voices from the parliamentary party, their comments were much less forceful than those of the president.[95]

In fact, they understated the importance of the new measures. According to those involved in the planning process, the Rapid Reaction Force was more powerful than French ministers let on. A French diplomat explained: "It was not merely a self-defense force if you look at how it was composed, what it could do, and the amount of artillery it had. This was very serious stuff about fighting a war."[96] The force's role, at least in France's eyes, was "not just to defend our soldiers, but if need be to prevent some action being taken by [Serb] forces on the ground. The idea was to reorganize the forces in a way that they could become operational."[97] This conception differed significantly from that of the British. Although the French were not the force's progenitors, Chirac was its most enthusiastic supporter and it developed a momentum of its own. The president's agenda was to secure the road over Mount Igman so as open a land route from the Sarajevo airport to Bosnian-controlled territory and be able to fire on the Serbs if they threatened the city, which UNPROFOR later did.[98]

The force had not been assembled by the time that Srebrenica fell. Chirac's response again was vigorous. A communiqué issued by the president called for a "firm, limited military action to put a stop to the abandonment of the enclaves," to which France was willing to commit elements of its Rapid Reaction Force. The next day Chirac went so far as to call for the recapture of Srebrenica by military means and threatened withdrawal if no action were taken.[99] Again those close to the process all refer to the president's personal reaction. An adviser to the defense minister said, "Chirac was terribly upset. He said, 'We have to react. We have to react.' The Serbs were taking over

94. In the *Journal officiel,* see François Guillaume (6 June 1995), pp. 429–430; Jacques Boyon (6 June 1995), pp. 435–436. "Premières dissonances sur la Bosnie au sein de la majorité en France," *Le Monde* (27 July 1995).

95. In *Journal officiel,* see Hervé de Charette (6 June 1995), p. 422; Alain Juppé (6 June 1995), p. 419.

96. Interview with the author (4 April 2001).

97. Interview with an adviser to the defense minister (19 March 2001).

98. Tim Ripley, *Operation Deliberate Force* (Lancaster, U.K.: Centre for Defence and International Security Studies, 1999), chaps. 8 and 13.

99. Ministry of Foreign Affairs Press Service, "Communiqué issued by the Presidency of the Republic," *Statements,* No. 143 (13 July 1995); Tardy (1999), *La France,* p. 293.

an enclave we were obliged to protect and we were not reacting."[100] Again Chirac's anger was based on embarrassment. "Srebrenica was not felt at that moment as a massacre but as a humiliation of the UN. Chirac was once again absolutely out of his mind, saying 'I do not want this to happen again.' He summoned Admiral Lanxade, the head of the armed forces, demanding to know what could be done," said a senior French diplomat.[101]

Chirac's calls for retaking the enclave were "only something to quiet the press," claimed Lanxade. "There was no military planning at all."[102] The president's pronouncements did pave the way, however, for a real plan to reinforce the existing enclaves. France proposed to contribute one thousand troops to the besieged city of Gorazde where three hundred British peacekeepers were struggling to hold off the Bosnian Serbs.[103] Since the operation would require use of American transport helicopters, a meeting of the heads of the British, French, and American armed forces was held. The British, wishing to leave Gorazde and doubting the credibility of the plan, dismissed it.[104] However, the proposal was a key factor in involving the Americans deeper in the resolution of the war. A senior American official credits the French initiative with forcing the United States to respond to the situation. Clinton had felt increasingly upstaged by Chirac, who derided America's lack of leadership.[105] The Americans thought that a bombing campaign to destroy Serb air defenses would anyway have to be the first step before reinforcing Gorazde by helicopter, and used that idea as an alternative to the French plan. The U.S. plan became the basis for the ultimatum to the Bosnian Serbs not to menace any of the remaining enclaves, a violation of which triggered the military operation of late August 1995 that contributed to the end of the war. And the artillery stationed at French initiative on Mount Igman dropped more ordnance on the Bosnian Serbs than NATO aircraft.

THE SECOND COHABITATION: PUBLIC DOUBTS, PRIVATE RESOLVE

France would not repeat this performance in Kosovo. Though Chirac was still president, the intervening three years had seen the election of a new

---

100. Interview with the author (5 June 2001).

101. Interview with the author (4 April 2001).

102. Interview with the author (18 April 2001).

103. Ministry of Foreign Affairs Press Service, *Statements*, No. 150 (19 July 1995); Ministry of Foreign Affairs Press Service, "Communiqué issued by the Presidency of the Republic," *Statements*, No. 152 (21 July 1995).

104. Interview with Jacques Lanxade (18 April 2001); Interview with Malcolm Rifkind (26 June 2001).

105. Ivo Daalder, *Getting to Dayton* (Washington: Brookings Institution Press, 2000). Also Halberstam (2001), pp. 305, 316; Bob Woodward, *The Choice* (New York: Simon and Schuster, 1996), p. 261.

parliamentary majority of the "plural left," composed of the Socialists, Greens, Radicals, Communists, and a new party formed by the former left-wing Socialist Jean-Pierre Chevènement, the Movement for Democratic Citizens. At the outset of the air war, the leftist coalition partners justified the war in inclusivist terms. Socialist prime minister Lionel Jospin stressed that force must sometimes be used to promote leftist goals, declaring: "If force without justice is always tyranny, justice without force is often impotence."[106] Speaking for the alliance of Greens, Radicals, and the Citizen's Movement, Roger-Gérard Schwartzenberg claimed that France was fighting to defend the rights of man and minorities in Europe, the values of the French Revolution. These were more important than the principle of sovereignty, which was gradually giving way to the "right of humanitarian intervention . . . with the understanding that humanity is one, transcending borders."[107] Unlike in Bosnia, the leader of the Socialists in government had the support of the head of the party, François Hollande.[108] France committed more aircraft to the operation than any other European ally.

The Socialists quickly ran into difficulties with the Communists, however. The Communists, like their German counterparts, the PDS, demanded an end to the air strikes and immediate negotiations just days after the operation began. Party leader Hue asked "what harm there is" in stopping the air strikes.[109] The initial inability of the air strikes to prevent Milosevic from retaliating against the Kosovar Albanians increased the unease in the left wing of the Socialist Party as well, as it had in Germany, by seeming to confirm the spiral model. Julien Dray, who had led the charge for the left wing in Bosnia, said that "nothing good" would come of the bombing campaign and wanted it to stop.[110] The argumentation of the opponents of the air strikes was identical to that of the extreme left in Britain and Germany. In parliament, Hue evoked the *engrenage,* or spiral, of violence. Bombing reinforced the extremists in Serbia and made coexistence more difficult in the future.

---

106. *Journal officiel* (26 March 1999), p. 2669.

107. *Journal officiel* (27 April 1999), p. 3634. Jospin agreed. See ibid., p. 3645.

108. "Jean-Pierre Chevènement dit sa préférence pour une solution politique du conflit; L'Hôtel Matignon minimise la différence exprimée par le ministre de l'intérieur," *Le Monde* (26 March 1999).

109. "Robert Hue: Cette guerre, c'est une connerie!" *Le Monde* (27 March 1999); "Déconvenues militaires et interrogations politiques: La majorité sous pression," *Le Figaro* (29 March 1999); "Mme Buffet, ministre communiste, se démarque de M. Jospin sur l'intervention en Yougoslavie," *Le Monde* (30 March 1999); "Robert Hue: Je pense que nous n'aurons pas à envisager le cas de figure d'une intervention terrestre," *Le Monde* (4 May 1999).

110. "Déconvenues militaires et interrogations politiques: La majorité sous pression," *Le Figaro* (29 March 1999); "Des députés socialistes et RPR s'interrogent sur l'efficacité de l'action militaire," *Le Monde* (31 March 1999); "De l'approbation à la critique ouverte, les quatre familles du PS," *Le Monde* (12 April 1999); "Une intervention terrestre menacerait la cohésion de la majorité en France," *Agence France Presse* (24 April 1999).

He quoted Mitterrand's warning not to "add war to war" and marshaled other arguments resonant with the left as well, demonstrating a low level of evaluative complexity. The war was illegal, and motivated not by humanitarian concerns but by NATO's wish to establish a precedent for intervention in Europe, thereby emasculating the UN. This was evident in the "selective arrogance and indignation" of the great powers."[111]

Unlike in Germany, however, the Communists were members of the government and could more directly influence policy through their seat at the table. Unlike in Britain, the extreme left clustered in a separate party organization that maximized its clout. The Communists expected to do just that, making it clear that they did not want to be "put outdoors."[112] That did not happen, at least in Socialist prime minister Jospin's public comments. Even though public opinion for an invasion was even stronger in France than in interventionist Britain, Communist pressure inhibited the Socialist-led government from sending signals of resolve.[113] The prime minister quickly put an end to the discussion of a ground intervention in Kosovo. One month after the campaign began, Jospin dissected and dismissed this option in parliament, arguing that Milosevic would have time to prepare and raising the specter of him using human shields. He also claimed that the NATO summit meeting in April 1999 had flatly ruled out the possibility. In the Senate, he was even more adamant, saying he "did not want" a land invasion.[114] Party leader Hue implied that the Communists were responsible for this language, saying the party was "not removed" from the decision on a ground invasion: "I am happy to say that after expressing my worries on the subject to the prime minister, the French government rejected the option entailing the deployment of a ground force."[115]

Jospin also went to great lengths to counter the left wing's other complaint, that France was blindly following the NATO strategy of accelerating the air strikes, with devastating effects on Serbian civilians. Chevènement and

111. Robert Hue, *Journal officiel* (26 March 1999), p. 2983. See also his comments in *Journal officiel* (26 March 1999), pp. 2982–2983; (27 April 1999), pp. 3628–3630. "Jean-Pierre Chevènement dit sa préférence pour une solution politique du conflit; L'Hôtel Matignon minimise la différence exprimée par le ministre de l'interieur," *Le Monde* (26 March 1999).

112. "L'engagement militaire de la France vu de l'Assemblée: 'Solidarité' à droite, trouble à gauche," *Le Figaro* (1 April 1999).

113. Simon Duke, Hans-Georg Ehrhart, and Matthias Karadi, "The Major European Allies: France, Germany and the United Kingdom," in Albrecht Schnabel and Ramesh Thakur (eds.), *Kosovo and the Challenge of Humanitarian Intervention* (Tokyo: United Nations University Press, 2000), p. 138.

114. For his comments in the National Assembly, see Lionel Jospin, *Journal officiel* (27 April 1999), pp. 3621–3622. For his comments in the Senate see "Jospin Reiterates Kosovo Land Operations Not Desirable," *FBIS* (29 April 1999).

115. "Robert Hue: Je pense que nous n'aurons pas à envisager le cas de figure d'une intervention terrestre," *Le Monde* (4 May 1999).

others accused the Socialists of *suivisme,* or "follower-ism." At his party's convention, the prime minister declared that France "would not be dragged along where it does not want to go."[116] Privately, France was taking issue with NATO's choice of targets. An adviser to Jospin said: "One thing that Matignon [the prime minister's office] did stick to was avoiding any degeneration of the situation so that the diplomatic pressure would give way to a military conflict. We wanted to make sure that the political goal was not changed by military objectives or targeting. The political goal was the retreat of Milosevic's army. We could not use the air war excessively or otherwise we would victimize the population."[117] A Defense Ministry official said: "We were among those very critical of any unnecessary targets that would exaggerate the risk of collateral damage."[118]

Another tool that the parliamentary government used to manage opposition was information. The coalition partners and the parliament in general were given unprecedented access to intelligence briefings. According to an adviser to the defense minister, the consultations changed long-standing practice in the conduct of foreign affairs and revolutionized the role of parliament in foreign policy. The intent was to minimize public criticism.[119] By giving minority members of the government information, opponents of the war would feel less able to present a one-dimensional view of the conflict. Differentiation would increase.

Despite his statements, Prime Minister Jospin was privately taking a very different position on the use of ground troops. He stressed to concerned Socialist deputies in closed-door meetings that he had not excluded a ground war in his statements at the party conference, but was accommodating the Communists.[120] Defense Ministry staff had done calculations similar to those of the British. "The question of ground operations was raised by the Brits, but here too we were thinking about how to enter Kosovo and be ready before the winter," said an adviser involved in the planning.[121] More precisely, according to an adviser to Alain Richard, the minister of defense, "You need ten weeks after you announce and then two or three more months to enter before

116. For the accusations see "Déconvenues militaires et interrogations politiques: La majorité sous pression," *Le Figaro* (29 March 1999); Robert Hue, *Journal officiel* (27 April 1999), p. 3630. For Jospin's denial, see "En France, pris à partie par ses alliés, Lionel Jospin s'efforce de rassurer," *Les Echos* (29 March 1999); "Mme Buffet, ministre communiste, se démarque de M. Jospin sur l'intervention en Yougoslavie," *Le Monde* (30 March 1999).
117. Interview with the author (9 April 2001).
118. Interview with the author (25 April 2001).
119. Interview with the author (25 June 2003).
120. "Lionel Jospin refuse d'exclure l'hypothèse d'une action terrestre de l'OTAN au Kosovo," *Le Monde* (1 April 1999); "Kosovo: Faut-il envoyer des troupes au sol?" *Le Monde* (1 April 1999).
121. Interview with Defense Ministry official (25 April 2001).

the winter. So we had to act between the 15th and 25th of June."[122] All interviewed claimed that France would have been a part of a ground operation. In fact, the French were worried that it was the Americans who could not be counted on, but stressed their resolve to go ahead nonetheless.[123] The prime minister's difficult domestic situation created constraints on his words but these did not affect the government's deeds, which were a better reflection of the real Socialist position.

Chirac's behavior was the opposite of Prime Minister Jospin's. Not needing to manage a restive parliamentary party due to his institutional position, the president was more careful not to create the impression that France would not invade on the ground. He was practicing compellence. Privately, the president was reportedly against a ground operation, but when publicly questioned, he responded: "By discussing this matter we give the Serbian authorities vital information. Do not count on me for such a thing."[124] A spokesperson for the Elysée said that France "will not oppose an updating" of NATO's plans.[125] In a television address Chirac menacingly referred to the possibility of needing "additional means."[126] Chirac also had a very different recollection of NATO's summit. According to him, the ground troop option was not dismissed as the Socialists claimed. It "did not arise."[127] He would later confirm that he had in fact been opposed to a ground war, but claimed that "We had to allow the uncertainty to remain only so as . . . not to encourage Milosevic to hold out any more."[128]

Left over Right: The Gaullists and the Greens

As in Bosnia, the French right was more supportive of the air operation than the British right because of the unique qualities of Gaullism. Nevertheless, there were dissenting voices, concentrated in the National Front and in the right wing of the Gaullists, where politicians could be expected to have the least interest in inclusive foreign policy. National Front leader Le Pen

---

122. Interview with the author (20 March 2001).

123. Interview with adviser to the defense minister (25 June 2003).

124. "Chirac Supports NATO Choice of Targets in Serbia," *FBIS* (23 April 1999).

125. "France 'Will Not Oppose' Updating of NATO Plans in FRY," *FBIS* (22 April 1999).

126. Alex Macleod, "Kosovo and the Emergence of a New European Security," in Pierre Martin and Mark R. Brawley (eds.), *Alliance Politics, Kosovo, and NATO's War: Allied Force or Forced Allies?* (Palgrave: New York, 2000), p. 122.

127. "Chirac Supports NATO Choice of Targets in Serbia," *FBIS* (23 April 1999).

128. "Excerpts from Interview of French President Chirac, June 10, 1999," in Philip E. Auerswald and David P. Auerswald (eds.), *The Kosovo Conflict: A Diplomatic History through Documents* (Cambridge: Kluwer Law International, 2000), p. 1150. Chirac's other public statements in the volume point out the importance of fighting human rights violations, but make a special point of not allowing them to occur in Europe, suggesting that the Gaullist president has a less universal conception of community than the left. See Ibid., pp. 516, 722–723.

called the Western powers "barbaric moralizers," and doubted reports about the deportation of Kosovar Albanians by the Serbs.[129] The right-wing Gaullist Pasqua's critique was more subtle, but its lack of evaluative complexity betrayed a genuine opposition. He doubted the efficacy of the bombing, questioned its legal basis, criticized France's dependence on NATO, and predicted a "chain of unforeseeable consequences."[130] The leader of the far right of the UDF, Philippe de Villiers, also condemned the action. More politicians joined the chorus when a ground intervention became part of the debate. The head of the RPR in the Senate, Christian Poncelet, signaled his opposition.[131] Phillipe Séguin, the head of the party organization, was also largely against.[132] In fact, no major Gaullist figure came out in favor of an escalation of the military campaign to include a land invasion. Again a possible increase in costs exposed a more pedestrian rightist ideology.

As in Britain, it was the leftist parties that began to lobby for a ground invasion. The Socialist head of the Defense Committee, Paul Quilès, was critical of the option's initial exclusion from consideration and argued that it was necessary to begin planning for it. He proposed the creation of a humanitarian exclusion zone in Kosovo secured by a peace force, which would require a ground intervention. The left-wing Socialist Melenchon approved.[133] Unsurprisingly, Kouchner, Europe's greatest proponent of a right of intervention, also endorsed a land invasion.[134] The real pressure, however, came from the Green Party. With a very different national history, the French Greens did not share the extreme antimilitarism of their German cousins. This meant that their more passionate commitment to equality translated into a more interventionist position. Despite their feeling that NATO was a "relic of the Cold War," the lack of a UN resolution, and their nonviolent tradition, the Greens most clearly expressed compellence logic in parliament. Marie-Hélène

---

129. "Un anti-américanisme renforce par le conflit du Kosovo," *Le Monde* (24 April 1999); "Jean-Marie Le Pen met en doute la déportation des Kosovars," *Le Monde* (28 May 1999).

130. Max Gallo and Charles Pasqua, "Pas de paix sans indépendance de l'Europe," *Le Monde* (2 April 1999).

131. "Une partie des responsables français contestent le cadre et les modalités de l'action de l'OTAN," *Le Monde* (27 March 1999);"Dans la majorité, des réactions discordantes aux propos du chef de l'Etat," *Le Monde* (31 March 1999); "Lionel Jospin reste ferme face aux opposants à l'intervention," *Les Echos* (31 March 1999); "Lionel Jospin refuse d'exclure l'hypothèse d'une action terrestre de l'OTAN au Kosovo," *Le Monde* (1 April 1999).

132. Richard McAllister, "French Perceptions," in Mary Buckley and Sally N. Cummings (eds.), *Kosovo: Perceptions of War and Its Aftermath* (New York: Continuum, 2001), p. 100. The author even argues that Séguin resigned from his post due to reservations about the war.

133. "Paul Quilès: Une mission claire pour nos soldats," *Le Figaro* (23 April 1999); Paul Quilès, *Journal officiel* (27 April 1999), p. 3640; "Des députés socialistes et RPR s'interrogent sur l'efficacité de l'action militaire," *Le Monde* (31 March 1999); "Lionel Jospin refuse d'exclure l'hypothese d'une action terrestre de l'OTAN au Kosovo," *Le Monde* (1 April 1999).

134. Macleod (2000), p. 122.

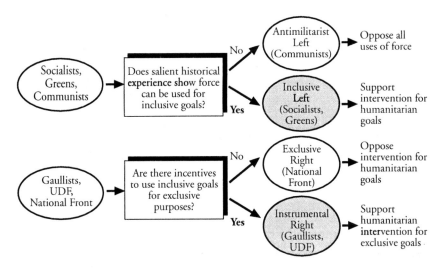

Figure 4. The French case

Aubert argued that Milosevic did not understand the language of negotiation, that Bosnia had damaged the noninterventionist position, and that France could not put itself in the position of being accused of not assisting people in danger. The particularly "cynical" strategy of refusing to send ground troops and of bombing from high altitudes to avoid casualties was not meeting this objective.[135] The environment minister, Dominique Voynet, also doubted the effectiveness of the air strikes in preventing ethnic cleansing and expressed disappointment that Jospin had ruled out ground troops. She was backed by prominent Greens Daniel Cohn-Bendit and Noel Mamère.[136] Aggravated by Prime Minister Jospin's call to keep a "cool head," which it interpreted as forbidding ground troops, the party openly called for a ground intervention that would prove effective in protecting the Albanian population. Jospin's strategy of only allowing air strikes was "cold-hearted," a "military gesticulation" that gave the signal that "the cleansing . . . can continue."[137]

Figure 4 shows the broad cleavage structure of French foreign policy on the issue of humanitarian intervention. The mainstream right, as in Germany, instrumentalized humanitarian intervention, although for a different purpose,

135. Marie-Hélène Aubert, *Journal officiel* (26 March 1999), pp. 2978–2982.
136. "Dominique Voynet se prononce pour une action au sol," *Le Monde* (1 April 1999); "Comment Lionel Jospin a imposé sa ligne aux communistes," *Le Monde* (2 April 1999); "Le trouble de la gauche plurielle ne se dissipe pas sur le Kosovo," *Le Monde* (21 April 1999); "Une prise de position de Dominique Voynet," *Le Monde* (25 May 1999).
137. Green Party, "Guerre au Kosovo: 'Tête froide,' coeur froid?" (28 March 1999).

that of maintaining a great power level of prestige and status. Only the far right National Front opposed peace enforcement, although the Gaullists' patience grew extremely thin in Bosnia. Were it not for the election of President Chirac and the hostage crisis, the right might have completely withdrawn French forces. The mainstream left Socialist Party and the Greens, without Germany's tragic history with militarism, approached the issue differently than its counterparts across the Rhine, and much like the British Labour Party. More so than in the other two cases, however, the actual policies pursued did not reflect these party positions. The Socialist Party did not have the institutional leverage to make President Mitterrand more interventionist in Bosnia. When the party as a whole enjoyed more influence, as was the case with cohabitation during the Kosovo war, it had to mute its public support of the air campaign to preserve coalitional unity. Unlike in Britain, the extreme left has an alternative political home. The Communist Party served as a bastion of antimilitarism that created headaches for the Socialists during Kosovo. However, the lack of fit between preferences and outcomes is not because parties did not have ideological preferences but rather because they had varying opportunities for voice. France, despite its exceptionalism, seems to prove the rule.

CHAPTER 6

European Army, Militarized Europe, or European Europe? The Domestic Politics of a Security and Defense Policy for the European Union

L ong a player in global trade, the European Union is becoming increasingly involved in matters of "high" politics, playing an important diplomatic role in resolving conflicts, promoting economic development, and fostering human rights in diverse areas of the world. Perhaps most significantly, its member states agreed, in a series of decisions from 1998 to 2000, on institutional arrangements that will allow the EU to politically direct military operations, making it the only international organization with the full range of means for conflict resolution at its fingertips—economic sanctions, humanitarian and development aid, diplomacy, and military force. In addition, the EU members have set a benchmark for improvements in their military capabilities, and created a Rapid Reaction Force of sixty thousand troops from voluntary contributions that is capable of intervening quickly in crisis areas.

A defense role for the European Union was first foreseen in the Treaty of Maastricht, signed in 1991. The treaty clearly used the language of compromise, mentioning the "*eventual* framing of a common defense policy which might *in time* lead to a common defense."[1] The treaty established a formal link between the EU and the Western European Union, a long dormant and redundant defense organization that France and Germany wanted to become the military arm of the EU. It identified the WEU as the institution that would "elaborate and implement" decisions of the EU.[2] The latter could request but not order that the former undertake operations on its behalf.

1. Treaty on European Union, Article J4, Paragraph 1 (emphasis added).
2. Ibid., Paragraph 2.

While progress was made to develop closer links between the WEU and NATO, a process known as the European Security and Defense Identity (ESDI), Britain's refusal to subordinate the WEU to the EU blocked any further steps toward a common EU defense policy for another seven years. The project seemed to be dealt another blow by the election of a leftist government in Germany that had a long-standing aversion to the "militarization" of the European Union. And both Britain and Germany had always been given pause by fears that France favored greater European defense self-sufficiency so as to weaken NATO. The British government, however, then backed two institutional and capability initiatives, now known as the European Security and Defense Policy (ESDP), that integrated the WEU into the EU and earmarked military capabilities for the latter. The red-green coalition in Germany followed loyally behind. A necessary but not sufficient condition for these changes was France's rapprochement with NATO during the 1990s. What changed in each country that made these developments possible? They were the result of the same factors that have figured heavily in previous chapters: party ideology, the instrumentalization of ideas, a more differentiated approach to the use of force, and the institutional prerogatives of presidential systems.

This chapter focuses primarily on Britain since it was that country that traveled the farthest in this area, was the originator of all the innovations to which France and Germany responded, and displayed most clearly the third continuum of partisan debate, that of unilateralism versus multilateralism. Culturalists argue that Britain is generally resistant to a deepening of European integration, a tendency reinforced in the security field by Britain's "special relationship" with the United States and the enhanced position it enjoys in NATO as a result. They claim there is a cross-party unilateralist consensus in Britain on European integration. These theorists stress a variety of reasons for this, including Britain's former colonial history, its unique understanding of parliamentary sovereignty, its isolated geographical location, and its historically positive experience with the nation-state. The result is a sense of identity that is incompatible with a European Union that makes national decisions a matter of interest to other members. This is supposedly true across the political spectrum. Thomas Risse writes: "The distinctive nationalist English identity is incompatible with federalist or supranationalist visions of European political order. It explains why British governments, *whether Conservative or Labour,* have consistently been reluctant to support a deepening of European integration."[3]

---

3. Thomas Risse, "A European Identity? Europeanization and the Evolution of Nation-State Identities," in Maria Green Cowles, James Caporaso, and Thomas Risse (eds.), *Transforming Europe: Europeanization and Domestic Change* (Ithaca: Cornell University Press, 2001), p. 199 (emphasis

In fact, unilateralism was a significant factor, but primarily for the Conservative Party, where it finds a strong basis in the Conservatives' less egalitarian ideology. Even though cooperation in the defense field within the framework of the European Union would preserve the right of countries to decide for themselves to commit their armed forces, the Conservatives resisted expanding the competencies of an organization that is taking on functions previously performed only by nation-states. The Conservatives feared the possibility of a "European army." Apprehensions of losing national sovereignty led the Conservative Party to a general rejection of European political integration, prevented them from evaluating each area of cooperation discretely, and thereby foreclosed for them certain institutional solutions to a problem identified by all British political parties: the inability of the Europeans to project military power abroad.

Although this seems to confirm the cultural argument about British distinctiveness, policy-making became more pragmatic when the Labour Party came to power. The different approaches to sovereignty of Labour and the Conservatives led them to very different conceptions of the national interest. While unilateralism was an ideological goal for the vast majority of the Tories, multilateralism was a concrete vehicle for the Labour Party to realize a number of policy objectives. Due to its ideology, the Labour Party was not inhibited by concerns that adding a competency in security to the EU would contribute to its development as an organization that threatens national decision-making autonomy. Labour's election created the opportunity for civil servants to develop proposals consistent with the party's overall strategy of engaging Britain's European partners again.[4] Without a turnover in government from the Conservatives to Labour, almost all analysts, civil servants, and politicians agree that this "revolution in military affairs" would not have taken place.[5]

Culturalists make very different predictions about German as against British behavior. Germany's history, they maintain, in addition to predisposing it to

---

added). For the most notable culturalist argument on Britain, see Stephen George, *An Awkward Partner: Britain in the European Union* (Oxford: Oxford University Press, 1998). Politicians often make reference to these arguments as well. See Malcolm Rifkind, "Speech to the French Chamber of Commerce," Paris (unpublished document, 23 February 1997).

4. I should make clear that this is not a determinative theory of sovereignty delegation. Rather I am simply trying to call attention to different approaches to sovereignty, which sometimes foreclose certain options and other times create room for political agency. Labour did not have to pursue the policies it did, but it could not have done so had it shared the Conservative approach to the European Union. Labour's multilateral approach plays a permissive role, a necessary but not sufficient condition. Also necessary was a perceived need to remedy the problem of force projection.

5. The phrase is taken from Jolyon Howorth, "Britain, France and the European Defence Initiative," *Survival*, Vol. 42, No. 2 (2000), p. 33; Philip Gordon, "Their Own Army? Making European Defense Work," *Foreign Affairs*, Vol. 79, No. 4 (2000), pp. 13–14.

antimilitarist solutions to international problems, leads it to consistently bind itself into multilateral and supranational institutions so as to avoid isolating itself again. The European Union and NATO help Germany prevent a new *Sonderweg* (separate path) or *Alleingang* (going it alone). Germany, more than Britain or France, has institutionalized a European identity, evident in the unwavering support of its political parties for further steps toward European integration.[6] While German parties as a whole are undoubtedly more willing to cede sovereignty to international institutions than their counterparts in other countries, again culturalists miss crucial partisan conflicts.

Due to the more extreme antimilitarism of the Social Democratic and Green parties, the left in Germany initially opposed the idea of adding security and defense to the European integration process, denouncing the "militarization" of the EU. While both parties supported political integration and even the creation of a federal European state, they believed that Europe, like Germany, should remain a "civilian power" concentrated on nonmilitary means of conflict resolution. They feared that subordinating the WEU to the EU would draw Germany into military interventions abroad and contribute to its normalization. They did not differentiate between multilateral operations for primarily inclusive purposes and unilateral missions in pursuit of narrower interests. The CDU government, by contrast, supported the development of a European rapid reaction capability as a way of enabling German participation in military interventions. The Christian Democrats endorsed EU defense cooperation as part of their broader strategy of making the use of force less controversial and restoring some degree of military sovereignty.[7] The combination of these two positions meant that the issue was fought along a hawk-dove continuum, as was the case with humanitarian intervention.

The antimilitarist position of the Greens and the SPD changed over the course of the 1990s, however. The two parties came to terms with European defense cooperation as part of their evolution on the question of humanitarian intervention more generally. Significant changes on peace enforcement and ESDP occurred simultaneously. In the SPD, foreign policy experts and the right wing of the party again initiated this reevaluation. The Greens, while maintaining a more antimilitarist political profile for electoral reasons, privately accepted the need for an EU defense capacity and raised no objections to developing it when they entered office. This was the dog that did not bark.

6. On Germany's multilateralist political culture, see Thomas Banchoff, *The German Problem Transformed: Institutions, Politics and Foreign Policy* (Ann Arbor: University of Michigan Press, 1999); Peter Katzenstein (ed.), *Tamed Power: Germany in Europe* (Ithaca: Cornell University Press, 1997). On identity, see Risse (2001).

7. Andrew Moravcsik and Kalypso Nicolaïdis, "Explaining the Treaty of Amsterdam: Interests, Influence and Institutions," *Journal of Common Market Studies*, Vol. 37, No. 1 (1999), p. 61.

Of the three countries, France's interest in ESDP is generally regarded as the least surprising. Central to de Gaulle's efforts at promoting French *grandeur* and *rang* was another fundamental principle considered unique to Gaullism— *indépendance*. In a bipolar world France could best increase its influence in international affairs through an "exit" as opposed to a "voice" strategy.[8] De Gaulle sought to make the superpowers compete for France's affections. He secured France's (at least symbolic) security independence through the creation of an autonomous French nuclear deterrent, the *force de frappe*. In terms of military strategy, France would not commit definitively to the defense of Germany in case of a Soviet attack. Most famously, in 1966 de Gaulle removed France from NATO's integrated military command structure and expelled the military alliance's headquarters from French soil. He also welcomed any step toward making Europe more self-sufficient in security. The creation of a "European Europe" was not so implicitly juxtaposed to an American one. His Fouchet Plan was an attempt to promote intergovernmental European cooperation free of American influence on issues of foreign policy and defense.[9] Although the left initially protested each of these policies, by the late 1970s they had become part of both the Socialist and the Communist platforms. An anti-NATO Gaullist consensus, it is argued, has deep roots in France and persists today.[10]

As long as promoting French influence meant weakening NATO, however, there would be only limited progress toward European defense cooperation, given that neither Germany nor Britain would countenance a weakening of the Atlantic Alliance. Only after the creation of a consensus based on a more pro-European and less anti-NATO approach could the major EU powers break the logjam. The end of the Cold War opened up a window of opportunity, since for the Gaullists promoting France's stature necessitated a rapprochement with NATO, the only organization capable of undertaking major crisis management tasks that the RPR identified as critical for maintaining France's relevance in world affairs. This allowed progress on ESDP as well. The unique element of Gaullist ideology, *grandeur,* made for a different

8. Albert O. Hirschman, *Exit, Voice, and Loyalty: Responses to Decline in Firms, Organizations, and States* (Cambridge: Harvard University Press, 1970). On independence, see Michael Harrison, *The Reluctant Ally: France and Atlantic Security* (Baltimore: Johns Hopkins University Press, 1981), p. 49.

9. Harrison (1981), p. 65; Anand Menon, "Defence Policy and Integration in Western Europe," *Contemporary Security Policy,* Vol. 17, No. 2 (1996), pp. 204–283. On the Fouchet Plan, see Andrew Moravcsik, *A Choice for Europe: Social Purpose and State Power from Messina to Maastricht* (Ithaca: Cornell University Press, 1999), pp. 175–190.

10. On the French position following the Cold War, see Philip Gordon, *French Security Policy after the Cold War: Continuity, Change, and Implications for the United States* (Santa Monica: RAND Corporation, 1992).

position than that of the British Conservatives, as it had on the Bosnian and Kosovo operations. Although a significant unilateralist and anti-European streak is also present in the Gaullist party, particularly in its right wing, the institutional autonomy enjoyed by President Chirac helped him negotiate the pitfall constituted by the "sovereignists" in his party who did not want the EU to expand into new areas of cooperation. President Chirac was then free to advance his party's long-standing interest in intergovernmental European defense cooperation in cohabitation with the Socialists, whose interest sprang from different sources, as was the case in the Balkans. Although both the moderate left and the moderate right agree on the necessity of ESDP, the Gaullists consider it another instrumental means of promoting French *grandeur*, while the Socialists emphasize its pragmatic operational functions as well as its contribution to the general process of political integration. As with humanitarian intervention, culturalists again mistake agreement on policy for agreement on values.

In the sections that follow, I explore the domestic politics of European defense cooperation in Britain, Germany, and France, particularly after Maastricht. Other studies have detailed the intergovernmental bargaining and technical details of the successive milestones in this process.[11] I focus therefore on the internal political dynamics critical for explaining major changes in national policy, as in Britain, and growing consensus where there previously was none, as in Germany. I also specify the very different motivations for supporting ESDP on the part of different political parties that are often lumped together under the label of "culture," particularly in the case of France. In addition to shedding light on a relatively theoretically neglected aspect of European integration, the identification of particular national processes identical to those seen in the earlier case studies on intervention strengthens the overall argument about parties and foreign policy.

From Unilateralism to Engagement: The Conservatives versus Labour

Unilateralism as Ideology: The Conservative Party, Sovereignty, and European Integration

Unilateralism dominated the Conservative Party's approach to European integration throughout the 1990s. While the party leadership has stressed the continued value of membership in the EU, it consistently resists efforts

---

11. The most recent contribution is Charles G. Cogan, *The Third Option: The Emancipation of European Defense, 1989–2000* (Westport: Praeger, 2001).

that might restrict decision-making autonomy. Tory foreign secretary Malcolm Rifkind asked rhetorically: "If . . . our membership of the European Union is a vital national interest, does that require us to submit to the inevitability of greater and greater loss of sovereignty and submersion into some incipient Euro-state?"[12] This unilateralist perspective has led the Conservatives to broadly reject initiatives thought to increase the authority of EU institutions. The party's 1997 manifesto pledged that it "will not accept other changes to the Treaty that would further centralise decision-making, reduce national sovereignty, or remove our right to permanent opt-outs."[13]

During the 1970s and 1980s, however, the Tories described themselves as the "party of Europe." What caused this change? I argue Tory opposition to the EU increased not so much because the party had changed, although its rightward drift contributed, but because the EU had been transformed. The Conservatives were originally Britain's most fervent EU supporters because they supported the free trade and deregulation program that were the key elements of integration.[14] The Maastricht Treaty marked a new supranational direction, however. In addition to identifying new areas for political cooperation such as a foreign and defense policy, the treaty pledged member states to the creation of a single currency governed by an independent European Central Bank. Even though Major opted out of European Monetary Union (EMU), the Conservatives divided between moderates who favored market-driven economic integration and limited political cooperation and a right wing that opposed any integrative efforts that limited British sovereignty.[15] The

12. Malcolm Rifkind, "Speech to the European Policy Forum," (unpublished document, London, 1 May 1996). The party opposes "the ratchet of unending institutional integration." Malcolm Rifkind, "Europe Fifty Years On: Speech at the Churchill Commemoration" (unpublished document, Zurich, 18 September 1996).

13. Conservative Party, *You Can Only Be Sure with the Conservatives* (1997 election manifesto). The party resists any efforts at extending qualified majority voting (QMV) in the Council of Ministers to any new issue areas so that Britain retains a veto. The Tories frequently refer to the paucity of democratic accountability in the EU, but they refuse to transfer any new powers to the European Parliament, although it is directly elected by EU citizens. Rifkind (1 May 1996) said that QMV has "gone far enough." On the democratic deficit, QMV and the European Parliament, see Malcolm Rifkind, "Europe: Which Way Forward? Speech at the Konrad-Adenauer Stiftung" (unpublished document, Bonn, 19 February 1997); Conservative Party (1997).

14. Their 1983 election manifesto stressed its economic, rather than political benefits. Conservative Party, *The Challenge of Our Times* (1983 election manifesto).

15. Numerous articles identify the association between right-wing domestic ideology and resistance to European integration. See David Baker, Andrew Gamble, and Steve Ludlam, "Whips or Scorpions: The Maastricht Vote and the Conservative Party," *Parliamentary Affairs*, Vol. 46. No. 2 (April 1993), pp. 151–166; John Garry, "The British Conservative Party: Divisions over European Policy," *West European Politics*, Vol. 18, No. 4 (October 1995), pp. 170–189; Philip Norton, "'The Lady's Not for Turning,' but What about the Rest? Margaret Thatcher and the Conservative Party 1979–89," *Parliamentary Affairs*, Vol. 43, No. 1 (January 1990), pp. 41–58; Matthew Sowemimo, "The Conservative Party and European Integration 1988–1995," *Party Politics*, Vol. 2, No. 1

Maastricht Treaty was only signed into law following a tortuous ratification procedure in which backbenchers attempted to scuttle it on the basis of its restrictions on national sovereignty. An adviser to Foreign Secretary Rifkind recounted: "Up until [the late 1980s], the EC had been a friendly economic organization. The party was not Europe lovers, but we accepted it as something necessary economically." Subsequent developments "allowed the party's instinct to awaken. Before all of this, there was not all of this talk about a superstate."[16]

Although the Tories were deeply divided on EMU, they were more unified against any significant step towards making the EU into a political actor. The EU should remain primarily an economic organization, as this was least threatening to British sovereignty. Restricting the EU to economic matters has been a consistent refrain of the party.[17] Unilateralism meant not just maintaining sovereignty in current areas of cooperation, but preventing the EU from claiming jurisdiction in new fields, even if they were strictly intergovernmental. The party's 1992 manifesto pledged to "resist pressure to extend Community competence to new areas," a theme often repeated by British officials.[18] Defense was one of those new areas. Although the Maastricht Treaty had laid the legal basis for providing an operational capacity for the EU in the form of the WEU, the Major government blocked any efforts to make the WEU into the Union's defense arm.

Ideology as Inhibition: The Conservatives in Office

The Conservatives tried to hide the ideological nature of their objections to European defense. They publicly advocated proposals "aimed at practical solutions to real problems," rather than those that were "an attempt

---

see David Baker, Andrew Gamble, and Steve Ludlam, "The Parliamentary Siege of Maastricht: Conservative Divisions and British Ratification," *Parliamentary Affairs*, Vol. 47, No. 1 (January 1994), pp. 37–60.

16. Interview with the author (10 July 2001). Rifkind echoed that sentiment about the post-Maastricht period in integration: "The process of integration was beginning to touch the essence of the nation-state: its borders; its currency." Rifkind (18 September 1996).

17. The party's 1999 manifesto for the European Parliament elections stated that the party wanted a "free enterprise Europe," but would not allow the "sacrifice" of "our national identity, institutions and *ability to govern ourselves*." Conservative Party, *In Europe, Not Run by Europe* (1999 European election manifesto), Foreword (emphasis added). See also Rifkind (19 February 1997). In *Hansard*, see comments by William Cash (23 November 2000), col. 519; John Maples (22 November 1999), col. 382.

18. Conservative Party, *The Best Future for Britain* (1992 election manifesto). "I am convinced that the future European Union will be more about doing better what we do already than about looking for new things to do." Malcolm Rifkind, "What Future for Europe: Speech at the Old Tweede Kamer," (unpublished document, The Hague, 19 March 1997).

to use those problems to advance some ideological European agenda."[19] In the government's White Paper stating its position on negotiations on defense matters at the 1996 Intergovernmental Conference, the Conservatives endorsed a "task-based approach" in which the countries would decide first what the Europeans would do together militarily before opening up discussions on institutional questions.[20] However, Foreign Secretary Rifkind and his advisers would later admit that their focus was hardly pragmatic, but ideological in its own right. They sought to keep the EU at bay. This was part of "our wider opposition to the degree of European integration that continental European countries were going for, in which defense was just part of a wider argument about single currencies and European harmonization across the whole spectrum," said Rifkind.[21] Adding defense, one of his advisers maintained, would "utterly change the nature of the European Union. . . . Defense goes to the heart of the nation-state." The WEU was not so much an effective option for undertaking military missions, but a "pawn, a political tool" in this larger battle.[22] Although neither characterizes this position as ideological, civil servants argue otherwise. A Cabinet Office official said: "It was always illogical of the previous government to insist on doing [crisis management operations] in the WEU," but it was "handicapped by prejudice."[23]

Some argue that Conservative policy reflected a pro-NATO rather than an anti-European reflex in the party.[24] The Tories are undoubtedly committed to NATO. The party endorsed arrangements that would allow the WEU to undertake operations using NATO assets when the United States did not take part. It agreed to the creation of a European chain of command within NATO—ESDI—that could detach from the organization in such an instance. That the majority of references to harming NATO are quickly followed by a plea to preserve sovereignty suggests, however, that this is a case of "belief system overkill," the tendency of ideological politicians to marshal all available arguments in favor of their positions. The 1997 Conservative Party manifesto said: "NATO will remain the cornerstone of our security. We will resist attempts to bring the Western European Union under the

19. Rifkind (19 February 1997).

20. Foreign and Commonwealth Office, *Memorandum on the United Kingdom Government's Approach to the Treatment of European Defence Issues at the 1996 Intergovernmental Conference* (London: HMSO, 1996).

21. Interview with the author (19 July 2001).

22. Interview with the author (10 July 2001).

23. Interview with the author (3 July 2001).

24. Dan Keohane, "The Approach of the British Political Parties to a Defence Role for the European Community," *Government and Opposition*, Vol. 27, No. 3 (Summer 1992), p. 306.

control of the European Union, *and ensure that defence policy remains a matter for sovereign nations.*"[25]

The Conservatives also cautioned that the EU included four neutral members that were not part of the WEU.[26] However, given that there were no plans for transferring the WEU's collective defense guarantee to the EU because the neutrals themselves did not want it, the argument seemed contrived.[27] The issue was crisis management operations, such as peacekeeping and the delivery of humanitarian aid. "Countries like Sweden and Finland make very useful contributions to those tasks, but parts of the previous government were deeply Europhobic," said a Cabinet Office official.[28] A defense ministry official recalled, "It was not a primary argument, but another reason to throw in the pot. If you were trying to come up with a list of arguments and points to make and defeat the case, that was another one to use. . . . They did not think of the EU as having a crisis management role at all."[29] The Tories deemed EU defense cooperation impossible because they did not want it, rather than the reverse.

The Conservative government vetoed ideas put forward by the civil service for the 1996 intergovernmental conference that would amend the Maastricht Treaty. The political director at the Foreign and Commonwealth Office, the civil servant Pauline Neville-Jones, developed a proposal to fuse the European Council and the WEU at the level of heads of government. At other levels, the organizations would remain separate. Since the European Council is not a formal body and not legally part of the EU, but instead a structure that facilitates informal intergovernmental meetings on EU matters, "We reckoned we could get around the theology that the EU would not have formal competence in this way," said Neville-Jones. After a warm reception in EU member states, she returned home to a meeting with Rifkind, then defense secretary, who rejected it. Neville-Jones claimed that he had "smelled the wind of the party and decided he was backing the Euroskeptic horse."[30] Unilateralism was leaving its mark. The party's ideological approach to sovereignty was hampering its ability to judge cooperation on defense

25. Conservative Party (1997) (emphasis added). In opposition, the party stressed that it supported the development of ESDI within NATO, but not outside of it. See comments in *Hansard* by Ian Duncan-Smith (1 November 1999), col. 739; (22 November 2000), col. 315; John Maples (10 June 1999), col. 812.

26. See FCO (1996), *Memorandum.*

27. For the government's position, see Foreign and Commonwealth Office, *Partnership of Nations: The British Approach to the European Union Intergovernmental Conference* (London: HMSO, 1996). On the neutrals, see Menon (1996), p. 277.

28. Interview with the author (3 July 2001).

29. Interview with the author (12 July 2001).

30. Interview with the author (19 July 2001). Aides said in interviews that it was not a real gamble as there was more of a consensus in the party on defense than on any other European issue.

independent of the European integration process in general. Only the removal of the party from office would lift the ideological barriers and allow the civil service to develop and implement ideas for more significant cooperation on defense policy.

Multilateralism as Means: Labour, Influence, and European Integration

The Labour opposition was not advocating a radically different approach from the Conservatives on the European defense issue. The Liberal Democrats had come out for the absorption of the WEU into the EU already in 1994.[31] Their primary leftist competitor, however, was lying low in the run-up to the election, not advocating new positions on integration except in social policy, which seems to support the cultural argument.[32] "We just played safe, did not think about it much," said a foreign and security policy adviser to Blair.[33] In brainstorming documents, the party came out against giving the EU a military competence, choosing instead to maintain the current WEU arrangements, but it did not do significant analysis.[34] The 1997 election manifesto did not mention the WEU. After trying to share thoughts with the Labour Party on foreign and security policy, a Liberal Democratic foreign policy expert said: "They had not done their homework. There was a reluctance to put flanks out there because they were shattered by the loss in the 1992 election."[35]

This lack of preparation was the main reason that the Labour government made no changes to Conservative policy in negotiating the Treaty of Amsterdam after coming to power. An adviser to Defense Secretary George Robertson asked rhetorically: "When was Amsterdam? June 1997. The election was one month before. They had not read the brief yet. . . . It would be slightly unreasonable to ask why you did not do a 180 degree turnaround in policy six weeks after arriving in power."[36] The Blair government maintained the Conservative line at Amsterdam, dubbing proposals for merging the EU and the WEU "an unrealistic common defence policy."[37]

Labour's reticence on European defense was therefore due more to sensitivity to a Euroskeptical electorate and to inattention than to a unilateralist

---

31. Liberal Democratic Party, "Shared Security: Security and Defence in an Uncertain World," *Policy Paper,* No. 6 (1994), p. 16.
32. George notes that anti-European rhetoric is popular in Britain during election campaigns. George (1998), p. 275.
33. Interview with the author (5 July 2001).
34. Labour Party, *Road to the Manifesto: Labour's Strategy for Britain in the Modern World* (1996).
35. Interview with Lord William Wallace (2 July 2001).
36. Interview with the author (24 July 2001).
37. Tony Blair, *Hansard* (18 June 1997), col. 314.

ideology. Both Labour and the Liberal Democratic Party take a very different approach to sovereignty from that of the Conservatives that reflects their egalitarian principles.[38] The Liberal Democrats are more explicit, claiming in their 1992 election manifesto that they "will take decisive steps towards a fully integrated, federal and democratic European Community. We believe that by sharing sovereignty and pooling power, Britain and its partners will be better able to achieve common goals for the economy, the environment, society and security than by acting alone."[39] The Labour government has been more cautious, laying out the pragmatic and instrumental case for sharing decision-making powers with Britain's partners. Prime Minister Blair said in a major address on Europe: "Above all, those opposed to Britain's role in Europe argue about sovereignty: that the gains we have made are outweighed by the fact that in many areas national sovereignty is no longer absolute. My answer is this: I see sovereignty not merely as the ability of a single country to say no, but as the power to maximise our national strength and capacity in business, trade, foreign policy, defence and the fight against crime. Sovereignty has to be deployed for national advantage. When we isolated ourselves in the past, we squandered our sovereignty—leaving us sole master of a shrinking sphere of influence."[40] According to Labour and the Liberal Democrats, by insisting on retaining sovereignty in the unilateralist, ideological sense, Britain was forsaking opportunities for collective action that would increase Britain's influence, even if control had to be shared with others.

A more pragmatic approach to sovereignty was an integral part of Labour's "internationalist" strategy, which distinguished it from the Conservatives in the 1997 election: "At present Britain is handicapped by a Conservative government that is insular in its mentality and isolationist in its foreign strategy. In international negotiation, they instinctively adopt a mode of confrontation rather than partnership. Their backbenchers and backwoodsmen increasingly articulate the language of a chauvinist, outdated nationalism rather than the realities of the modern world."[41] This idea was present long

---

38. Their more multilateralist approach can also be seen in calls to expand QMV into some areas of decision-making, in contrast to the blanket rejection of the Conservatives. As part of their inclusive emphasis on democratic participation, both parties advocated strengthening the European Parliament vis-à-vis the less transparent Council of Ministers and European Commission. See *New Labour because Britain Deserves Better* (1997 election manifesto). On Liberal Democratic policy, see *Changing Britain for Good* (1992 election manifesto). Also, Liberal Democratic Party, "Meeting the European Challenge: Proposals for the 1996 Intergovernmental Conference," *Policy Paper*, No. 19 (February 1996).

39. Liberal Democratic Party (1992).

40. Tony Blair, "Speech at the Opening of the European Research Institute," (unpublished document, Birmingham, 23 November 2001). See also Tony Blair, "Speech at the Lord Mayor's Banquet," (unpublished document, London, 22 November 1999).

41. Labour Party (1996). See also Labour Party (1997); Labour Party, *Policy Handbook* (unpublished document, 2001), chap. 20.1; Tony Blair, "A New Doctrine of the International Community"

before the election in comments by the shadow foreign secretary and has been the government's most common refrain as concerns European politics since entering office.[42] The contrast with the Conservatives is striking. Labour foreign secretary Robin Cook's predecessor had made a point to stress that influence is not synonymous with interests. "While the accretion of influence is the stuff of diplomatic life and particularly important to a power like Britain, we must constantly remind ourselves that influence is a means, not an end in itself," argued Rifkind in a keynote speech.[43] Influence might have to be foregone for the sake of interests. Labour, with its more multilateralist approach, did not see the conflict.

What had changed for Labour? The party had called for withdrawal from what was then the European Community (EC) in its 1983 election manifesto. However, this did not imply that Labour was approaching sovereignty in an ideological way. Labour's opposition to the EC reflected the incompatibility of membership with its Keynesian economic program of fiscal and monetary stimulation. The party discovered in the 1970s that it could not pursue such policies without serious balance-of-payments deficits if Britain belonged to a free trade area.[44] Membership of the EC restricted decision-making autonomy, but Labour's dissatisfaction was with how it inhibited reaching specific policy goals, not with the loss of sovereignty for its own sake.[45] Labour's rapprochement with the EC began when the party moderated its economic

---

(unpublished document, Chicago, 22 November 1999); Robin Cook, "Shaping the Future of Europe: Speech to the Portuguese Ambassadors," (unpublished document, Lisbon, 6 January 2000).

42. The pre-election critique was: "Under the Conservatives Britain's influence has waned." Labour Party (1997). Jack Cunningham, when shadow foreign secretary, said "Britain with a Labour government will be at the centre of all European decisions and policy debates . . . Influence comes from co-operation not isolation." Jack Cunningham, "Britain in a New World," *Report of Conference* (Annual Conference 1994/Special Conference 1995), p. 177. See statements by ministers after the election in *Hansard:* Tony Blair (13 December 1999), col. 22; Robin Cook (25 May 1999), col. 186; Geoffrey Hoon (22 November 2000), col. 317.

43. Malcolm Rifkind, "Principles and Practice of British Foreign Policy: Speech to the Royal Institute of International Affairs" (unpublished document, London, 21 September 1995).

44. "The next Labour government, committed to radical, socialist policies for reviving the British economy, is bound to find continued membership a most serious obstacle to the fulfillment of those policies. In particular the rules of the Treaty of Rome are bound to conflict with our strategy for economic growth and full employment, our proposals on industrial policy and for increasing trade, and our need to restore exchange controls and to regulate direct overseas investment. . . . We emphasise that our decision to bring about withdrawal in no sense represents any weakening of our commitment to internationalism and international co-operation." Labour Party, *The New Hope for Britain* (1983 election manifesto).

45. Some members of the left wing of the party showed little enthusiasm for the EU, but their concern was with the undemocratic and opaque nature of much of EU decision-making. The faction's leader, Tony Benn, said in Parliament, "I do not know what sovereignty is. . . . We are talking about democracy." Tony Benn, *Hansard* (20 November 1991), col. 333.

policies and the EC began to expand beyond economic cooperation and develop into a political organization. Neither the left wing nor the moderates protested against an enhanced EU role in defense.[46]

Pragmatic Policy-Making: Labour in Office

As part of its strategy of engagement in Europe, the office of the prime minister queried various ministries about possible proposals for a new European initiative shortly after taking office.[47] Richard Hatfield, the policy director at the Ministry of Defence (MOD), proposed that the government might consider the defense field. The MOD had little confidence in the WEU, and had therefore advised against Britain playing a role in a small, Italian-led operation in Albania in 1997. The institutional organization was unwieldy. A more efficient arrangement was possible, according to Hatfield and others. He testified before Parliament's Defence Committee:

> You had a system where the EU, as one political organisation . . . was going to, if it got into crisis management . . . avail itself of another organisation, the WEU, which had a very limited military infrastructure and capability, which in turn, would turn to a third organisation, which we all think is a very good organisation—NATO. . . . Essentially the institutional changes are to say that if you are in that sort of position . . . you would do the whole debate inside the EU as a consistent thing involving defence and foreign policy, as you would nationally. . . . That played into a wider debate that was going on inside the government.[48]

Hatfield confessed that the bureaucracy had been "conscious of the problem in the previous administration," but that under the Major government it had been too politically controversial.[49] Ideology interfered with pragmatism.

---

46. See supportive comments in *Hansard* by Michael Gapes (25 May 1999), col. 218; Laura Moffatt (22 March 1999), col. 14; Dari Taylor (3 July 2000), col. 4. All are considered members of Labour's left wing. David Winnick, another member of the party's left wing, said the issue was not controversial for the party. "Not in Labour. More with the Tories. This is all part of European integration [for them]. Kosovo showed after all that European armies working together can serve a useful purpose." Interview with the author (24 July 2001). Another member of the party's "soft left," Martin O'Neill, former defense spokesperson, agreed. "To be honest, it was not a big issue. Nobody wants their troops dispatched abroad unless there was a good reason. But I do not think they were concerned whether it was the EU or the WEU. That is the simple truth of the matter." Interview with the author (27 June 2001).

47. Interviews with current and former MOD officials (14 June 2001 and 24 July 2001).

48. Defence Committee of the House of Commons, *European Security and Defence*, Eighth Report (19 April 2000), Minutes of Evidence, p. 4. Similarly, a FCO official asked, "Why have the WEU between two effective organizations?" No. 10 Downing Street agreed. A defense policy adviser to Blair asked: "And the WEU, why have a third organization?" Interviews with the author (5 July 2001).

49. Interview with the author (14 June 2001).

"I think everyone could see this was a logical thing to do and the bureaucrats were frustrated that the previous government had been unwilling to go that far," said one high-ranking civil servant.[50] In the Blair administration, the civil servants' practical ideas and party politics converged. "The Prime Minister's wish to position Britain better in Europe has been central to this. But the Foreign Office and MOD had wanted something like this under the previous government. So it was very easy to move relatively quickly," said a Cabinet Office official.[51]

ESDP served another practical function. In addition to adapting the institutional structures and helping Britain play a more constructive role in Europe, giving the EU a defense competence would also reinforce the Union's political role in international affairs by backing its Common Foreign and Security Policy (CFSP) with a credible threat of force. Both CFSP and ESDP would fall under the second "pillar" of EU decision-making, so that those directing any possible military operation under the latter would also be managing the former, giving it much more weight. "There is a specific political objective in this, that the EU should be a more serious player in world affairs, and that involves being able to deploy force," said a Cabinet Office official.[52] This was thought to be in Britain's interests as well, as it would simultaneously increase Britain's influence in world affairs. Even though the Conservatives had noted the necessity that the CFSP "call on all of the resources of the EU—its economic muscle as well as its diplomatic skills," they had not wanted defense to be included.[53]

The result of the convergence of bureaucratic and partisan ideas was the St. Malo Declaration. At a Franco-British summit in 1998, the two powers announced their commitment to give the EU "the capacity for autonomous action, backed up by credible military forces, the means to decide to use them, and a readiness to do so, in order to respond to international crises."[54] This was a shock to Britain's partners and Britain's anti-European political culture. "Here the Brits, the usual backmarkers on this, were suggesting we might be able to do something on this. If we were able to make it work, it was going to play well politically in Europe," said a senior MOD official who

---

50. Interview with Cabinet Office official (3 July 2001).

51. Interview with the author (12 July 2001).

52. Interview with the author (3 July 2001). Blair said: "At Amsterdam, European leaders agreed on new political instruments—a so-called Mr. CFSP and a new planning capability. They will certainly help. But they will not be enough. Diplomacy works best when backed by the credible threat of force. The maxim applies to Europe too." Tony Blair, Speech to the North Atlantic Assembly (unpublished document, Edinburgh, 13 November 1998).

53. Malcolm Rifkind, "Common Foreign and Security Policy: Speech to the Institute Français des Relations Internationales," (unpublished document, Paris, 5 March 1996).

54. For a compendium of the St. Malo and other key documents in the ESDP process, see *From St. Malo to Nice,* Chaillot Paper No. 47 (Paris: Institute for Security Studies, 2001).

was integrally involved in the process.[55] The momentum behind the bilateral initiative was channeled into the European Union as a whole. In June 1999, the European Council agreed in Cologne on a set of new EU institutions to make decisions on and direct military operations, either autonomously or borrowing NATO assets. A new Political and Security Committee (PSC) of permanent representatives to Brussels replaced the Political Committee of national representatives who met only once or twice a month. The PSC was charged with politically directing any operation as well as managing the Union's Common Foreign and Security Policy on a daily basis. It relies on the strategic planning capacities of a European Military Staff and a Military Committee. NATO was the model, but the ESDP was not directed against NATO. Any anti-NATO sentiment apparent in Labour's unilateralist nuclear policies in the 1980s had faded as the alliance took up a new role of intervening militarily for humanitarian purposes that the party heartily endorsed. Instead, its pragmatic approach to European integration merely meant it did not regard progress in ESDP as detrimental to NATO.

Bringing defense under the EU was also seen by the Labour administration as a way of marshaling the political will to spend more on defense, a solution foreclosed for the Conservatives by their ideology. Former Tory foreign secretary Rifkind complained of the St. Malo initiative: "You can create all the new structures you like. You can give it all the fancy names you wish. . . . But if you have not provided more resources, then it is highly improbable you will have significant increased capability."[56] Yet NATO efforts to pressure states to increase defense spending had been a "complete fiasco,"[57] so the Labour government turned the continental commitment to European integration to its own advantage. A senior official explained: "The fact is that the international political organization that has clout, the organization that people across the government and influential movers and shakers are all aware of, is the European Union. It was recognized here that the political profile you could get in the EU would help this underlying desire to improve capabilities."[58] The government believed that making defense part of the EU portfolio would make it easier for member countries to advocate increases in spending, and that a public commitment at the European Council would make failure much more costly politically.[59] With this in mind, the Blair government proposed

55. Interview with the author (14 June 2001).
56. Interview with the author (19 July 2001).
57. Interview at the Prime Minister's Office (5 July 2001).
58. Interview with MOD official (12 July 2001). Others mentioned the same strategy. "There is a massive desire for the EU to move on." Interview with MOD official (14 June 2001).
59. "The best and most powerful incentive we have is peer pressure, credibility, and face. Having got heads of government to do this Headline Goal, there is then quite a premium on the defense ministers coming up with the means to do it." Interview with Cabinet Office official (3 July 2001).

the Headline Goal, the creation of a Rapid Reaction Force of sixty thousand troops capable of fulfilling the full range of crisis management tasks. The project was agreed to by the EU at the Helsinki Summit in December 1999.

Cultural Circumvention: Labour and the Conservative Opposition

A stress on capabilities created particular headaches for the government, however. The Conservative leadership, bolstered by the right wing of the party, labeled the Rapid Reaction Force a "European army."[60] The MOD soon regretted the use of the term "Rapid Reaction Force," which was used as media shorthand but created the impression of a standing force rather than of units earmarked to be deployed voluntarily by member governments in the event of a crisis. The frontbench spokespersons of the opposition stressed that they opposed the initiative because it would undermine NATO, but anti-European feeling was transparent in their statements, as it had been during their time in government. An MOD official involved in controlling the political damage said: "The current opposition spokesperson is rabidly anti-European, not only on defense. . . . This debate is hugely distorted by British politics. [They] are waging a political campaign, not really about European defense but more about Europe in general in which this was a convenient weapon to use."[61]

The Conservatives continued to invoke the ideological goals of the French and Germans of creating a political Europe, and raised the prospect of a slippery slope leading toward federalism. The right-wing Tory Michael Howard, formerly one of the Major cabinet's senior Euroskeptics and now shadow foreign secretary, said, "The agenda of the integrationists on the continent of Europe is clear: one currency, one tax policy, one employment policy, one legal area, one army—what else is needed to create a single European state? Why do the integrationists here deny it?"[62] The party's shadow defense secretary, John Maples, said: "Clearly at present, that is a separate pillar of the European Union, and it will require unanimity to do anything, but we have been

---

"We wanted to put down metrics for the measurement of the generation of capability, recognizing it is difficult to measure and even more difficult to get people to live up to it. To a certain extent, you put out a league table to embarrass people. That was what was in our minds." Interview with adviser to George Robertson (24 July 2001).

60. Ian Duncan-Smith, *Hansard* (13 December 1999), col. 25. The label was particularly liked by right-wing members of the party. In *Hansard*, see Geoffrey Clifton-Brown (22 November 2000), col. 327; Michael Howard (2 November 2000), col. 909; John Redwood (19 March 2001), col. 143.

61. Interview with the author (14 June 2001).

62. *Hansard* (25 May 1999), col. 190. See also Michael Howard (2 November 2000), col. 909. For the argument that it would undermine NATO, see comments by Ian Duncan-Smith (1 November 1999), col. 739; (22 November 2000), col. 315; John Maples (10 June 1999), col. 812.

down that road a few times before on other subjects."[63] Criticism did not only come from the traditional Euroskeptics, however. Even Malcolm Rifkind and John Major continued to oppose ESDP out of office, in spite of being freed from the constraints placed on them by the backbenchers. This suggests a solid consensus in the party and discounts the possible argument that the Conservatives, had they remained in office, would have read the geopolitical situation similarly to Labour and followed the same policy. Yet, as in the case of Kosovo, not all of the opposition was disloyal. The Liberal Democrats, similar ideologically to Labour, went so far as to publish a joint statement with the Labour government endorsing ESDP.[64]

The Labour Party did not engage the Conservative criticism directly, demonstrating the power of the predominantly anti-European political culture in Britain. To avoid the "European army" line of argumentation, the government dodged questions on the institutional innovations behind the initiative and stressed the continuities with the previous government's policy during almost every discussion in Parliament.[65] The defense secretary, George Robertson, argued, "It was, after all, my predecessor, Michael Portillo, who signed up to the European security and defence identity at the Berlin summit."[66] The government neglected to note that the purpose of ESDI was to make NATO assets available to the WEU, and excluded EU involvement. ESDP was not ESDI, but the government manipulated the confusing set of acronyms. Robertson's remark drew a rebuke from former Prime Minister Major, who called his characterization a "grotesque distortion."[67] The debate over ESDP was fought on unilateralist-multilateralist lines, but this was not always evident in the public discussion.

FROM ANTIMILITARISM TO ENGAGEMENT:
THE CDU VERSUS THE RED-GREEN COALITION

Multilateralism as Means: The CDU, Normalization, and the Instrumentalization of European Defense Cooperation

In Germany, the issue of European defense became intertwined with the broader question of German participation in out-of-area military operations.

63. John Maples, *Hansard* (10 June 1999), col. 811. On the Franco-German agenda, see comments by Ian Duncan-Smith (1 November 1999), col. 743; Caroline Spelman (13 December 1999), col. 4.
64. Interview with Lord William Wallace (2 July 2001).
65. For the avoidance of the institutional question, see comments in *Hansard* by Robin Cook (22 June 1999), col. 912; George Robertson (22 March 1999), cols. 814–815. On continuity, see Tony Blair (13 December 1999), col. 29; Geoffrey Hoon (13 December 1999), col. 13; (22 February 2000), col. 1401; (22 November 2000), col. 324.
66. George Robertson, *Hansard* (21 June 1999), col. 747.
67. John Major, *Hansard* (22 November 2000), col. 318.

Instead of being framed as a unilateralist-multilateralist debate, it was another front of the battle between a hawkish right committed to making the use of force normal again and a dovish left that initially opposed this. The integration of the WEU into the EU found its strongest support from the CDU. As culturalists correctly argue, the ideological attraction of unilateralism for the German right was much less pronounced than in either France or Britain. The experience of the Second World War had a direct impact on the party system, discrediting the German conservative parties that had previously located themselves to the right of the more moderate and centrist Christian Democrats. The CDU has a broader European identity than the more nationalist British Conservatives and French Gaullists due to its Christian fundamentals, which are seen as being shared across Western Europe and demarcating the continent from non-Western countries. The CDU also has a strong social Catholic wing, committed to creating more equality among social classes, that moderates its rightist leanings.[68] These factors contributed to a level of comfort with European defense cooperation on the part of the CDU in comparison to other rightist parties.

While the CDU is genuinely committed to the European Union playing a stronger role in foreign and defense policy internationally, the CDU believed that this agenda would also have the effect of increasing Germany's military sovereignty.[69] As was demonstrated in Chapter 4, the Kohl government pushed for *Handlungsfähigkeit,* the ability to take military action, which was the right's code word for military sovereignty. The CDU extended this concept to Europe, arguing that Germany had to be *europafähig,* capable of acting with European allies, as well.[70] As the unilateral use of force is prohibited by Germany's antimilitarist constitution even in the eyes of the CDU, European defense cooperation could help free Germany from internal constraints by creating a mechanism by which it could quickly and legally team up with others. It served the CDU's strategy of making German participation in military operations possible, an option that any hawkish party wants to have available.[71] The more centrist FDP supported this goal, but as in the debate over out-of-area interventions, it was insistent that the WEU obtain a UN

68. On the CDU and Europe, see Risse (2001), pp. 203–204. This is true of Christian Democratic parties in general, who are found to be more pro-European than Conservative parties. See Gary Marks and Carole Wilson, "The Past in the Present: a Cleavage Theory of Party Response to European Integration," *British Journal of Political Science,* Vol. 30, No. 3 (2000), pp. 451–455. For the party's social policies, see CDU, *Freiheit in Verantwortung: Grundsatzprogramm der Christlich Demokratischen Union Deutschlands* (1994).

69. Interview with adviser to the former German defense minister (13 May 2004).

70. See CDU (1994), p. 94. On the Eurocorps, see G. Wyn Rees, *Western European Union at the Crossroads: Between Trans-Atlantic Solidarity and European Integration* (Boulder: Westview Press, 1998), chap. 4.

71. Interview with adviser to the former German defense minister (13 May 2004).

mandate for any operation, a restriction, as seen before, the more hawkish CDU rejected.[72]

The CDU's foreign and security policy committee advocated the full integration of the WEU into the EU with the exception of the WEU's collective defense guarantee, which would have been unacceptable to the neutral members of the EU and would have caused consternation in NATO.[73] The putative antimilitarist consensus did not put much of a brake on conservative plans. The government was planning for EU military operations even before the constitutional issue was resolved. In May 1992, two years before the Constitutional Court declared multilateral operations beyond the NATO area to be legal, the rightist government and France announced the creation of a joint Franco-German Eurocorps composed of fifty thousand troops that would provide the WEU with the operational capacity to intervene both inside and outside of Europe. The 1993 plan for the Bundeswehr and the 1994 White Paper on security policy stated the government's commitment to making the armed forces more mobile so as to be able to project power abroad in WEU operations, among others—again many months before the Constitutional Court settled the issue.[74]

Already in June 1992, before the international community was fully invested in Yugoslavia, the government was laying out a European defense agenda. In remarks before the WEU assembly, Defense Minister Rühe was making the connection between the CDU's normalization strategy and European defense cooperation:

> Germany has only been able to agree to the Eurocorps' mission subject to what its current constitutional situation permits it to accept. As regards this, we Germans are facing the question to what extent our security policy is capable of assuming a European dimension. . . . Being a normal state, Germany must be in a position to exercise all of its rights and fulfill all of its obligations in safeguarding and restoring peace and international security.

The WEU was another means to do so. Germany, he went on, needed to be able to use "all political and economic instruments available to us" in order to provide security for Europe. If it did not change the constitution to allow for deployment in service of European organizations, Germany would

72. FDP, *Liberal denken. Leistung wählen* (1994 election manifesto), p. 121; See also FDP, "Für ein europäisches Deutschland: Leitsätze der FDP zur Europawahl" (unpublished document, 22 January 1994), p. 16.

73. For the party caucus view, see Bundesfachausschußes Außen- und Sicherheitspolitik der CDU Deutschlands, "Die Weiterentwicklung der Gemeinsamen Außen-, Sicherheits- und Verteidigungspolitik der Europäischen Union in der Regierungskonferenz" (unpublished document, 1996).

74. Bundesministerium für Verteidigung, *Die Bundeswehr der Zukunft—Bundeswehrplan '94* (1993); Bundesministerium für Verteidigung, *Weißbuch* (1994), pp. 91–93.

"lose our credibility as a European nation."[75] Credibility, as seen earlier, is a consistent marker of a hawkish foreign policy.

Multilateralism as Militarization: The German Left and European Defense Cooperation

At the beginning of the 1990s, both the SPD and the Greens opposed the incorporation of defense matters into the EU, calling this a "militarization" of what had previously been a civilian organization. Due to Germany's history, the German left was first and foremost antimilitarist. The SPD contested the creation of the Eurocorps and the decision to expand the possible scenarios for WEU intervention to include crisis management operations. Both leftist parties accused the coalition of trying to cloak the Bundeswehr's deployment in military missions around the world in the "robe of West European integration," a process which was widely accepted in Germany.[76] A statement by the SPD party executive read, "The world asks in astonishment how many competing structures the federal government wants in order to make possible the out-of-area deployment of the Bundeswehr."[77] The government's efforts to change the constitution and promote the WEU were "two sides of the same coin."[78] The Greens and Social Democrats put forward instead vague proposals to build the Organization for Cooperation and Security in Europe (OSCE) into a pan-European collective security system without any recourse to intervention forces.[79] The left's objections to humanitarian intervention and European defense cooperation were also intertwined, however. Christian Sterzing, the Green spokesperson on European affairs, echoed Wieczorek-Zeul's characterization of the partisan cleavages during the out-of-area debate when he wrote that the negotiations for the Treaty of Amsterdam presented "the choice between the transformation of the EU into a military power or the continuation of the EU as a civilian power."[80] This time, the left was resisting military means at the supranational level.

75. WEU Parliamentary Assembly, *Official Report of Debates,* 38th Session (3 June 1992), pp. 164–172.

76. Bündnis 90/Die Grünen, *Lieber Europa erweitern als Demokratie beschränken"* (1994 European election manifesto), p. 33; SPD, *Sofort-Programm* (Bonn, 16–17 November 1992); SPD Parteivorstand, "Antrag A 1: Perspektive einer neuen Außen- und Sicherheitspolitik," *Protokoll,* SPD Party Conference (Wiesbaden, 16–19 November 1993), p. 990.

77. *Presseservice der SPD,* No. 438 (23 June 1992).

78. Fraktion der Bündnis 90/Die Grünen, "Eckpunkte für eine Reform der Gemeinsamen Außen- und Sicherheitspolitik," in *Perspektiven für Europa: Materialen zur Integrationsdebatte* (1997).

79. SPD Vorstand, "Regierungsprogramm," in *Protokoll,* SPD Party conference (Halle, 22 June 1994), p. 203; Fraktion der Bündnis 90/Die Grünen (1997).

80. Christian Sterzing, "Eine Zwischenbilanz der Europäischen Regierungskonferenz," in *Perspektiven für Europa: Materialen zur Integrationsdebatte* (1997), p. 64.

The position of the left should not be misread as an overall rejection of European integration, as with the British right. Criticism of the Maastricht and Amsterdam treaties from both leftist parties centered on the government's inability to push through more significant steps toward political integration, in particular greater powers for the European Parliament and the introduction of majority voting on matters pertaining to the Common Foreign and Security Policy.[81] In terms of institutions, the left was more integrationist than the right. The SPD had gone as far as proposing an amendment to the constitution that would establish the creation of a United States of Europe as the end goal for Germany.[82] Due to their leftist program of redistribution and environmentalism, the Greens condemned European integration in the form it had taken to date as "radically free-market, monetaristic, unsocial, and centralistic."[83] But the increasing possibilities in the field of political integration caught their imagination. Green European spokesperson Sterzing said: "It is becoming clearer to the public that the Greens are an integration-friendly party, but that was not the case in the 1980s. We criticized the Europe of big business, tendencies that are also present in other European green parties. However, now the perspective of a political union has become much more important. We have always supported that, not least because it meant overcoming the nation-state in the European area."[84]

So as not to play into the hands of increasingly intense rightist and unilateralist critiques of integration, the Greens began to take a more constructive tone. Sterzing said: "We have fundamental criticisms of the Common Agricultural Policy and the democratic deficit, but we had to prevent this critique from being instrumentalized by the anti-European forces. When one says there is not enough democracy in Europe, one can say 'enough of Europe,' or one can say 'we have to fight for this democratization.'"[85] In the early to mid-1990s, however, adding a defense capacity for the European Union was a red line for both parties. In an article on European foreign and security policy at the time, Sterzing wrote that the party could not support

---

81. For a review of the SPD's critique of the CDU, see Andrew Denison, "The European Dilemmas of the German Left: the Social Democratic Party and West European Security Cooperation" (Ph.D. diss., Johns Hopkins University, 1996), chap. 4. For a review of Green policy, see Ludger Volmer, *Die Grünen und die Außenpolitik: Ein Schwieriges Verhältnis* (Muenster: Westfälisches Dampfboot, 1998), pp. 476–492. Another statement of SPD policy is SPD Parteivorstand, "Wir brauchen Europa" in *Protokoll,* SPD Party Conference (Mannheim, 14–17 November 1995). For the Greens, see also Bündnis '90/Die Grünen (1994).

82. Denison (1996), p. 350. See also SPD Parteivorstand, "Europapolitische Perspektiven der SPD," *Protokoll,* SPD Party Conference (Bremen 28–31 May 1991).

83. Volmer (1998), p. 485.

84. Interview with the author (5 February 2001).

85. Ibid.

integration "at any price," indicating the tension felt between conflicting goals of antimilitarism and multilateralism.[86]

With the reflection process triggered by Bosnia, however, both parties began to reappraise their position. Since the left's objection to an EU role in defense was to the use of force in general, policies changed in lockstep with the evolution of Social Democratic and Green positions on humanitarian intervention. The SPD, being a more moderate party and therefore more predisposed as a whole toward differentiated positions on the use of the military, began to move first. The reevaluation was spearheaded by those who were in the vanguard of the change in position on intervention in Bosnia: the foreign and defense policy experts such as Norbert Gansel, Walter Kolbow, and Karsten Voigt, as well as the party's right wing, led by Hans-Ulrich Klose. The foreign policy spokesperson for the right-wing Seeheim Circle, Dieter Schloten, ridiculed the party's ideas for the OSCE as unrealizable.[87]

Those most opposed to an EU role in defense were from the left of the party—those who had figured prominently in battle over out-of-area interventions and had initially taken an undifferentiated position on the use of the military. They included Heidemarie Wieczorek-Zeul, Katrin Fuchs, Herman Scheer, Konrad Gilges, and Gernot Erler.[88] The official position of the left-wing Frankfurt Circle was that the WEU should be dissolved, leaving the OSCE responsible for European security.[89] As it had done before, the left wing marshaled other arguments in pursuit of its antimilitarist goals. Like the British Conservatives, the SPD's left played on its country's attachment to NATO by evoking fears that a European role in defense would duplicate military structures and weaken the alliance. The transparency of this argument was even clearer than in the United Kingdom considering that the same left-wing politicians favored the alliance's dissolution in the future.[90]

As the SPD's absolute rejection of military intervention weakened, so too did its objections to European defense cooperation. In its manifesto for the 1994 election, in which it limited its endorsement of the use of the Bundeswehr

86. Sterzing (1997), p. 64.
87. "Dokumentation eines Entwurfs für den Seeheim-Kreis zur Außen-, Europa- und Sicherheitspolitik der SPD," *tageszeitung* (19 January 1995); Denison (1996), pp. 404–405; Walter Kolbow, "Problemfelder und Fragestellungen für die Arbeit der Projektgruppe Außen-, Friedens- und Sicherheitspolitik, Europa beim Parteivorstand" (unpublished document, 1991).
88. Denison (1996), p. 371; Johannes Rau and Heidemarie Wieczorek-Zeul, Preliminary report submitted to the SPD Projektgruppe "Internationale Politik" (unpublished document, 24 July 1992).
89. Frankfurter Kreis, "Orientierung für eine sozialdemokratische Friedenspolitik," *Sozialdemokratische Pressedienst* (21 November 1991); Denison (1996), p. 371; Rau and Wieczorek-Zeul (1992).
90. June 1992 draft of program by SPD *Projektgruppe,* quoted in Denison (1996), p. 397.

strictly to peacekeeping, it rejected any participation of German armed forces under the WEU and instead called in vague terms for the creation of a collective security system in Europe by integrating the OSCE, NATO, and the WEU.[91] The real change occurred following Srebrenica. The two major party documents on foreign policy subsequent to the massacre embraced the idea of integrating the WEU into the EU for the first time. These were the also the first explicit endorsements of peace enforcement by the party.[92]

Although the Greens did not modify their public statements, claiming in their 1998 manifesto that the EU "needed no military arm" and that the WEU should "in the continual process of civil European integration be dissolved," this position was no longer as strongly held as before.[93] As it had done on the issue of humanitarian intervention, the party was clinging for electoral reasons to a political profile that did not accurately portray the views of its parliamentarians. Quickly following the election, the Greens abandoned the platform in their coalition negotiations with the SPD, in which they pledged to further develop the WEU. Their reversal left the PDS as the only party in Germany that opposed the creation of an EU military capability.[94] Therefore, when the Social Democrats and Greens took office in 1998, no major changes in German policy were made. The red-green coalition promised, as did Britain and France, to provide twenty thousand troops to the Rapid Reaction Force, a third of its strength.

Nevertheless, because of the sensitivity of the Greens and their voters to military matters due to Germany's particular historical experience with force, the party still downplays the military aspects of the process. Sterzing, the Green spokesperson on EU affairs, said, "You will never notice any particular excitement about the Headline Goal in all of our papers and resolutions. Instead we focus on the civilian aspects."[95] Almost all statements on ESDP are accompanied by references to its preventive and civilian components, including the decision to create a unit of five thousand police officers capable of restoring order quickly in crisis regions. Privately the parties are

91. SPD Vorstand (1994).

92. For the 1994 programme, see SPD Vorstand (1994), p. 203. For 1998, see Schwerpunktkommission Außen- und Sicherheitspolitik, *Sozialdemokratische Außenpolitik im Übergang zum 21. Jahrhundert* (2 May 1997); "Beschlußübersicht A1: Außen-, Sicherheits- und Entwicklungspolitik" *Presseservice der SPD*, (3 December 1997).

93. Bündnis 90/Die Grünen, *Grün ist der Wechsel: Programm zur Bundestagswahl '98* (1998 election manifesto).

94. SPD and Bündnis '90/Die Grünen, *Aufbruch und Erneuerung: Deutschlands Weg ins 21. Jahrhundert* (20 October 1998). On PDS policy, see PDS, *Für einen Kurswechsel in Europa: Das Europa des 21. Jahrhunderts braucht Frieden, Arbeit und Demokratie* (13 June 1999), p. 21. The party calls for the WEU's dissolution and the reform of the OSCE just as the SPD and Greens did earlier.

95. Interview with the author (5 February 2001).

no different.[96] SPD deputy defense minister Kolbow stressed that the ESDP is "not just peace enforcement, but also peacekeeping, humanitarian help, and the development of civil prevention methods. Military means are a last resort."[97] With this emphasis, the government has been able to ensure the support of its backbenches, particularly on the left. Erler, Eberhard Brecht, Uta Zapf, and Winfried Nachtwei all mentioned this as extremely important to their parties.[98] As long as civilian means are given priority in a comprehensive approach, the government is assured of left-wing support. According to the key foreign policy figure on the Green left, Ludger Volmer, who became deputy foreign minister in 1998, "I always said when we were in opposition that at the moment when crisis prevention and civilian conflict resolution were implemented, the question of military intervention as a last resort would be completely changed."[99]

Despite this civilian emphasis, the red-green government has welcomed the agreements between the British and the French that gave new impetus to the European defense process, even if it has done so in muted tones.[100] Privately, politicians give the same reasons as the British Labour Party for their endorsement. The Headline Goal gives the means to undertake missions if the United States chooses not to engage. Kolbow said: "The Headline Goal will fill gaps in capabilities that the Americans have, and is necessary if something like Kosovo happens. They will certainly not always be ready to intervene. Bosnia and Kosovo would not have been possible without the Americans."[101] This finds broad agreement in the left of the SPD and Greens as well. Erler said, "It is dangerous to be dependent on American participation in such an instance as Kosovo. It could have happened that for some domestic political reason, Clinton could have decided 'we are not going to do this with you. Kosovo does not concern us.' Then the Europeans would not have been able to do anything militarily."[102] Nachtwei said the same: "We cannot be dependent on whether Washington or the American public is willing to support such an operation."[103]

In those cases in which the United States is involved, the ESDP will allow the Europeans more say by adding weight to the CFSP. Aachim Schmillen,

96. "Beschlußübersicht A1: Außen-, Sicherheits- und Entwicklungspolitik" *Presseservice der SPD*, (3 December 1997); Fraktion der Bündnis '90/Die Grünen, *Die Bundeswehr reformieren* (6 June 2000); SPD Bundestagsfraktion, *Die Zukunft der GASP: Sozialdemokratische Perspektiven für die Gemeinsame Außen- und Sicherheitspolitik der Europäischen Union* (2000).

97. Interview with the author (25 January 2001).

98. Interviews with the author (2000–2001).

99. Interview with the author (18 May 2001).

100. Joschka Fischer, "Speech at the 37th Munich Conference on Security Policy" (3 February 2001).

101. Interview with the author (25 January 2001).

102. Interview with the author (7 February 2001).

103. Interview with the author (15 February 2001).

the Green head of policy planning, said: "Without an ESDP and the military means, everything is determined by the Pentagon and the White House." He cited the Kosovo experience: "Those countries that have the capacities made the decisions."[104] On the left of the Greens the opinion is the same. "If the EU really wants to be able to act within the CFSP, that does not work without military capabilities," said Nachtwei. "Without this capacity for military conflict resolution there will be no real partnership with the U.S."[105]

FROM INDEPENDENCE TO ENGAGEMENT: THE GAULLISTS AND THE PLURAL LEFT

Multilateralism as Means: The RPR, *Grandeur,* and the Instrumentalization of European Defense Cooperation

This reasoning, common to the European left, was also the basis of Gaullist thought, but so long as it was taken to be indicative of anti-American feeling, it had been one of the major impediments to European defense cooperation, as it was seen to threaten NATO. As one French diplomat explained, "France's partners, even within the fifteen EU countries, would never join a European project if they had not seen that France had reconciled itself with NATO."[106] Ironically, rapprochement with the alliance was given its biggest boost with the election of the conservative RPR-UDF coalition in spring 1993 and of a Gaullist president in spring 1995. In December 1995, with the right in control of both parliament and the presidency, France rejoined the Atlantic Alliance's North Atlantic Council and its Military Committee, although it did not go so far as to reintegrate into the military command structure.

Roland Tiersky considers this a significant departure from Gaullist principles, but he mistakes Gaullism for a general anti-Americanism. It is another example of policy-seeking behavior in the face of a changing international environment.[107] Gaullism is first and foremost a policy that maximizes French influence over world affairs. As argued in the previous chapter, in the post–Cold War world, France's independent nuclear deterrent was significantly devalued, and there were no longer two superpowers to play off of one another. The RPR's way of keeping France relevant in international affairs was to make it a major player in crisis management.

104. Interview with the author (11 May 2001).
105. Interview with the author (15 February 2001).
106. Interview with the author (11 April 2001). French foreign minister Hubert Védrine also identified this a precondition for progress. See Hubert Védrine, "Vers une Europe de la sécurité et de la défense," *Le Monde* (3 December 1999).
107. Roland Tiersky, "A Likely Story: Chirac, France-NATO, European Security and American Hegemony," *French Politics and Society,* Vol. 14, No. 2 (1996), pp. 1–7.

By the time of the right's election, however, it had become clear that no purely European institution, such as the WEU, was capable of serving as a vehicle for this goal. The EU's early record in dealing with the Bosnian war had been abysmal, and according to Defense Minister Charles Millon was central for convincing France of the need for an effective military organization capable of dealing with crises on the European continent.[108] NATO was the only alternative. A French official in a senior post at NATO during that time said: "NATO is the only credible military organization. If we need NATO for peace operations and if France is supposed to take part in every peace operation in Europe, it is not logical that we are not a member of the institutions of NATO. That led us in December 1995 to announce we were considering a step-by-step approach."[109]

This new direction was simply a change in strategy, using "voice" to increase French influence in a changing geopolitical environment in which an "exit" strategy no longer worked.[110] Like the German right, the RPR adjusted its thinking to changing geopolitical realities. If France wanted to pursue *grandeur* through peacekeeping and peacemaking operations, having a say in the management in these new types of military conflicts meant literally taking a seat at the table of the organization best equipped to conduct them. Rejoining would allow both increased political control and military interoperability. "The idea was to make sure that the French military was able to function properly with NATO and that France would exercise its full influence within NATO on matters that pertained to our men," said an adviser to the French defense minister.[111]

This new approach led to France's first steps toward assuming a more normal role in NATO. Already in January 1994, in the era of cohabitation, France announced that the defense minister and head of the armed services could take part in NATO meetings "if questions concerning French forces are taken up."[112] The course was bumpy. As with Bosnia, the conservative coalition had to solicit the approval of Mitterrand, who sometimes blocked the attendance of senior officials at NATO meetings.[113] His replacement by Chirac removed

---

108. Charles Millon, "France and the Renewal of the Atlantic Alliance," *NATO Review,* Vol. 44, No. 3 (1996), pp. 13–16. See also Robert P. Grant, "France's New Relationship with NATO," *Survival,* Vol. 38, No. 1 (1995), p. 63; Adrian Treacher, "New Tactics, Same Objectives: France's Relationship with NATO," *Contemporary Security Policy,* Vol. 19, No. 2 (1998), pp. 97–98.

109. Interview with the author (13 March 2001).

110. Treacher (1998).

111. Interview with the author (19 March 2001). This is also the conclusion reached in Michael Brenner and Guillaume Parmentier, *Reconcilable Differences: U.S.-French Relations in the New Era* (Washington, D.C.: Brookings Institution Press, 2002), p. 48. Parmentier was a key government official during this time.

112. Grant (1996), p. 62.

113. Ibid., p. 64.

the remaining obstacles. Chirac stated before his election in 1993 that playing a role in NATO "can only take place from the inside."[114]

By normalizing relations with NATO, progress became possible in European defense cooperation. France has gone through its own, if more subtle, "revolution," said a senior diplomat at the foreign ministry. "For the first time, a project of European defense construction is not a project to build European autonomy against NATO. It is pro-European, accepting the NATO factor as a part of it. It is no longer viewed as a zero-sum game."[115] Rapprochement had the effect of "defusing the theological questions" of NATO versus the European Union and allowing for more "practical" policies in the EU area.[116] It yielded immediate and positive results on French goals of creating a "European pillar" within the alliance. The United States agreed at the Brussels NATO summit in 1994 to ESDI—the possibility of European-led operations using NATO assets under a European-led chain of command, further elaborated in Berlin in 1996.[117] French agreement to build a European defense structure within NATO and the election of the Labour government in 1997 opened up the way to the St. Malo Declaration.

The European Union was another vehicle for promoting Gaullist goals. Chirac has adapted traditional Gaullist language to justify the new endeavor. While de Gaulle had "a certain idea of France," Chirac had "a certain vision of Europe in the world." Europe, he argued, should be a political actor in "the *first rank* of great states of the world."[118] Therefore, as was the case in the debates over military intervention, the unique qualities of Gaullist ideology, in particular the pursuit of *grandeur* and *rang*, lead the French Gaullists to take a different approach toward European defense cooperation than the British Conservatives.

Again, however, those differences should not be overstated. The pursuit of *indépendance* is not uniquely Gaullist, but a general unilateralist tendency of parties on the right. De Gaulle's uniqueness lay in his linking it to the promotion of French *grandeur* and *rang*. He and his party resisted supranational integration as vehemently as they did NATO domination of European security policy. The Gaullist "open chair policy" had provoked the Luxembourg Compromise, preserving the veto right of member states in European Community affairs and checking the sovereignty-ceding momentum of European integration.[119] This is still a strong tendency in the RPR. As in Britain, it

---

114. Ibid., p. 63.

115. Interview with the author (11 April 2001).

116. Interview with defense ministry official (2 April 2001).

117. David S. Yost, *NATO Transformed* (Washington: United States Institute of Peace Press, 1998), pp. 207–217.

118. Jacques Chirac, "Le besoin d'une Europe forte," *Regard européen* (August 2000) (emphasis added).

119. Moravcsik (1999), pp. 193–196.

intensified with the significant steps toward political integration in the 1990s.[120] The RPR's 1993 electoral programs called for France to avoid the "federalist temptation" and "guarantee against an uncontrolled expansion of areas of the Community."[121]

The party was deeply divided over the Maastricht Treaty, abstaining from the final ratification vote. Anderson estimates that two-thirds of the party opposed the treaty's provisions on Common Foreign and Security Policy, even though they are located in a separate "pillar" in which decision-making is almost completely intergovernmental and predicated on unanimity.[122] The fight against the treaty was organized by two figures from the right wing of the party, Charles Pasqua and Phillipe Séguin. The latter led the charge in parliament, proposing an amendment that would sink the treaty that received the votes of almost half the Gaullist deputies in the National Assembly. His was a unilateralist critique akin to that in Britain. "One is sovereign or one does not exist!" declared Séguin. Sovereignty could not be shared or limited. Maastricht amounted to the "anti-Luxembourg compromise."[123] The treaty provisions in the areas of foreign and security policy would not remain inter-governmental for long, he said, raising the specter of a slippery slope leading toward a federal European state.

Yet unlike in Britain, these objections did not inhibit progress on ESDP. Chirac is sensitive to sovereignty concerns as well, and has recently backed a vision of Europe as a federation of nation-states preserving the independence of its members. However, he is inclined to support collaboration in defense provided it remains intergovernmental. The president's wish for France to play an influential role in crisis management, clear in his efforts

120. Guyomarch et al. write: "The passage of the SEA with surprisingly little debate reflects the presentation of the Single Market programme as its central feature. In contrast, there was no possibility of packaging the Maastricht Treaty as essentially about the abolition of non-tariff barriers. Its highly symbolic features—a European Union, European citizenship, the voting rights for non-French nationals, a single European currency, a common foreign and security policy, the co-decision making between the Council and the European Parliament—could not be ignored by any strong nationalist within the Centre-Right." See Alain Guyomarch, Howard Machin, and Ella Ritchie, *France in the European Union* (New York: St. Martin's, 1998), p. 120.

121. Rassemblement pour la Republique, *Avec le RPR* (1993 election manifesto); Rassemblement pour la Republique, *20 réformes pour changer la France* (1993).

122. Stephanie B. Anderson, "The Amsterdam CFSP Components: A Lowest Common Denominator Agreement," *Current Politics and Economics of Europe*, Vol. 10, No. 2 (2000), p. 110.

123. See Philippe Seguin, *Journal officiel* (5 May 1992), p. 865. Sixty-three deputies abstained from the vote, while only one voted against Seguin's proposal. See Annexe au procès-verbal, *Journal officiel* (5 May 1992), p. 884. On the right's campaign against Maastricht see Andrew Appleton, "Maastricht and the French Party System: Domestic Implications of the Treaty Referendum," *French Politics and Society*, Vol. 10, No. 4 (1992), pp. 1–18; Byron Criddle, "The French Referendum on the Maastricht Treaty," *Parliamentary Affairs*, Vol. 46, No. 2 (1993), pp. 228–238; James Shields, "The French Gaullists," in John Gaffney (ed.), *Political Parties and the European Union* (London: Routledge, 1996).

to reform the French military to make it more rapidly deployable, is more important than potential future threats to French decision-making autonomy.[124] His cause is helped by the wide prerogatives of the French president in foreign affairs and his insulation from partisan pressure. As was the case in Bosnia, the institutional autonomy of the *domaine réservé* allows him to deflect right-wing criticism in a way the British government could not. A senior civil servant said, "The real problem is the 'sovereignists.' They think that Europe is antagonistic to the continued existence of the French nation." The sovereignists include Séguin, Pasqua, and the head of the far right National Front, Jean-Marie Le Pen. However, their influence on the president, for whom "the need to use Europe as another channel of influence is not questioned," is "marginal."[125]

Multilateralism as Means and End: The French Left and European Defense Cooperation

The Socialists justify their support for ESDP differently, focusing on its pragmatic functions but also situating it in a larger multilateral strategy of building Europe. Socialists claim not to be interested in *grandeur* and *rang*. Defense Minister Richard's adviser said: "If our goal was to gain influence, we would do it through NATO, which is not our intention. Encouraging European defense is our normal reflex to reinforce Europe because in military operations, like in currency questions, reinforcing France alone makes no sense."[126] For this reason, the party is now more skeptical of NATO than its rightist counterparts, putting it in line with the antimilitarism of other leftist parties, although this is a more mainstream sentiment in France. The Socialists largely opposed the RPR's steps toward rapprochement. In reaction to the right's participation in NATO bodies, Paul Quilès, one of the most influential defense experts in the party, complained that if France were to give up some of its military sovereignty, it should do so in service of the European Union. He complained that no efforts were being made to integrate the WEU and the EU.[127] However, if the Socialists had won the 1993 and 1995 elections there is, paradoxically, strong reason to believe that ESDP would have never moved forward, given that improving relations with NATO were a precondition for this.

124. On the president's European vision, see Jacques Chirac, *Mon engagement pour la France* (2002 presidential election manifesto). On military reforms, see Sten Rynning, "French Defence Reforms and European Security: Tensions and Intersections," *European Foreign Affairs Review*, Vol. 4, No. 1 (1999), pp. 99–119.

125. Interview with the author (25 April 2001).

126. Interview with French official (20 March 2001)

127. Paul Quilès, "Défense européenne et OTAN: La dérive," *Le Monde* (11 June 1996); Bremer et al. (2002), p. 61.

The consensus on European defense cooperation is therefore not a Gaullist one, but, as in Bosnia and Kosovo, the proverbial coalition of Baptists and bootleggers. Advisers to Prime Minister Lionel Jospin and Defense Minister Richard both rejected the characterization of ESDP as the realization of a long-standing Gaullist goal. The former said: "European defense is more Socialist than Gaullist. It was the Gaullists who broke up the European Defense Community in 1954. The impetus was provided by Mitterrand with the Eurocorps and Maastricht. The Socialists are quite at ease with the concept of a European defense." In fact, according to the latter, "What is ironic is that it is a Gaullist president who is heading this, not that Socialists are creating a more autonomous Europe." They are cynical about Chirac's motivations. "You have to be pro-European to get elected president today in France," said Richard's adviser about the president's support for European defense.[129]

The Socialists' more multilateral approach toward Europe manifests itself in their support for "shared sovereignty" and political integration, including the strengthening of European institutions such as the European Parliament and the introduction of majority voting into the Common Foreign and Security Policy.[130] This belief in adding military matters to the broader process of European integration formed part of the Socialists' public marketing of the initiative as well and differentiated them from the Gaullists.[131] As in Britain and Germany, this perspective on international politics opens up possibilities for addressing certain practical problems. Defense Minister Richard's adviser pointed to Kosovo: "The Americans were hesitating, and the Europeans realized that they had no means to implement alone a decision taken by their own heads of state and government. That is simply politically unacceptable to the European Union, to be in a position to make decisions according to the Amsterdam Treaty but not to be in a position to implement them without somebody else."[132] This means that the "European Union needs more than a plastic sword. We want Europe to have a minimum capability to take autonomous decisions and execute them," said Jospin's aide.[133] The Socialists would use this capacity for inclusive purposes. The influence of the Second Left's notion of a right of interference can be seen in recent party

128. Interview with the author (9 April 2001).

129. Interview with the author (20 March 2001).

130. Parti Socialiste, *Le contrat pour la France* (1993 election manifesto); Lionel Jospin, *Changeons d'avenir* (1995 presidential election manifesto); Parti socialiste and les Verts, *Texte politique commune* (28 January 1997).

131. Védrine (1999).

132. Interview with the author (20 March 2001).

133. Interview with the author (9 April 2001). See also the interview with Richard in "Défense européenne: L'ardente obligation," *Politique internationale,* No. 85 (Autumn 1999).

documents that pledge to establish a "global doctrine of intervention" for the EU in cases of human rights violations.[134]

At the beginning of the 1990s, France's more extreme leftist parties, like the more antimilitarist German leftist parties, were skeptical of a defense role for the European Union. The Greens expressed a vague desire for a "security community" in Western Europe predicated on disarmament and a strengthening of the OSCE.[135] The Communists criticized European plans for rapid reaction forces, claiming that the principles underlying France's security must rest on more than the use of force. Again, the party opposed military means, not humanitarian missions. Its parliamentary leader, Georges Hage, said: "A rapid reaction force, yes! An intervention force, no!"[136] Again the OSCE was a more attractive option.

As with the German left, however, this perspective evolved as a result of the experience that the Greens accumulated during the 1990s. The Greens' position changed as the party's antimilitarism waned. This allowed their more intense multilateralism, a reflection of their more extreme egalitarianism, to come through. By the time of the Kosovo war, the Greens were advocating going further than the Socialists in terms of political integration, calling for an integrated European armed force under the permanent control of the United Nations for humanitarian interventions. Like the German Greens they also insisted on an accompanying civilian policing capacity.[137] This meant that European defense cooperation was easily accepted by the plural left coalition when it became a possibility in 1999.

The empirical evidence lends further credence to the partisan argument discussed earlier in the context of humanitarian intervention. Developments in Britain, Germany, and France were necessary conditions for moving forward. A less unilateralist, and therefore more pragmatic, British Labour Party was able to maneuver around the constraints set by a largely Euroskeptical political culture to establish the structures for intergovernmental cooperation in crisis management that the Conservative Party had opposed. The German left could support such cooperation because of the lessons drawn from Bosnia and the fact that it did not rely purely on military means but also included civilian elements. For the German right, ESDP furthered normalization. British and German fears about France's intentions were

---

134. Conseil national du Parti socialiste, *Le projet internationale des Socialistes* (6 October 2001).

135. *Protocole d'accord entre les Verts et Génération Ecologie* (17 November 1992). This was repeated in a common platform with the Socialists. Parti socialiste and les Verts (1997).

136. Georges Hage, *Journal officiel* (31 May 1995), pp. 431–432. See also (12 April 1994), pp. 694–695.

137. Marie-Hélène Aubert, *Journal officiel* (26 March 1999), p. 2980; "Plus sérieuse, plus proche des Français et quasi exclusivement centrée sur les problèmes de défense," *Les Echos* (15 April 1999); "Les socialistes et les chevènementistes confirment leur alliance," *Le Monde* (11 April 1999).

assuaged by the Gaullists' reinterpretation of their strategy for realizing the longstanding goal of international influence—rapprochement with NATO. Pursuing ESDP in France was made easier by the institutional insulation of the presidency from right-wing sensitivities about national sovereignty. The French left followed along, but for reasons that more closely resembled the British left than its Gaullist opponents.

Somewhat expectedly, the targets for improving defense capabilities have not been met in a time of fiscal austerity in Europe, but three operations overseen by the Political and Security Committee under ESDP have already been launched in 2003. The EU took over the NATO mission designed to create the conditions for peace in Macedonia. Under the leadership of France it launched a peacekeeping operation with a robust mandate in the Bunia region of the Congo to improve the humanitarian situation. It also began its first civilian operation aimed at improving law enforcement capabilities in Bosnia. This flurry of activity demonstrates that the EU is serious about putting ESDP into effect. After ten years of little progress, ESDP finally succeeded, precisely because it was neither a "European army" nor a mere "militarization" of the European Union, nor a bid for a more "European Europe."

CHAPTER 7

Parting Ways

A true liberal democracy without political parties is practically unimaginable. But what does this mean for foreign policy? That democracies are unique actors in international affairs has been confirmed by an enormous literature on the behavior of democracies in the security arena.[1] Nevertheless, the key emphasis has been on the distinction between democratic and nondemocratic *polities*, not on democratic *politics*. Democratic institutions allow for the alternation of governments. They open up the possibility of political debate. Just as important as what type of institutions regulate politics within a given country is who actually governs in democratic countries and what they stand for. What do politicians and parties do with the opportunities that free elections provide?

This book has tried to begin to answer that question. The literature on regime type and international security does not fully open the "black box" of structural arguments to look at the domestic politics inside. It only points to a variety of boxes. I have found that democratic states travel in very different directions and that a sharper focus on internal politics is necessary to account for their paths. Below I review the main theoretical findings and their substantive support. I also include evidence drawn from the approach of four other countries to humanitarian intervention: the United States, Canada, Italy, and Japan. These additional cases show that the political dynamics at work in Britain, France, and Germany are also seen in the other countries of

1. For a thorough review, see Bruce M. Russett and Harvey Starr, "From Democratic Peace to Kantian Peace: Democracy and Conflict in the International System," in Manus I. Midlarsky (ed.), *Handbook of War Studies II* (Ann Arbor: University of Michigan Press, 2000), pp. 93–128.

the G-7, the most advanced industrial democracies in the world. Finally, I apply the partisan argument to the transatlantic and intra-European differences over the war in Iraq in order to show that the explanation fares well in nonhumanitarian contexts.

Analysis of the responses of Britain, France, and Germany to the Bosnian and Kosovo crises and their policies toward European defense cooperation reveals six themes.

At the country level, historical experience is critical for determining the left's choice between antimilitarism and protecting human rights.

Peace enforcement poses a severe value conflict that can lead parties on the left side of the political spectrum in polar opposite directions. Their humanitarian or what I call inclusive impulses spring from their commitment to equality. Leftists have a larger conception of political community than rightists. At home this is seen in their fight for income redistribution and against discrimination. Abroad it is manifest in their support for international development aid, promoting democracy, and granting multilateral institutions some voice in sovereign decision-making when it serves leftist purposes. Peacekeeping causes no problems and finds almost universal acceptance on the left. But peace enforcement violates those same egalitarian values and the left's libertarian tendencies as well. To use force is to compel behavior, to drive wedges between nations and peoples, and to decide through physical violence who is right and who is wrong. Armed action, even with the best of motives, can itself be regarded as a human rights violation, particularly when there is a danger of harming innocent civilians in the process. There is also a belief that it may not be effective, or may lead to an escalatory counterattack.

In these situations, leftists must choose whether antimilitarism is an end in itself or if exceptions are to be made in cases in which human rights are at risk. I found that in those countries with a more positive historical experience in armed conflict, the left *differentiated* between different types of operations and generally came down in favor of peace enforcement. Most salient for all countries under study was the experience of the Second World War. In the victorious Allied countries, Britain and France, the left used the language and logic of deterrence and compellence, stressing the importance of showing resolve and keeping promises to demonstrate credibility. In Germany, where armed conflict is associated with destruction and guilt, the left at least initially eschewed any participation in peace enforcement. It denied any value conflict, arguing that violence inevitably begets more violence, and therefore is an ineffective and morally inappropriate instrument for resolving conflicts, even if the motivation is primarily humanitarian.

Britain's Labour and Liberal Democratic parties drew from their country's victory over fascism in the Second World War. They believed that force could have positive results and criticized the government for "appeasing" the Bosnian Serbs as the British Conservatives had done in the 1930s with Hitler. Both Labour and the Liberal Democrats made an explicit connection between the values they stood for domestically and peace enforcement. While conflicts such as the Cold War and Gulf War were more controversial within the left because of the presence of more exclusive or strategic motivations, Bosnia was an operation it could support. In opposition during the early 1990s, Labour and the Liberal Democrats argued the justness and practicality of more forceful military action, and pleaded with their government to make good on commitments to protect the safe areas for Bosnian Muslims and to refrain from public discussions of withdrawal so as to avoid sending signals of weakness. This was the language of deterrence that had once been the province of the Conservatives.

When in office, the Labour Party was the most vehement advocate of the air war against Milosevic to stop the repression of the Kosovars within Yugoslavia. Human rights and democratic values, Labour reasoned, were universal, and their promotion should not be confined within Britain's borders. In the face of the initial failure of the air war, Britain was the first to escalate both rhetorically and militarily by pushing for a ground campaign and advocating a new right of intervention that trumped sovereignty. This steeled NATO and likely contributed to Milosevic's decision to capitulate. The Liberal Democrats supported the Blair government at every step, sometimes even exceeding the government's enthusiasm since they did not have to manage a hesitant NATO coalition. The British left's conception of a broader political community was also evident in its support for European defense cooperation, the creation of a formal EU institutional framework and set of capabilities for undertaking crisis management operations. This process had been stalled for years before Labour was elected.

The cases of the United States and France provide further support for the argument about the impact of historical experience on the left. The U.S. Democratic and the French Socialist parties were also committed to engaging in the Balkans, with force if necessary. The Clinton and Mitterrand presidencies' policies are reviewed later, but Congressional Democrats and parliamentary Socialists and Greens based their defense of peace enforcement in Bosnia on long-standing ideas about the special role that the United States and France, respectively, have to play in the world as the guardians of freedom and human rights because they were the world's first democracies.[2] In both countries, the self-conception of their nation is not only the protector of its own interests, but also the selfless guarantor of its universal values abroad.[3]

The French left developed the concept of a right of intervention in the internal affairs of other states to promote leftist values, and it set out to convince Socialist president Mitterrand of the need for a stronger policy in Bosnia. The Socialist Party leader and deputies advocated earlier intervention and supported every new mandate that UNPROFOR added. Like the British left, it decried any public discussions of withdrawing peacekeepers as undermining deterrence. The U.S. Democrats also conceived of the national interest broadly and inclusively. Ron Dellums, the former chair of the House Armed Services Committee, argued during a Bosnia debate against "the notion of *narrowly construed vital national interests*" and claimed a responsibility to risk American lives to save those of others in Bosnia.[4] The Democrats' broad conception of community was also evident in comments by Senator Barbara Boxer: "If it is not in the national interest to stop the most god-awful ethnic cleansing since Hitler . . . I do not know what is. We are human beings first and foremost."[5] As in Britain, many others identified upholding human rights as an explicit part of the national interest.[6]

The United States had demonstrated this selfless commitment in its victories in two world wars, particularly in the Second World War when it "saved Europe from fascism."[7] The necessity of American intervention to restore stability to Europe earlier in the century also reaffirmed the indispensable leadership role that the United States must play in Bosnia and Kosovo.[8] There

2. On America's special historical role, see comments in the *Congressional Record* by House minority whip David Bonior (14 December 1995) p. 14861; Senator Ted Kennedy (13 December 1995), p. 18457; Representative Nita Lowey (14 December 1995), p. 14863; Representative John Olver (28 April 1999), p. 2419; Representative Robert Torricelli (14 December 1995), p. 14867.

3. The struggle between exclusivist isolationists on the right and idealistic internationalists on the left is nicely documented by Jeffrey Legro, "Whence American Nationalism?" *International Organization,* Vol. 54, No. 2 (2000) pp. 253–289; Robert Endicott Osgood, *Ideals and Self-Interest in America's Foreign Relations: The Great Transformation of the Twentieth Century* (Chicago: University of Chicago Press, 1954); John Gerard Ruggie, "The Past as Prologue? Interests, Identity, and American Foreign Policy," *International Security,* Vol. 21, No. 4 (1997), pp. 89–125.

4. *Congressional Record* (17 November 1995), p. 13244 (emphasis added).

5. *Congressional Record* (3 May 1995), p. 4531.

6. See comments in the *Congressional Record* by Senator Joseph Biden (13 December 1995), p. 18496; Representative Benjamin Cardin (14 December 1995), p. 14862; Representative Rosa DeLauro (28 April 1999), p. 2447; Representative Nita Lowey (14 December 1995), p. 14863; Representative Nancy Pelosi (13 December 1995), p. 14856.

7. Representative James Moran, *Congressional Record* (14 December 1995), p. 14862. See also Representative Sheila Jackson-Lee (28 April 1999), p. 2426; Senator Ted Kennedy (13 December 1995), p. 18457.

8. David Bonior, *Congressional Record* (14 December 1995), p. 14861. See also Representative Nita Lowey (14 December 1995), p. 14863.

was a token antimilitarist opposition to the Kosovo war, to be discussed later, but the overwhelming majority of the American left opted for defense of human rights rather than a pacifistic rejection of force. Support from Democrats for both the Bosnia and the Kosovo operations was extremely high. Forty-five of 46 senators and 179 of 197 representatives voted in December 1995 to deploy twenty thousand American peacekeepers to Bosnia to guarantee the Dayton Accords. Forty-three of 45 Democratic senators and 181 of 211 representatives voted to support the air campaign in Kosovo.[9]

So far as Bosnia was concerned, the German left's initial position could not have been more different from that of its British and U.S. counterparts. Due to the tremendous destruction of the Second World War and the attendant guilt about the Holocaust, the German left was an antimilitarist left. German history, the Social Democrats and Greens argued, had shown the futility of all wars. They adopted an undifferentiated position on the use of force. The two parties held that the use of force in Bosnia would only escalate the misery in the region, leading to a spiral of violence, and rejected not only German participation but even peace enforcement measures by Western allies. Both parties fought bitterly against any change to the German constitution that would allow the deployment of the military "out of area" in UN peace enforcement operations, regardless of whether the objective was humanitarian or strategic. While the SPD condoned peacekeeping with significant restrictions, the Greens opposed even this. Both described any further steps as a "militarization" of German foreign policy. They preferred instead for Germany to remain a "civilian power," committed to the peaceful resolution of international disputes. This antimilitarist conception of the national interest was also seen in both parties' opposition to creating a military arm for the European Union.

The broader applicability of the argument about the interaction of negative historical experience and party ideology can be seen in the case of Japan. The Japanese left, sharing with its German counterpart a similar historical experience of military defeat and destruction, has also defined itself as an antimilitarist opponent to the right. It initially opposed rearmament and a defense treaty with the United States after 1945 that might embroil Japan in a military conflict. Following the end of the Cold War, it objected

9. On Bosnia, see House Roll Call no. 858 on House Resolution 306 and Senate Roll Call no. 603 on Senate Joint Resolution 44 in the 104th Congress, 1st session. The House debate can be found in the *Congressional Record* (13 December 1995), pp. 14860–14869. The Senate debate can be found in the *Congressional Record* (13 December 1995), pp. 18449–18548. On Kosovo, see House Roll Call no. 103 and Senate Roll Call no. 57, both on Senate Concurrent Resolution 21 in the 106th Congress, 1st session. The House debate can be found in the *Congressional Record* (28 April 1999), pp. 2385–2451. The Senate debate can be found in the *Congressional Record* (23 March 1999), pp. 3110–3118. All text is available at http://thomas.loc.gov/.

vigorously to an expansion of Japan's military role.[10] The Socialist Party argued that the constitution forbade overseas deployment of the Self Defense Forces (SDF) and initially opposed bills proposed by the government to allow for participation in peacekeeping, even resigning in symbolic protest from the legislature before one vote.[11] Like the German Greens, the Japanese Socialists proposed instead an unarmed civilian corps to perform noncombatant tasks.

The Socialist Party and the more moderate Democratic Socialist Party modified their policies over the course of the 1990s, accepting peacekeeping operations as a way of contributing to humanitarianism while demonstrating Japan's peaceful intentions. Socialist Prime Minister Tomiichi Murayama presided over the dispatch of Japanese forces to Cambodia. However, even after the Socialist Party entered office its Executive Committee did not remove the freeze on Japanese participation in the military aspects of peacekeeping such as patrolling borders and disarming warring factions. Unsurprisingly, leftist parties have opposed deployments to provide logistical help to combat operations in Afghanistan and Iraq. The left still considers itself a "pacifist watchdog," but it has attracted little attention given its decimation in the parliament in recent years.[12]

The importance of historical experience is further confirmed by an examination of the debates over peace enforcement in two other countries. While Britain, France and the United States mark the positive extreme and Germany and Japan the negative, Canada and Italy have more ambiguous histories. Consequently the left in both has more ambivalent policies. Canada is proud of its role in the victorious coalition in both world wars. It is therefore not marked by fears that the use of force will prove disastrous. Nevertheless, Canada is a relatively minor power without a strong sense of its ability to make a significant contribution to the military resolution of conflicts, and it has carved out a distinctive niche since the end of the Second World War as the peacekeeper par excellence. Former foreign minister Lester Pearson was the originator of the idea of an impartial police force of interposition between two formerly warring parties. For this solution to the Suez crisis of 1956, he won the Nobel Peace Prize.[13] Since then the Canadians have

10. Thomas Berger, *Cultures of Antimilitarism: National Security in Germany and Japan* (Baltimore: Johns Hopkins University Press, 1998), chaps. 3, 7.

11. Peter J. Woolley, *Japan's Navy: Politics and Paradox, 1971–2000* (Boulder: Lynne Rienner, 2000), p. 120.

12. Aurelia George Mulgan, "International Peacekeeping and Japan's Role: Catalyst or Cautionary Tale?" *Asian Survey*, Vol. 35, No. 12 (December 1995), pp. 1106–1107.

13. On Pearson's efforts, see Barry Cooper, "Canadian Discourse on Peacekeeping," in Michael Keren and Donald Sylvan (eds.), *International Intervention: Sovereignty vs. Responsibility* (London: Frank Cass, 2000).

been a participant in almost all of the dozens of UN peacekeeping operations, contributing over 100,000 troops. In terms of a proportion of its armed forces, it is the largest supplier of blue helmets, a fact noted with pride by Canadian ministers.[14] There is even a national monument dedicated to Canadian peacekeepers. As a result, there is a strong feeling of Canada having a special calling as a neutral force, "a sort of honorary North American Sweden," which finds its most significant support on the left.[15]

It can be argued that this conception of Canada as peacekeeper initially predisposed the Canadian left, dominated by the Liberal Party, toward the peaceful, diplomatic resolution of ethnic conflicts and civil wars during the post–Cold War period, with Canada acting as an honest broker between conflicting sides rather than as an enforcer of just settlements. Unlike Germany, Canada's history did not give it pause about every use of the military. The Liberal Party pressed the more reluctant Progressive Conservative government to send peacekeepers to Bosnia, reminding it of Canada's commitment to human rights.[16] Yet after the Liberals assumed power in late 1993 they were wary of peace enforcement, in particular of air strikes against the Bosnian Serbs. In his justification of Canada's reluctance to use NATO air power for purposes other than the protection of UN peacekeepers, Minister of Foreign Affairs André Ouellet referred to the Canadian "approach to peacekeeping . . . which seeks to promote the prevention of conflicts before they begin, and the peaceful resolution of conflicts already under way."[17] The Liberal Party made its maintenance of eight hundred troops in Bosnia contingent on maintaining that impartial role and cited this as a reason for not retaking Srebrenica. More strikingly, when the hostage crisis made at least the safety of the nation's soldiers in Bosnia a matter of national interest in the exclusive sense for the right in Britain and France, the Canadian left offered no additional troops to the Rapid Reaction Force, even thought its primary purpose was to protect the peacekeepers.[18]

Due to Italy's history, it was even more predisposed than Canada to an antimilitarist approach to peace enforcement. Italy had had virtually no experience since the end of the Second World War in deploying its forces overseas, and its history before that was largely one of military inefficacy.

---

14. Joseph T. Jockel, *Canada and International Peacekeeping* (Washington, D.C.: Center for Strategic and International Studies, 1994), p. 2. For a long list of the missions, see comments by the Minister of National Defense, David Michael Collenette, in the Canadian version of *Hansard* (21 April 1994), cols. 1835–1840.

15. Jockel (1994), p. 21.

16. "Tories Blasted for Inaction over 'Slaughter' in Bosnia," *Toronto Star* (12 August 1992).

17. *Hansard* (25 January 1994), col. 1035. For comments on air strikes, see col. 1100.

18. *Hansard* (21 April 1994), col. 1805. For comments on air strikes, see col. 1805–1810; "No snap Decision on Bosnia, Minister Says," *Toronto Star* (14 July 1995).

The Italian left did not, however, associate the military with disaster and guilt like its counterparts in Germany or Japan. The country had switched sides late in the war, avoiding the tremendous destruction of the other fascist states and allowing it to claim that at least the official government had aided the Allies. Nor did it commit the same sort of atrocities as the other Axis powers. Accordingly, the major leftist party in Italy had serious reservations about peace enforcement, but they were not as severe as in Germany. Italy was not involved in UNPROFOR as UN rules excluded countries neighboring on conflict zones from contributing troops. However, the Democratic Party of the Left, a group of reformed Communists, demanded a pullout of Italian troops from Somalia when the operation escalated beyond peacekeeping. The Greens and the residual Communists concurred. The three parties supported only a purely humanitarian and impartial mandate.[19] Thus, the Canadian and Italian lefts fell somewhere between the German and Japanese lefts on the one hand and the British, French and American on the other as a result of their more ambiguous historical experiences, with the Canadians leaning toward the attitude of the victors and the Italians toward that of the vanquished. They did not reflexively oppose humanitarian intervention as they supported the goals, but could not always will the means.

The first theme deals with differences in leftists across countries. Yet the argument also helps account for differences within the left.

At the individual or party level, placement along the ideological continuum also affects the intensity of leftist politicians' foreign policy preferences and their choices between antimilitarism and human rights.

Individuals at the extreme end of the political spectrum hold on to values more intensely, and therefore have a more difficult time admitting value conflicts. Therefore, in all the countries I examined, even those with a more positive view of the military due to past successes, a portion of the extreme left does not differentiate between humanitarian and strategic military operations, and opposes all uses of force. Their arguments are based on the spiral model. Antimilitarism provides a way of avoiding the trade-offs between protecting human rights and resolving conflicts peacefully. They can logically assert that since violence is both immoral and ineffective, there is no trade-off in non-intervention. In Britain's Labour Party, this group was led by Tony Benn, a long-time leader of the party's left wing; in France by the Communists; and in the United States by a small number

19. "Fabbri Defends Troops' Role in UN Actions in Somalia," *FBIS,* Western Europe (21 June 1993).

of liberal Democratic legislators organized by Dennis Kucinich.[20] In Bosnia, these groups supported the delivery of humanitarian aid and balked at any suggestion of withdrawing the peacekeepers but opposed any expansion of the blue helmets' mission to include enforcement tasks. In Kosovo, they opposed the initiation and escalation of air strikes and pleaded for a resumption of diplomatic negotiations. However, in these countries, these factions were small and outnumbered even on the extreme left.

While individuals with undifferentiated approaches to the use of force are found almost solely on the extreme left, the extreme left is not exclusively antimilitarist. In those countries in which politicians tend to differentiate, intensity of support for peace enforcement generally increased steadily toward the left of the political spectrum, where commitments to equality are stronger. The most strident proponents of military action against the Bosnian and Yugoslav Serbs were also from the extreme left. In Britain, Robin Cook and Clare Short were their leaders during the Bosnian war, and both were in the Cabinet during the Kosovo war. In France, the Greens urged for stronger action, including a ground war in Kosovo so as to effectively protect the civilian population. In the United States, the proportion of members of Congress voting for deployments to the Balkans increased as ADA scores, a barometer of liberalism, rose.[21] In Canada, the more extreme New Democratic Party demanded a strengthening of the UN mandate in Bosnia to allow for an increase in ground forces to protect the safe areas from Bosnian Serb artillery.[22] In the cases in which these parties were in government, this made for a solid political basis of support for robust intervention.

In those countries in which military action has more of a negative association, the opposite was true. The left was predominantly antimilitarist, and opposition to involvement in peace enforcement increased toward the extreme end of the political spectrum. As previously mentioned the German Greens but also the former Communists in the PDS refused even peacekeeping, while the Social Democrats attached numerous conditions. In Italy, the Communists were the strongest opponents of military deployment abroad. An Italian-led operation to restore order in Albania following the country's economic collapse in 1997 provoked the single most significant crisis in the coalition of leftist parties led by Romano Prodi. The Communists objected to the use

20. For American antimilitarists, see in the *Congressional Record,* Representative Tammy Baldwin (28 April 1999), p. 2396; Representative Rod Blagojevich (28 April 1999), p. 2450; Representative John Conyers (28 April 1999), p. 2410; Representative Dennis Kucinich (28 April 1999), p. 2408; Senator Paul Wellstone (3 May 1999), pp. 4516–4520.

21. Scores can be found at http://adaction.org/voting.html.

22. See comments in *Hansard* by Svend Robinson, the foreign affairs spokesperson (25 January 1994), cols. 1150–1200, as well as Simon de Jong (21 April 1994), col. 1915; (29 May 1995), col. 2215; Nelson Riis (21 April 1994), col. 1910.

of the military for even humanitarian and police purposes. Following their departure, the Prodi government had an easier time approving NATO's October 1998 decision to use air strikes against Yugoslavia. By the time the air war began, however, the Communists had returned to the leftist "Olive Branch" coalition, this time under Prime Minister Massimo D'Alema. Along with the Greens, they demanded pauses in the bombing and threatened to resign from the coalition at several points during the war.[23]

The previous propositions refer to the static parts of the argument. There is also a dynamic element that emerges naturally from the logic of the claim that parties are ideological policy-seekers.

In order to stay true to their values, parties and individuals change their positions in response to new and salient events that seem to disconfirm key elements of their belief system. Nevertheless, significant historical experiences remain crucial for understanding how parties react to new information.

Party positions are not fixed and policy change is not indicative of an abandonment of principles. In fact, the opposite is true. Bosnia was an initial deterrence failure. The experience of the war undermined the belief of the antimilitarist left that protecting human rights and promoting antimilitarism were inextricably linked. This was brought home most vividly by the fall of the safe areas and the subsequent massacres in 1995. Impartial peacekeeping troops were not able to prevent the killing of thousands of civilians. This prompted a painful reorientation of the German Social Democrats and Greens on the question of military intervention, although only for humanitarian purposes. These parties began internal discussions about what it meant to be on the left in foreign policy that triggered important and enduring changes in their foreign policies.

Party members did not move as blocs, however. The process was led by moderates and foreign policy experts in both parties, individuals that cognitive psychologists have identified as being more predisposed toward differentiation. Experts, by virtue of knowing more about an issue, are less inclined to apply general rules to all situations. In both parties, these individuals more quickly discarded an all-encompassing pacifism for a more nuanced approach. Moderates can more easily accept value trade-offs because they are not as

---

23. Rosa Balfour, Roberto Menotti, and Ghita Micieli de Biase, "Italy's Crisis Diplomacy in Kosovo, March–June 1999," *International Spectator*, Vol. 34, No. 3 (1999), p. 70–71; Maurizio Cremasco, "Italy and the Management of International Crises," in Pierre Martin and Mark R. Brawley (eds.), *Alliance Politics, Kosovo, and NATO's War: Allied Force or Forced Allies* (New York: Palgrave, 2000), p. 172; Osvaldo Croci, "Forced Ally? Italy and 'Operation Allied Force,'" in Mark Gilbert and Gianfranco Pasquino (eds.), *Italian Politics: The Faltering Transition* (New York: Berghahn Books, 2000), p. 42.

passionately committed and consequently more able to see the implications of salient events for their previously held beliefs. For this reason, the Social Democrats changed their official policy more quickly, abandoning their opposition to peace enforcement following Srebrenica, while the Greens struggled over the issue for several more years. This reevaluation got a further boost when the red-green coalition entered office in 1998, another factor that induced more differentiation by creating direct responsibility for the consequences of action or inaction. This enabled the vast majority of parliamentarians in both parties to commit to sending German aircraft to Yugoslavia as well as to supporting European defense cooperation. The critical effect of salient events can be seen in sharper relief when compared to Japan. Although the left in that country initially responded identically to peace enforcement in the early 1990s, without the direct experience that the Germans underwent in the Balkans, the Japanese left has not been under the same pressure to question its antimilitarist principles.

Bosnia also seemed to have a galvanizing effect on the Liberal Party government in Canada, although the experience was not nearly as tortuous. The left's previous conception of Canada was as a peacekeeper, not as a civilian power opposed to all use of the armed forces. After Bosnia, the party was heavily influenced by the thinking of Minister of Foreign Affairs Lloyd Axworthy who had been advocating the notion of "human security" as the basis for Canadian foreign policy.[24] At its heart was a focus on individual well-being as opposed to interstate relations. It provided a rationale for attacking a sovereign state akin to Blair's doctrine of international community and figured prominently in the government's justification for intervening in Kosovo. Although Canada only provided eighteen aircraft, these 2 percent of coalition planes undertook 10 percent of the missions with a much higher average of success than other countries. Although not as strident as the Labour government in Britain, the Liberals did begin to openly plan and argue for a ground invasion quite early in the conflict, far ahead of the NATO curve.[25]

In Kosovo, the NATO countries quickly did what they had struggled for years to do in Bosnia, namely to use overwhelming air power against the Serbs. Yet the Kosovo war was an initial compellence failure. The situation on the ground for the Kosovar Albanians deteriorated significantly in the first weeks of the conflict as Yugoslavia raised the ante with an ethnic cleansing

24. Lloyd Axworthy, "Canada and Human Security: The Need for Leadership," *International Journal*, Vol. 52, No. 2 (1997), pp. 183–196.

25. Wesley K. Clark, *Waging Modern War: Bosnia, Kosovo and the Future of Combat* (New York: Public Affairs, 2001), p. 261; Kim Richard Nossal and Stéphane Roussel, "Canada and the Kosovo War: The Happy Follower," in Martin and Brawley (2000) pp. 183–188.

campaign that drove millions from their homes. If Bosnia had seemed to indicate the importance of credibility and resolve, Kosovo initially showed that force was no panacea. Leftist politicians again adjusted their policies to stay true to their ideology. Those who had only recently embraced peace enforcement were less willing to wait to see if the air war would have an effect and quickly called for NATO to return to the table with Yugoslavia. For them, the air campaign confirmed their worst fears about spiraling, escalating violence. The German Green Party called for a bombing pause. The Social Democrats balked at this but ruled out a ground invasion.

However, in those countries with more positive histories with the use of force, resolve generally stiffened as the atrocities convinced the left of the justness of the cause, most notably in Britain. The same occurred in more muted form in France and the United States for reasons discussed below. Historical experience was again critical, this time for determining whether the left remained interventionist and inclusive or shifted back to pacifism. In the United States only a few individuals such as liberal Senator Paul Wellstone made this change. In Canada, with a more ambiguous history to draw from, the turn away from war encompassed an entire party but did not reach far into the center-left. The New Democratic Party backed the Kosovo war at the outset, but the ethnic cleansing and the ineffectiveness of air strikes gave the party pause. Three weeks into the war, party representatives began to call for a return to diplomacy and a complete halt to the bombing with fewer conditions than NATO had stipulated.[26] Thus, the endurance of leftist parties during peace enforcement operations is also a function of the historical experience of their countries.

Unless rightist parties instrumentalize a humanitarian intervention for other purposes, they generally oppose peace enforcement since it is not considered to be a vital national interest. Any support they do offer is shallower since it is not grounded in ideological commitment. Their usual emphasis on demonstrating credibility and resolve is not nearly as pronounced.

Rightist parties have a more exclusive conception of the national interest and do not feel the same extent of obligation to those in other countries as do leftist parties. This is in keeping with their less inclusive domestic policy agenda. For instance, they generally guard against the extensive use of

26. For the initial position, see comments by foreign affairs spokesperson Svend Robinson, *Hansard* (24 March 1999), col. 1530–1540. See later comments by Alexa McDonough, the head of the party (12 April 1999), cols. 1425–1640; Svend Robinson (12 April 1999), cols. 1945–1955. Also Bill Blaikie (12 April 1999), cols. 2520–2635; Libby Davies (12 April 1999), cols. 2950–2955; Yvon Godin (27 April 1999), cols. 1130–1140; Peter Mancini (27 April 1999), col. 1610; Lorne Nystrom (27 April 1999), col. 1155; Judy Wasylycia-Leis (27 April 1999), col. 1555.

the state for redistributive purposes, although this varies significantly among different types of rightist parties. They are also less concerned with preventing discrimination on the basis of gender, sexual preference, or race. This weaker commitment to equality translates into a general opposition to extensive involvement in righting wrongs in other countries by force. Although some members of rightist parties feel a compunction to rally around the troops once they are committed, this does not overcome their distaste for peace enforcement as a whole.

This exclusive ideology is of crucial importance for understanding Britain's response to the crises in the Balkans. With the support of moderates in the party, the Conservative Major government was willing to dispatch a few thousand peacekeepers to the Balkans, but the deteriorating situation in Bosnia translated into increasing discontent among backbenchers, particularly in the right wing. They argued primarily that a war in the Balkans did not justify endangering British soldiers but added other arguments to buttress this central contention. Intervention would not help in a civil war in a region bedeviled by ancient ethnic hatreds where all sides were guilty of atrocities and military action was impossible. As pressure to do more grew, the government embraced this rhetoric of the right wing. The Tory government was almost always the least enthusiastic in deliberations in the Security Council and NATO about how much enforcement to add to UNPROFOR's mandate. For instance, the Tory government helped water down the concept of protection in the safe area resolution so that it applied only to the peacekeepers themselves. The soldiers were not safe, however, and the government refused to reinforce them for fear of provoking the Bosnian Serbs. The right was only worried about credibility and sending strong signals in cases in which tangible national interests were at stake. This narrower conception of political community also meant that the Conservatives were opposed to a European Union competence in defense because of fears that it would encroach on sovereign decision-making.

This lack of resolve, however, contributed to a situation that put British soldiers at risk, most clearly in the hostage crisis of May 1995. Only once the safety of troops was tangibly threatened, a true national interest in the exclusive sense, did the Conservatives take action by sending thousands of reinforcements with heavy weapons. The government passed on an opportunity to use this force to warn the Bosnian Serb forces about further offensives against the safe areas, however. It did not even leave the Rapid Reaction Force's mandate ambiguous. Instead, ministers publicly claimed that it was purely for the protection of the peacekeepers. They accompanied these statements with public musings about withdrawal. The party exhibited this same lack of concern with credibility in the Kosovo war when it demanded that the Labour government rule out the use of ground forces at the very beginning of the conflict, derided Blair's notion of a right of intervention, and criticized every NATO misstep.

The British Conservatives were not unique on the right. In the early 1990s, the partisan debate in the United States and Canada over a Bosnian intervention was similar to that in Britain. The Republican George H. W. Bush administration showed no interest in sending troops to Bosnia, even as peacekeepers, and couched their objection in terms familiar on the right. Former national security adviser Brent Scowcroft explained that engagement in Bosnia was not justified for an administration that was "heavily national interest–oriented." He added, "If it stayed contained in Bosnia, it might have been horrible, but it did not affect us."[27] Secretary of State James Baker put this exclusivist opposition more colorfully when he declared that the United States "does not have a dog in this fight."[28]

The George H. W. Bush administration's exclusive conception of the national interest led to the familiar characterization of the conflict as an ancient feud in which all sides had committed great crimes, taking place in a region whose geography forbade military action.[29] The administration settled first on the lack of a vital interest, then worked backward to justify its course. It even refused to recognize the existence of detention camps until an intrepid journalist exposed them.[30] This was not for lack of intelligence but because of lack of interest, according to a former State Department aide: "The intelligence community is responsive to what the bosses want to know. . . . [W]hen the higher-ups are blaming the killings on the victims, you aren't going to get much intelligence."[31] Although public support for a peacekeeping operation was around 80 percent and the Democratic Senate had approved funding, the president balked.[32] This introduced an asymmetry in the exposure of American and European soldiers to risk that was perhaps the primary obstacle for the Clinton administration in defining a common transatlantic position over the next three years.

The lack of a vital national interest in the Balkans was the overwhelming reason cited by Congressional Republicans as well, even in the case of peacekeeping. The House Republicans campaigned in 1994 against extensive commitments of U.S. forces to UN missions, promising to "ensure that U.S.

27. Samantha Power, *"A Problem from Hell": America and the Age of Genocide* (New York: Harper Collins, 2002), p. 288.

28. Elizabeth Drew, *On the Edge: The Clinton Presidency* (New York: Simon and Schuster, 1994), p. 139.

29. Power (2002), p. 283.

30. David Halberstam, *War in a Time of Peace: Bush, Clinton, and the Generals* (New York: Simon and Schuster, 2001), pp. 130–134.

31. Power (2002), p. 281.

32. Ibid., p. 283.

troops are only deployed to support missions in America's national security interests." Their manifesto, the *Contract for America,* accused the Clinton administration of "raiding the defense budget to fund social welfare programs and UN peacekeeping programs," equal nemeses for a party taking a decisive turn to the right.[33]

Almost every single Republican speaker in both houses during the debates over Bosnia and Kosovo objected to the lack of tangible American concerns in the region. Phil Gramm, a Republican candidate for president, derided President Clinton for running "our Nation's foreign policy as if it were social work," recognizing the left's link between domestic and foreign policy and dismissing both.[34] The right had a narrower conception of political community and consequently a narrower conception of the national interest than the left. Republicans frequently stated that they could not justify the loss of American lives to save Bosnians.[35] Only interests like stability and access to oil in the Gulf signified threats critical enough to justify the use of force.[36] As in Britain, Republicans noted the foreign policy realignment of the post–Cold War era and expressed perplexity over the fact that many Democratic members of Congress who had opposed the Gulf War would want to send troops to Bosnia and Kosovo, even those on the left who were usually antagonistic to the armed forces.[37] U.S. Republicans utilized numerous other arguments against participation identical to those of the Tories about the practicality, legality, and morality of intervention. These arguments tended to be brought up by Congress's most conservative representatives, including Dan Burton, Phil Gramm, Tom DeLay, and John Ashcroft, suggesting that marshaling numerous arguments was a sign of intense opposition and that the lack of vital U.S. interests in the Balkans was the real objection.[38]

33. Ed Gillespie and Bob Schellhas (eds.), *Contract with America: The Bold Plan by Rep. Newt Gingrich, Rep. Dick Armey, and the House Republicans to Change the Nation* (New York: Times Books, 1994), pp. 91–92.

34. *Congressional Record* (13 December 1995), p. 18455.

35. See, for instance, comments in the *Congressional Record* by Representative Jay Kim (17 November 1995), p. 13245: "[B]osnian lives are not worth more than American lives." Also Senator Kay Bailey Hutchinson (13 December 1995), p. 18449: "I remain to be convinced that we have a greater moral obligation to the Bosnians than we do to our own soldiers and their families."

36. In the *Congressional Record,* see Representative Dan Burton (28 April 1999), p. 2388; Representative Randy Cunningham (28 April 1999), p. 2416; Senator Dan Coats (13 December 1995), p. 18452; Representative Henry Hyde (14 December 1995), p. 14864.

37. Representative Stephen Buyer said sarcastically: "When vital national security interests are at stake, vote no. But vote yes to send troops in harm's way to an ill-conceived, poorly defined and highly dangerous mission." *Congressional Record* (17 November 1995), p. 13244. "Those from the left attempt to use a vehicle they neither support, understand or even loathe at times." Randy Cunningham (28 April 1999), p. 2416. See also Bob Dornan (13 December 1995), p. 14840.

38. In the *Congressional Record,* see Senator John Ashcroft (13 December 1995), p. 18494; Representative Dan Burton (28 April 1999), p. 2388; Senator Dan Coats (13 December 1995), pp. 18452–18453; Representative Tom DeLay (28 April 1999), p. 2415; Representative Bob Dornan (14

Once they won legislative majorities in 1994 they attacked the Clinton administration with a vengeance. Not only did the House Republicans vote 219 to 11 against deploying peacekeepers to Bosnia, they passed a resolution preventing the use of Defense Department funding for such an operation.[39] Although it had no effect without Senate passage, House Resolution 2606 served as a powerful signal of Congressional opposition to an American security presence for those negotiating the Dayton peace accords at the time. The timing of the initiative shows that Republicans were concerned less about the credibility of American commitment during the talks than about preventing deployments of American armed forces for humanitarian purposes they did not support.

The Kosovo war led to a reprise of these events. The House refused a resolution supporting the campaign even well after it had started, with 187 of 222 Republicans voting against even though this could have been construed as a tangible lack of resolve at a crucial time in the conflict.[40] Concurrently 127 House Republicans, over half, opposed the war enough to vote in favor of a resolution whose object was to remove U.S. forces from the operation altogether.[41] Another resolution to withhold funding for any possible ground invasion found almost unanimous Republican backing and passed after the onset of hostilities with only 16 Republicans opposed.[42] The opposition was organized by the right-wing party whip, Tom DeLay, and according to some reports against Speaker Dennis Hastert's will. Senate opinion was less opposed to war, which has led some observers to mistakenly argue that there was a firm bipartisan consensus. However, the bedrock of that support was a group of only three Republicans—Richard Lugar, Chuck Hagel, and John McCain. All were not coincidentally members of the Senate Foreign Relations Committee, those politicians who consider all angles of a particular conflict due to their high level of knowledge about international affairs. They weighed not only whether safeguarding human rights in Kosovo was

---

December 1995), p. 14866; Senator Bill Frist (13 December 1995), p. 18472; Senator Phil Gramm (13 December 1995), p. 18455; Senator Tim Hutchinson (3 May 1999), pp. 4521–4523; Senator James Inhofe (3 May 1999), p. 4537.

39. For the peacekeeping deployment vote, see Roll Call no. 858 in the 104th Congress, 1st session. The House debate can be found in the *Congressional Record* (13–14 December 1995), pp. 14825–14869. On cutting off funding, see Roll Call no. 814 and H.R. 2606 in the same Congress. The debate is in the *Congressional Record* (17 November 1995), pp. 13222–13247.

40. See Roll Call no. 103 on Senate Concurrent Resolution 21 in the 106th Congress, 1st session. The House debate can be found in the *Congressional Record* (28 April 1999), pp. 2385–2400.

41. See Roll Call no. 101 on House Concurrent Resolution 82 in the 106th Congress, 1st session. The House debate is in the *Congressional Record* (12 April 1999), pp. 2414–2441.

42. See Roll Call no. 100 on H.R. 1569 in the 106th Congress, 1st session. The House debate is in the *Congressional Record* (12 April 1999), pp. 2400–2413.

in the national interest, but also how success or failure would affect other, more vital, U.S. interests. As expected, these three rightist politicians voiced their concerns loudest after the United States committed its forces, arguing that losing the war would severely damage American and NATO credibility and that no option could therefore be taken off the table.[43] They were, however, overshadowed and outnumbered by Republican opponents, particularly in the House, whose actions likely had a significant influence on Clinton's Balkans policy, as I will discuss later.

The same processes were at work in Canada as well. The center-right Progressive Conservative Party government under Prime Minister Brian Mulroney committed Canadian peacekeepers in fall 1992, but the party imploded in the 1993 elections and its place on the right side of the political spectrum was filled by the more ideological Reform Party, later renamed the Canadian Alliance. The party initially called for a withdrawal of Canadian troops in conjunction with a complete multilateral removal of UNPROFOR. However, as the situation in Bosnia worsened, the party embraced a unilateral move.[44] Spokesperson Bob Mills echoed British Prime Minister John Major when he declared during the hostage crisis that to leave "would in no way be a humiliation for Canada," and followed the example of British Foreign Secretary Malcolm Rifkind when he raised the specter of an escalation if more force was applied.[45] Also present was the now familiar refrain about the fighting abilities that the Serbs had demonstrated against the Germans in the Second World War, the multitude of hot spots across the globe not receiving attention, the thousand-year history of Balkan grievances, the ethnic cleansing on both sides, and the internal character of the war.[46] The party protested against the air campaign in August 1995 again for fear of escalation and, like the U.S. Republicans, opposed even the use of Canadian peacekeepers in IFOR following the conclusion of peace talks.[47]

In Kosovo, the party was no more resolute. Like the British Conservatives, the Reform Party leadership pledged support for the air campaign, but almost all backbench speakers expressed their distaste for the war. To the almost identical litany of arguments against intervention, they added the additional points

---

43. Ivo Daalder and Michael O'Hanlon, *Winning Ugly: NATO's War to Save Kosovo* (Washington: Brookings Institution Press, 2000), p. 132.

44. "Canada's Peacekeeping Dilemma: Reform MP Wants Deadline Set for Pulling Troops Out of Bosnia," *Toronto Star* (6 January 1994); "Mission Impossible?: The Mythology of Canada's Blue Berets Is under Attack," *Toronto Star* (1 July 1995).

45. *Hansard* (29 May 1995), col. 1930.

46. In *Hansard* see Jack Frazer (25 January 1994), col. 1140; (21 April 1994), col. 1825; Jim Hart (21 April 1994), col. 1935; Allan Kerpan (21 April 1994), col. 1905; Ian McClelland (29 May 1995), col. 2155; Bob Mills (25 January 1994), col. 1155; John Williams (29 May 1995), col. 2050.

47. "Canada's Role in Attack Criticized," *Vancouver Sun* (31 August 1995); "NATO Team Arrives in Bosnia," *Vancouver Sun* (5 December 1995).

that Serbia was a sovereign country and that NATO should remain a defensive alliance.[48] Even the remnants of the more moderate Progressive Conservative Party were overwhelmingly negative.[49] It is almost certain that the Canadian right, uncomfortable with an air campaign, would have opposed a land invasion of Kosovo. Therefore, Reform's persistent calls for a debate on a possible ground deployment almost from the beginning of the air war were likely a vehicle to speak against such an action even after the war had begun. As with the British and American right, credibility and signaling mattered to Reform only in interventions that served strategic goals.

Peace enforcement can serve purposes other than simply protecting minorities against repression or stopping civil wars that might justify a more forceful posture. A number of such interests were involved in the countries under study. The German right would have likely favored intervention in Bosnia in any case due to the large number of refugees the country took in and the implications for stability in a region more significant for Germany than for any other country except perhaps Italy. It is not a coincidence that these two countries were the only ones in which all sections of the right accepted at least some degree of intervention. More importantly for Germany, participation in UN operations, such as those in Yugoslavia and Somalia, opened a convenient avenue for gradually reducing constitutional and political restrictions on deploying the armed forces overseas. The European Union was also seen as an instrument for military intervention abroad. Contrary to culturalist claims that pacifism was historically rooted in the German political system, the antimilitarist consensus on German foreign policy only firmly encompassed the left. The rightist CDU and Christian Social Union played hawk to the Greens and Social Democrats' dove.

The conservative coalition quickly changed its interpretation of the constitution almost immediately following the end of the Cold War, claiming that it allowed German participation in UN or NATO operations. It gradually escalated the scale of involvement, including monitoring the embargo in the Adriatic against Serbia and enforcing the no-fly zone over Bosnia, in hopes of establishing precedents and provoking a constitutional ruling it believed would go in its favor. It also hoped to habituate a wary German public to the

---

48. For negative views, see in *Hansard* remarks by Diana Abloncz (12 April 1999), col. 2445; Reed Elley (12 April 1999), cols. 2830–2835; Ken Epp (27 April 1999), col. 1715; Paul Forseth (12 April 1999), cols. 3025–3030; Deborah Grey (27 April 1999), col. 1415; Jay Hill (27 April 1999), col. 1530; Bob Mills (27 April 1999), cols. 1050–1100; Deepak Obhrai (12 April 1999), cols. 3055–3100; John Williams (12 April 1999), col. 3015; Ted White (27 April 1999), cols. 1030–1040, 1705–1710. Only Leon Benoit spoke in favor (27 April 1999), col. 2325.

49. For negative views, see in *Hansard* (12 April 1999) comments by Scott Brison, cols. 2740–2750; Norman Doyle, col. 2215; Charlie Power, col. 2305; David Price, col. 2055. They used the same arguments as the Reform Party. For a positive view, see only Peter MacKay, col. 1660.

idea of actively using the Bundeswehr internationally. After its legal victory, the CDU continued this process. It contributed aircraft as part of the Rapid Reaction Force to help detect and eliminate Bosnian Serb air defenses. The conservative coalition dispatched peacekeepers to IFOR in December 1995 and the next year went as far as to allow German ground troops on Bosnian soil. Their presence in an area where German soldiers had committed grave crimes fifty years before was the culmination of an incredibly rapid normalization process. The right's more interventionist position persisted following the success of its "habituation" strategy primarily because Germany, more than other European countries, was affected by an influx of refugees and regional instability—additional instrumental considerations.

As with the left, the parallels between the Japanese and the German right are striking, showing that the party ideology argument stands up well. Culturalist scholars argued that as with Germany, the end of the Cold War would lead to no significant change in Japan's hesitance to deploy the SDF abroad, citing again the cross-partisan consensus on national security.[50] Article 9 of the Japanese constitution forbids the use of Japanese armed forces for purposes other than self-defense, which has subsequently been interpreted as generally forbidding the overseas deployment of the SDF in a combatant role. Yet the Japanese right began to remove political restrictions on the dispatch of the SDF almost immediately after 1989, a process driven by a group of "neoconservatives" who explicitly aim, like the German Christian Democrats, to make their country normal again.

The rightist Liberal Democratic Party (LDP), the dominant political force in Japan, first proposed in October 1990 a United Nations Peace Cooperation Bill to govern the use of the Japanese armed forces in overseas missions in a noncombatant capacity so as to allow Japan to contribute to the coalition in the first Gulf War. The bill's chief engineer was the LDP's secretary general, Ichiro Ozawa, who later headed a special LDP study group on Japan's role in the international community, charged with providing an intellectual foundation for the position that Japan should gain a higher foreign policy profile. Ozawa and other conservatives such as Nakashini Keisuke, a former director of Japan's Defense Agency, have argued, like prominent German Christian Democrats, that no constitutional change is necessary for Japan to participate in the full range of UN activities, including peace enforcement operations. For these conservatives, humanitarian interventions are instruments for reaching a different goal.[51]

50. Peter J. Katzenstein, *Cultural Norms and National Security: Police and Military in Postwar Japan* (Ithaca: Cornell University Press, 1996), pp. 124–128; Berger (1998), pp. 178–185.

51. On this political faction, see Mulgan (1995). Also Aurelia George, "Japan's Participation in U.N. Peacekeeping Operations: Radical Departure or Predictable Response?" *Asian Survey*, Vol. 33, No. 6. (June 1993), pp. 560–575.

A bill allowing participation in limited peacekeeping activities was passed in 1992, clearing the way for Japan's first international deployment of over seven hundred soldiers to the UN mission in Cambodia.[52] This was followed by smaller presences in Mozambique, Rwanda, and the Golan Heights. In December 2001, the conservative coalition lifted a freeze that had limited SDF participation to those activities least likely to lead to military engagement such as election monitoring, administration, medical provision, and reconstruction, and expanded soldiers' ability to use force to protect others under their control, such as refugees, UN personnel, and other peacekeeping forces.[53] More significantly, in October 2001 the coalition gained passage of an antiterrorism bill that enabled Japanese forces to provide logistical support for the U.S. war against the Taliban in Afghanistan. This was the first Japanese deployment in a military operation other than peacekeeping. The conservative government is providing logistical support for U.S. occupying troops in Iraq, and there is growing discussion about a constitutional amendment removing restrictions on a combat role. Culturalist expectations have not held up.

The French right also supported the interventions in the Balkans and European defense cooperation for instrumental purposes, but these differed from those of Germany and Japan. Participation in multilateral peace operations was part of a new twist on a long-standing Gaullist goal of maintaining French influence in foreign affairs. In the immediate post–Cold War period, resolving ethnic conflicts and civil wars were among the most important international issues on the agenda, and the Gaullists were determined for France to remain relevant. Therefore what appeared to the British and American right as a somewhat trivial matter was of keen importance to the French right. Finding peace in Bosnia and Kosovo resonated well with Gaullist rhetoric, which had always blended leftist and rightist themes and trumpeted France as having an exceptional role to play in the world. Building an EU capacity for undertaking these type of operations would also help to increase Europe's and therefore France's voice on the international stage. Only the extreme right, primarily the National Front, argued forcefully against involvement in the Balkans and European defense cooperation.

After the French right trounced the Socialists in the 1993 parliamentary elections, the parliamentary coalition of the RPR and the UDF put France front-and-center on the Bosnian issue. Foreign Minister Alain Juppé brokered two of the more important Western initiatives, the creation of the safe areas and the Sarajevo ultimatum. There were limits to the uniqueness of the

52. For a good review of the bills, see Woolley (2000).
53. "Diet Approves Bill That Boosts SDF Role as Peacekeepers," *Japan Times* (8 December 2001).

French right, however. Less conspicuously, the Gaullists began to draw down French troops in the Balkans almost immediately following their election. As the costs mounted, the right's policy increasingly resembled that of rightist parties elsewhere. This trend was only stopped by President Chirac's personal intervention in Bosnian affairs after French peacekeepers were taken hostage shortly after his election in spring 1995. This brings us to the next major finding.

Parties can more easily implement their will in parliamentary systems as these institutions give party members a voice in foreign policy. Presidential systems lessen the accountability of the head of state to his party and can (but do not necessarily) reduce partisanship in foreign policy, depending on whether the president departs from the ideological wishes of his party.

Institutions affect the degree to which ideological inputs become policy outputs. The pattern of partisanship was clearest in parliamentary Britain where an exclusive right did battle with an inclusive left. While the Conservative government did not want to get more deeply militarily involved in Bosnia, it conceded that this would have been politically impossible anyway. Vociferous backbenchers, particularly on the right of the party, would not have allowed it. Parliament provided effective voice to the larger party. When the government turned over, the Tories were replaced by a much more interventionist Labour Party that had the almost unanimous support of its backbenchers for peace enforcement. This enabled it to play the role of NATO's strongest hawk during the Kosovo War. The party also set in motion the process that led to major steps forward in the European Security and Defense Policy blocked previously to a large degree by Conservative backbenchers.

In Germany, the need for coalition partners to gain a majority in parliament provided a consistent source of influence for junior partners. In Germany, the Christian Democrats would have pursued a much more aggressive normalization policy had the centrist, and consequently less hawkish, Free Democrats not insisted on the necessity of a constitutional amendment. This allowed the SPD to hold the government's out-of-area policy hostage given that a two-thirds majority was necessary for such a change. During Kosovo, the Greens used their voice to bring about a German-led effort at resolving the conflict diplomatically. The Fischer peace plan was at least partly intended to convince the Greens that Germany was doing its utmost to bring about an end to the bombing. Without it, the coalition would have likely broken apart. In France, the presence of an antimilitarist Communist Party meant that the Socialists had to tone down their rhetoric during Kosovo. While Labour was pushing for a land invasion, French ministers publicly dismissed such an option even though they were planning to be a part of it.

NATO's credibility would have been much stronger if the French left had stood beside the British.

The ability of smaller coalition parties to force changes in policy and public rhetoric is not unique to France and Germany but also apparent in Italy's behavior during the Kosovo war. Prime Minister D'Alema's statement just hours into the conflict that diplomacy should recommence was generally regarded as a way of soothing the concerns of the more extreme leftist members of his coalition.[54] So too was the resolution passed by the parliament on 26 March 1999 that pledged the government to end the war as soon as possible, begin immediate diplomatic initiatives, and restrict Italian participation to the defense of NATO planes and troops, excluding offensive operations against Serbia.[55] This was the price the moderate Democrats of the Left, the senior coalition party, had to pay just to keep the Communists in the coalition; the latter did not vote for the motion.[56]

The Democrats of the Left lived up to the public part of the bargain. Foreign Minister Lamberto Dini watered down NATO's five conditions for an end to the campaign to only three, excising the unimpeded return of refugees and a Yugoslavian commitment to reopen political talks with the Kosovar Albanians.[57] In a plan similar to Fischer's, D'Alema proposed a bombing pause on 16 May that would follow the passage of a UN resolution imposing the withdrawal of Yugoslav forces and the return of refugees.[58] Periodically throughout the crisis, Dini questioned the wisdom of escalating the bombing, suggested that the Serbs were not completely in the wrong, and ruled out Italian participation in a land war.[59] All of this could be seen as a lack of resolve on the part of the Italian government were it not for the fact that behind the scenes the Italians did in fact participate in offensive operations and were planning on being a part of any land operation.[60] It seems that in Italy as in France, the antimilitarist left forced a particular public stance, but did not decisively affect behavior.

Partisanship is less prominent in presidential systems such as France as these eliminate opportunities to express opposition. Socialist president François Mitterrand was able to refuse pleas for stronger military intervention in Bosnia from the majority Socialist parliamentary caucus, the Socialist Party organization, prominent foreign and defense policy experts in his party, and the

---

54. Balfour et al. (1999), pp. 70–71; Cremasco (2000), p. 172; Croci (2000), p. 42.

55. Balfour et al. (1999), p. 71; Cremasco (2000), p. 171.

56. Martin Clark, "Italian Perceptions," in Mary Buckley and Sally N. Cummings (eds.), *Kosovo: Perceptions of War and Its Aftermath* (New York: Continuum, 2001), p. 130.

57. Balfour et al. (1999), p. 74.

58. Ibid., p. 76; Cremasco (2000), p. 175.

59. See Croci (2000).

60. Balfour et al. (1999), p. 73; Clark (2001), pp. 300, 305.

most interventionist public opinion in Europe. Due to the unique nature of Gaullism, he even had the support of the right to a degree not true of the United States or Britain. Those close to the decision-making attribute his policy to his personal feelings, in particular his affection for the Serbs due to their historical friendship with France. It was only when the 1993 election swept the Gaullists into power in parliament that policy changed as cohabitation increased the influence of the foreign and defense ministries over what had been to that point a presidential prerogative. As described above, this led to higher diplomatic but lower military involvement.

The latter trend only ended with the election of Chirac and the contemporaneous hostage-taking episode. The end of cohabitation marked a decline in the influence of the Gaullist parliamentary coalition in foreign policy and a return to presidential decision-making. Chirac was by all accounts personally outraged by the audacity of the Bosnian Serbs. In a way not true in Britain or other parliamentary systems, policy emanated from the president's office with little input from the party. Although the Gaullist parliamentarians were uneasy, Chirac skillfully played on the humiliation of the French, which had an enormous impact on a rightist party that had its origins in de Gaulle's efforts to restore French standing after the dual disgraces of military defeat and collaboration. Chirac's bold gestures such as demanding the recapture of Srebrenica and the reinforcement of Gorazde, although not always practical, did force the Americans to develop their own plan and were therefore critical for bringing about the end of conflict.

The story of the U.S. approach to the wars in the Balkans resembles the French case in many ways, suggesting that the argument made here has broader generalizability. Foreign policy can be just as partisan in presidential systems if the president articulates a policy in keeping with his party's ideology. However, the U.S. president can buck the trend in his party in a way that a prime minister cannot, unless the latter is prepared to pay high political costs. Bill Clinton, the Democratic nominee for president in the November 1992 elections, seized on the Bosnia issue in a campaign otherwise dominated by domestic matters. He framed the debate as one in which an inclusive left was fighting for human rights and democracy against an uninterested, exclusive right. Clinton advocated bombing Bosnian Serb units that were besieging Sarajevo and using force to facilitate the delivery of humanitarian aid and the opening of camps to inspection.[61]

However, by the time of Clinton's inauguration in January 1993, the situation on the ground was much different, and interventionists' hopes for

---

61. Drew (1994), p.138; Richard Holbrooke, *To End a War* (New York: Modern Library, 1999), p. 41; Powers (2002), p. 275.

a decisive new policy were disappointed. The Bosnian Serbs controlled almost three-quarters of Bosnia-Herzegovina by the time Clinton took office and the staggering difficulties for the outgunned blue helmet mission were already clear. The window of opportunity for a U.S. ground presence had effectively closed during the Republican presidency, putting the Americans and Europeans in very different structural positions. Now in office, the Democratic team was forced to consider not just the rightness of their cause, but also the desires of the European allies. The Democrats had to consider their policy from more angles. Accountability led to more differentiation, according to national security adviser Anthony Lake—to consideration of not just the inclusive-exclusive and hawk-dove aspects, but also of the unilateral-multilateral dimension.[62] Multilateralist fears of endangering the transatlantic relationship led the Democrats to drop their idea of lifting the arms embargo so as to give the Bosnian Muslims a more level playing field and simultaneously striking at Bosnian Serb positions from the air. The Europeans resisted as this would endanger their troops while the Americans remained safely in the sky.[63]

As in France, Bosnian policy was determined largely by the personal engagement of the president rather than by the Democratic Party. The first two years of the Clinton presidency were marked by periodic fits of activity depending on the president's mood. In spring 1993, he was apparently influenced by Robert Kaplan's book *Balkan Ghosts,* which traces the roots of the Bosnian war to deep-seated and ancient grievances. At this point the administration described Bosnia as a "morass of ancient hatreds" and insinuated that the Bosnian Muslims were themselves committing genocide against the Bosnian Serbs.[64] Later, however, Clinton was shocked by television images of the suffering in Sarajevo in July 1993.[65] His outrage led to the first involvement of NATO as a possible means to punish the Bosnian Serbs.[66]

Others knew there would be no solution unless Clinton was fully engaged. Anthony Lake took advantage of the president's rising anger at the events of the summer of 1995 to articulate an "endgame strategy."[67] The national security adviser's intention was to capitalize on the president's frustration in

---

62. Halberstam (2001), p. 199.

63. On the "lift and strike" proposal, see Ivo H. Daalder, *Getting to Dayton: The Making of America's Bosnia Policy* (Washington, D.C.: Brookings Institution Press, 2000), pp. 15–16; Drew (1994), pp. 154–158; Power (2002), pp. 303–304.

64. Drew (1994), p. 162; Power (2002), p. 308.

65. Halberstam (2001), p. 228; Bob Woodward, *The Choice* (New York: Simon and Schuster, 1996), p. 157

66. Drew (1994), p. 275.

67. On Clinton's explosions in front of aides, see Daalder (2000), p. 91; Halberstam (2001), p. 316; Woodward (1996), p. 261.

order to get his approval for a bold new commitment to finding a diplomatic solution and if that failed, to force the withdrawal of UNPROFOR and to implement lift-and-strike to help the Bosnian government retake Serb-held territory.[68] For the first time, the president was fully attentive, which meant that he was prepared to insist on a firm policy of drawing a line at Gorazde at the London conference following the fall of Srebrenica.[69] The U.S. plan, to respond to Serb aggression against any safe area with massive air strikes across all of Bosnia, was the key military element to bringing about peace.

Another factor pushing for an increased commitment in Bosnia was growing Congressional criticism. Unlike in France, the American legislature plays an influential role in foreign policy, not by holding the president accountable to the wishes of his party, but by establishing another center of decision-making authority, most importantly through its power of the purse. Therefore, the administration's position on any particular issue was to some degree a function of Congressional preferences. Senate Majority Leader Robert Dole was attracting increasing bipartisan support for his bill to begin arming the Bosnian Muslims. The two parties had different reasons for backing the initiative. For the Democrats it was way of forcing the administration to take some action that might help the Bosnian Muslims, generally regarded as the victims of the war. However, the Democrats wanted the arming of Muslims combined with an American commitment to use air power. In May 1994, Democratic Senator George Mitchell managed to pass without a single Republican vote an amendment to Dole's initial arms embargo bill that pledged the U.S. to add NATO air power to any effort to lift the ban on exporting weapons.[70]

The Republicans were looking for a cost-free alternative that would not involve American air or ground troops. Dole said: "We're talking about lifting the embargo with no American involvement—it would seem to me a big difference."[71] Speaker of the House Newt Gingrich had the same idea.[72] By summer 1995, the balance of power in both chambers had shifted to the Republicans, and Dole pushed his bill through the House and Senate in July. Clinton vetoed the measure, but with a veto-proof, two-thirds majority, the threat of a Congressional override was credible. The Europeans made known they would withdraw if more weapons flowed into the region, which would have triggered the deployment of twenty-five thousand American forces to extricate them, a commitment that a multilateralist Democratic

---

68. See Daalder (2000), pp. 99–101.

69. Halberstam (2001), pp. 313, 326.

70. See Roll Call no. 110 in the 103th Congress, 2nd Session on S. Amdt. 1696. *Congressional Record* (10 May 1994), pp. 5468–5479.

71. Power (2002), p. 426.

72. Holbrooke (1999), p. 71.

administration had every intention of honoring. This undoubtedly motivated the Americans to find a diplomatic resolution to the war.

Without the asymmetry of commitment from the outset, American policy was much more in line with that of the Europeans during the Kosovo crisis. Nevertheless, Republican control of the Congress again posed a significant
constraint for the second Clinton administration at every step along the way.
U.S. envoy Richard Holbrooke brokered a last-minute deal with Milosevic
in October to avoid the onset of air strikes, but due to feared Congressional resistance to providing U.S. peacekeepers, could only offer unarmed
OSCE observers.[73] Only after the massacre at Racak galvanized the interventionists in the administration did the president request four thousand troops
for a possible peacekeeping force predicated on a diplomatic agreement at
Rambouillet in February 1999. Led by Madeleine Albright, the proponents
of military action in the administration did constant battle with the more
resistant Pentagon, whose secretary of defense, William Cohen, was a former
Republican senator who had voted against the Bosnian deployment.

The shadow of the Republican Congress and its power to cut off funding
loomed over the major decisions of the war. In his speech to the nation after
the failure of diplomatic talks and the beginning of air strikes, the president declared: "I do not intend to put our troops in Kosovo to fight a war."
The statement, a clear signal of uneasiness in Washington, did not sit well
with the resolute message coming from other NATO members, most notably
Britain, but Labour was not operating under the same constraints. National
security adviser Sandy Berger later claimed that the sentence was necessary
to win the war, as the Republican Congress needed to be reassured that there
would be no land invasion of Kosovo. The narrow margin of victory just for
peacekeepers had shown the danger.[74] Although Prime Minister Blair convinced the United States to begin to secretly plan for a land war, American
hesitance persisted throughout the campaign as the administration knew that
any ground war would need political support from Congress, which it feared
it would not obtain.[75] Clinton would gradually escalate his rhetoric, claiming that all options were on the table, but never went as far publicly as the
British. This likely lengthened the war significantly.

*Parties base their foreign policies on principles, not on their electoral impli-
cations, although fears of endangering party chances of remaining or obtaining power often affect the timing and the extent to which true preferences are
revealed.*

73. Clark (2001), p. 138; Daalder and O'Hanlon, p. 43; Halberstam (2001), p. 442.
74. Daalder and O'Hanlon (2000), p. 97, Halberstam (2001), p. 424.
75. Clark (2001), p. 306.

Although electoral considerations are undoubtedly present and influential in many political decisions, in the cases I studied parties frequently passed up opportunities to inflict political damage on their opponents. In Britain, because of right-wing opposition, Labour and the Liberal Democrats provided the parliamentary support necessary to keep British peacekeepers in Bosnia. This gave the opposition significant leverage to provoke a crisis in the government by rescinding its backing. However, the left, which wanted peacekeepers to remain, refrained. A similar process occurred in Italy where the leftist coalition needed the parliamentary support of the right to authorize the war in Kosovo because of antimilitarist coalition partners. Forza Italia, the primary rightist party, as well as the extreme right, supported the war because of its implications for regional stability and refugee flows, concerns that were more urgent for Italy than for any other country except Germany, due to its geographical proximity to the crisis zone.

In Germany, the changing positions of the Social Democrats and Greens were the result not of finger-to-the-wind prognostications but of inner reflection based on reactions to events. Although the SPD had an electoral incentive to become more interventionist as part of a move to the center, it passed up such a chance in 1994 because it was not yet convinced of the merits of peace enforcement. Only the final chapter in Bosnia helped convert the party. Although the leadership, which would benefit most, was eager to make the change, the process was driven by experts and moderates. When in jeopardy during the Kosovo war, the SPD leadership turned to party ideals, not their followers' interest in remaining in power, to hold the government together. In France, the president's relative insulation from voter sanctions did not make France consistently more hawkish than countries with parliamentary systems, as office-seeking arguments predict. In the United States, Clinton proceeded with his endgame strategy even though he recognized that it might undermine his presidency just a year before his reelection campaign.[76]

Office-seeking concerns did often lead parties to postpone initiatives and policy announcements until circumstances were propitious. The British Labour Party may have toned down its critiques of Tory Bosnia policy for fear of appearing too casual with soldiers' lives. It certainly avoided any discussion of European defense cooperation until after it was elected. The German Greens obscured the evolution of their thinking on both humanitarian intervention and ESDP in their election materials so as to retain an antimilitarist profile. In all of these cases, however, the parties could not hide their true preferences forever. In those instances in which parties never did admit their preferences so as not to endanger coalition relations that might result in a

76. Halberstam (2001), pp. 313–314; Power (2002), p. 441; Woodward (1996), pp. 265, 328.

loss of power, as was true of the French and Italian center-left in Kosovo, they dutifully pushed their real agenda behind the scenes at significant risk.

Epilogue: Contesting the National Interest in Iraq

Was partisanship in foreign and defense policy in the 1990s just an interlude? Has political culture reasserted itself in the face of more perilous threats to national security? The recent transatlantic controversy over the war in Iraq seems to have confirmed long-held views about the foreign policy approaches and interests of the three major European powers. Britain is consistently loyal. France is unfailingly obstructionist. Germany is instinctively pacifist. Beneath the surface, however, are less monolithic positions. The partisan argument has stood up well. Almost all of the advanced democracies that supported the United States—Australia, Denmark, Italy, Japan, the Netherlands, and Spain—were governed by rightist parties. Primary opponents—Belgium, Canada, Germany—were mostly leftist.

The Iraq war itself was another partisan intervention. Unlike the war against the Taliban in Afghanistan, it could not be justified using traditional notions of self-defense that would muster broad, truly bipartisan support. It seemed a departure for the American right. Governor George W. Bush campaigned in 2000 against "nation-building," claiming that the purpose of the military was to fight and win wars, not to put countries back together following ethnic strife and humanitarian disasters. This was completely consistent with the exclusive policy of his party in Congress throughout the 1990s. Yet the administration's interventionist policies after the terrorist attacks in September 2001 were consistent as well. The security environment had changed but Republican ideology had not. Three principles have marked President Bush's foreign policy, each of which corresponds to an ideological dimension that I identify as organizing partisan conflict. The Democrats have defined their opposition along these three continua.

The first characteristic of Bush's policy is that it is driven primarily by self-interested motivations, what I call an exclusive foreign policy. Although a strong humanitarian case could have been made against Saddam Hussein, the president and his advisers unabashedly stressed his possession of weapons of mass destruction and his possible links to terrorist organizations intent on harming the United States, at least prior to the war. Neoconservatives in the government might genuinely believe in the benefits of and chances for democracy promotion in the Middle East, but Republicans tend to support such action only in areas of vital strategic interest. Their half-hearted response to the crisis in Liberia illustrates the point. This focus on strategic interest has created particular problems for the administration given the difficulty it has had in finding evidence of those weapons. Attempts to reframe the war as primarily humanitarian have been met with skepticism.

The second feature of Republican policy is its belief in the efficacy of force as a way of demonstrating U.S. resolve, particularly to adversaries in the Middle East. Nor is the Bush administration shy about announcing its willingness to use force, as evident in the president's doctrine of preemption. The corresponding Democratic criticism is that the administration is too quick to pull the trigger, not allowing enough time, for instance, for the weapons inspectors in Iraq to confirm the danger of Iraq's weapons programs. This tendency has created particular problems for the administration in the form of the controversy over how the administration used somewhat ambiguous intelligence in making the case for war. Information was selectively used to justify a war that the Bush administration wanted, regardless of the facts, goes the critique. The experience of the Bosnian and Kosovo wars, however, shows that this is not altogether unique.

The third feature of the Republican foreign policy of the Bush administration is its focus on sovereignty. This has exposed it to what is perhaps the most commonly repeated Democratic criticism, that it too often acts unilaterally. Many cited the President's willingness to bring in the United Nations in September 2001 as a major concession to multilateralism, but the administration's message did not vary: if the UN would not act, the United States would. The United States would welcome the UN and others if they would like to come along, but it would not grant any international organization or state the ability to override American interests. This focus on sovereignty can also be seen in the administration's removal of President Clinton's signature from the International Criminal Court, its withdrawal from the Antiballistic Missile Treaty, and the manner in which it abandoned the Kyoto Protocol.

The German left seems to have taken the Bush administration at its word, that the war's primary motive was to disarm Saddam Hussein, not to liberate the Iraqi people. The Social Democrats and Greens had come around to humanitarian intervention, but only in cases in which there was no clear self-interested rationale, let alone one to be realized by means of a preemptive war. In such a case, even a mandate from the Security Council would be insufficient to justify German involvement, as Chancellor Gerhard Schröder clearly stated. In interviews several years ago, before the new security environment had evolved, politicians of both leftist parties always stated that, even given the left's evolution, their support for another war against Iraq would be unthinkable. They were right. Some have argued, and President Bush is thought to believe, that Schröder's position was determined by his precarious electoral position in the summer of 2002. The chancellor might have played on public opposition to win an election, but his coalition's position was determined long before. There is nothing in my partisan explanation that argues that leaders will not take electoral advantage of policies to which their parties and supporters are genuinely committed.

Many have since mistaken the red-green coalition's strong stance against a war in Iraq as a return to an innate German pacifism. However, in justifying their refusal to join the war, coalition leaders took great pains to stress Germany's deployment of thousands of troops in other theaters abroad, noting that Germany was second only to the United States in this regard. As is always the case when politicians oppose wars, they stressed how the conflict could spiral, creating instability in a volatile region including in Palestine, and serving as a lightning rod for terrorist recruiting efforts.[77] Yet Germany's history was barely mentioned. The left's objection was to the exclusivist goals of the United States, and was not based on antimilitarism per se. Somewhat counterintuitively, the war showed how far the left has evolved in Germany.

The war in Iraq put the Christian Democrats in the uncomfortable position of supporting a policy of solidarity with the United States that the overwhelming majority of the German public did not believe in, and doing so in an election year. They responded in the same way that other parties did in the early 1990s when public preferences and private positions diverged— by trying to dodge the issue. The compellence logic that marks their thinking on strategic and exclusive matters enabled them to criticize the red-green policy without explicitly endorsing German participation in the war. All leading CDU politicians stressed that a credible threat of war was actually the only path to peace, as only the likelihood of armed conflict would induce Iraq to come clean about its weapons programs. For this reason, they focused their ire on the chancellor's statement that Germany would support no military action regardless of the circumstances, since it removed any incentive for Iraq to comply with UN resolutions. The very presence of UN inspectors in Iraq, the CDU argued, was due to U.S. policy.[78] This was classic hawkish thinking about the efficacy of force, which distinguished the right from the left while allowing the former to duck charges of warmongering. After the election, however, the CDU did introduce a resolution in parliament that

77. On Germany's contributions to other military operations, see comments in the *Plenarprotokoll* by Gerhard Schröder, 15/25 (13 February 2003), pp. 1874–1875; Peter Struck, 15/25 (13 February 2003), p. 1894; Ursula Mogg, 15/24 (12 February 2003), p. 1856. On the possible destabilizing effects of war, see comments by Gerhard Schröder, 15/25 (13 February 2003), p. 1875; Ludger Volmer, 15/25 (13 February 2003), p. 1900; Uta Zapf, 15/24 (12 February 2003), p. 1854.

78. In *Plenarprotokoll*, see comments by defense experts Glos and Schmidt and party leader Merkel: Michael Glos, 15/25 (13 February 2003), p. 1893; Angela Merkel, 15/25 (13 February 2003), pp. 1880–1881; Christian Schmidt, 15/24 (12 February 2003), p. 1854.

called for Germany to provide numerous measures of military support to the United States in case of war.[79] There were real party differences.

The diplomatic alliance of France and Germany has done more to reinforce the impression of a solid European bloc against the war than any other factor. Yet French policy was driven by very different and seemingly contradictory motivations—the desire to promote French stature and influence by checking U.S. power while at the same time leaving the door open to being a part of any military operation. The French right took back the parliament in 2002, and the reelected President Chirac therefore enjoyed complete preeminence in foreign affairs. He sounded the same familiar themes of international law and the UN's monopoly on decisions regarding the use of force that Germany did, but there is substantial reason to doubt that this was a genuine conversion to multilateralism. As was argued in Chapter 5, the French right discovered the utility of the UN only in the 1990s when it suited traditional Gaullist interests. Pushing decisions on major issues through the Security Council enhanced France's stature and influence. Iraq was no different. The inspectors were so important to the French right because they served as impartial arbiters of whether Saddam Hussein had weapons of mass destruction. They served as a check on U.S. power. The Americans would not be the ones to determine whether Iraq was a threat to international security.

Just as importantly, if the inspectors verified that the weapons programs existed, they also offered a way for France to fight alongside in the war without appearing to be American lackeys. The French right would want to be involved in the most significant action in international affairs in a decade. Ultimately this did not come to pass, but we should not infer from the course of events that it was not possible. Chirac was very careful not to rule out French participation in a military action and explicitly contrasted the French position with that of Germany, to the chagrin of the French left which was more ideologically opposed to the war.[80] The French-German axis would have been even more passionately antiwar had the French Socialists been in power. The French government's opposition became more implacable as it became clearer in the early months of 2003 that the Americans would not allow the inspectors to be the ultimate judges of Iraq's intentions. France could not participate if the inspectors did not find weapons of mass destruction.

Perhaps the most puzzling aspect of the European response to the war in Iraq was the British Labour government's solid support for it. Some of this should be attributed to the fact that the party had undergone a substantial

---

79. *Bundestag Drucksache* 15/434 (13 February 2003). See also *Bundestag Drucksache* 15/421 (11 February 2003).

80. "French Leader Offers America Both Friendship and Criticism," *New York Times* (9 September 2002).

ideological reorientation during the early 1990s. This was New Labour, a more centrist party with a more exclusive conception of the national interest than the old left. It was certainly more right-leaning than its counterparts in Europe. In Bosnia and Kosovo, this had not been a factor, as the moderates and left-wingers within Labour were in broad agreement. Predictably, however, in the conflict with Iraq the prime minister lost the support of many of his colleagues who had been most ardently interventionist in the Kosovo war. It also appears that Britain under Labour was pursuing a conscious strategy of moderating U.S. policy privately with influence gained by showing public support, making the United States more multilateral.[81] Nevertheless, despite this and the centrist caste of his party, much causal weight must be placed on the personal commitment of the prime minister to risking a war without the solid support of his party.

Due to the particular institutional parameters in which Blair was working, he paid a heavy price. Here the partisan argument is vindicated. Unlike in presidential systems, parliamentary governments cannot buck their parliamentarians without serious consequences. Antiwar Labour backbenchers proposed a resolution stating that the case for war had not yet been proven. In one of the most significant backbench revolts in British parliamentary history, the resolution garnered 139 Labour votes. Although Blair's tenure has been marked by reform of many cherished and previously untouchable leftist policies, the war has been by far his greatest challenge and has brought him the closest he has been to losing power. Only a fraction of the rebels were Labour's traditional pacifists. Many, including one of the junior ministers who resigned in protest, made an explicit point of alluding to their support of the Bosnia and Kosovo interventions.[82] Again the primary point of opposition was the lack of a solid inclusive rationale.

The government's policy was only possible with the support of the right, which heartily endorsed the war. Generally opposed to humanitarian intervention, the Conservatives embraced a military action that they believed advanced Britain's vital interests. Tory party leader Ian Duncan-Smith noted that Hussein had a terrible human rights record and was in breach of UN resolutions, but explicitly contrasted those facts with the primary Conservative rationale for the war: "[T]he main reason why we will be voting for the motion is that it is in the British national interest. Saddam Hussein has the means, the mentality and the motive to pose a direct threat to our national security."[83] Recently ousted party leader William Hague made almost iden-

---

81. The prime minister and the foreign secretary claimed to have such an intent. See comments in *Hansard:* Tony Blair (18 March 2003), cols. 770–771; Jack Straw (18 March 2003), col. 896.

82. See comments in *Hansard* by John Denham (18 March 2003), col. 798.

83. *Hansard* (18 March 2003), col. 775.

tical remarks: "[A]lthough there are legal arguments on either side, we are not morally obliged to take action—if we were, we would have to take action against many other countries. . . . We should take action because it is in the national interest."[84]

The war in Iraq was therefore a mirror image of that in Bosnia, where Labour support had been critical for maintaining the British peacekeeping presence in the face of right-wing pressure to withdraw, even while Labour wanted to do more. The leftist Liberal Democrats had also backed the government then, whereas in Iraq, they joined with the Labour rebels. In policy-seeking fashion, the Conservatives avoided any temptation to weaken the Blair government, instead pledging total support to Blair for an exclusive pursuit they could rally behind. As they had in the early 1990s, Conservatives expressed confusion over how Labour politicians could support the wars in the Balkans and not action against Iraq. The comparison then had been the first Gulf War and Bosnia. During the second war against Iraq, former shadow defense secretary John Maples, criticizing humanitarian intervention, stated: "Those who will oppose the government tonight out of their principles cannot have been acting on the same principles when they supported the Government on Kosovo."[85] I have shown that this is in fact possible.

Foreign policy, the empirical record reviewed above has shown, is partisan. The national interest is contested. The partisan nature of foreign policy has both a positive and a negative face that parallel the two most fundamental understandings of what it means to be ideological. To be led by an ideology is to have principles. My finding is that, as concerns humanitarian intervention, parties are indeed struggling over what the national interest is in the post–Cold War period. There is no binding culture that prevents new alternatives from being presented. They are trying to decipher what is best for their nations, and not merely for themselves. That parties use values to articulate different foreign policy programs, present them to the electorate, and attempt to implement them following their election, is a good sign for democracy in general. Voters can have an influence on the course of international affairs. This does not mean, however, that parties are completely up front about what motivates them. As I have shown, rightist parties in particular often use these interventions for other purposes.

More negatively, almost all politicians, even those driven primarily by humanitarian considerations, define their policies first on the basis of ideological instincts, then work backwards to create arguments that justify their

84. *Hansard* (18 March 2003), col. 792.
85. *Hansard* (18 March 2003), col. 839.

preferred courses of action. For interventionists, the aggressor is clear, the price low, the operation legal, the problem solvable, and the cause just. For opponents, it is just the opposite. The tendency is more pronounced at the extreme ends of the political spectrum but exists among moderates as well. This is the downside of ideological politics—the absence of a cold and calculated weighing of costs and benefits and the tendency to believe what one wants to believe despite the sound arguments of others.

Yet it is not clear whether such a calculus is even possible. Military planners can provide assessments about the likelihood of reaching goals, but all operations provide surprises. Bosnia and Kosovo were no exception. At best the chances and costs of success can only be roughly estimated and this provides significant room for partisan debate. Will military action improve or inflame the situation? Even if such judgments were precise, politicians would still be at a loss. When distilled to its essence, peace enforcement requires politicians to make judgments about whether saving lives in other countries justifies exposing their own citizens to peril, and about whether violence can be effective in preventing more violence. How many soldiers' lives should be sacrificed to protect individuals suffering repression in foreign lands? There is no formula for such a calculation absent values, and values differ across parties. In an attempt to muster solid national support, politicians frequently argue, as House Minority Leader Richard Gephardt did during the Kosovo war, that there "is not a Republican Army or a Democratic Army or a Republican Air Force or a Democratic Air Force."[86] This is an echo of Kaiser Wilhelm from almost a century before, and it is no more true now than then.

86. *Congressional Record* (28 April 1999), p. 2444.

Index